CHEAP LABOUR AND RACIAL DISCRIMINATION

Cheap Labour and Racial Discrimination

RALPH FEVRE
Department of Sociology and Anthropology,
University College,.
Swansea

Gower

Published by
Gower Publishing Company Limited,
Gower House, Croft Road, Aldershot, Hampshire GU11 3HR, England

and

Gower Publishing Company,
Old Post Road, Brookfield, Vermont 05036, U.S.A.

British Library Cataloguing in Publication Data
_____

Fevre, Ralph
  Cheap labour and racial discrimination.
  1. Minorities—Employment—England—Bradford (West Yorkshire)
  2. Textile workers—England—Bradford (West Yorkshire)
  3. Race discrimination—England—Bradford (West Yorkshire)
  I. Title
  331.6   HD8398.A2

Library of Congress Cataloging in Publication Data
_____

Fevre, Ralph
  Cheap labour and racial discrimination.

  Bibliography: p.
  1. Discrimination in employment--Great Britain   2. Race
discrimination--Great Britain   3. Area labour--Great Britain
4. Textile workers--Great Britain   I. Title
HD4903.5.G7F48 1984   331.6'2'0941   84-1522

ISBN 0-566-00683-9

Contents

List of tables   vii

Preface   ix

1   Asians in wool textiles   1
        Tables   8

2   Cheap labour in the first
    capitalist industry   11

3   The postwar crisis   17
        The employers' crisis   17
        The workers' crisis   21
        The employers' failure   25

4   Working in wool textiles   32
        Pay and conditions   32
        Change in the labour process   44
        Conclusions   52

5   Labour supply and Asian recruitment   55
        Tables   66

6   The division of labour   68
        The distribution of Asian workers
           between firms   68
        The distribution of Asian workers
           within firms   74
        Change and resistance   81
        Recent trends   84
        Conclusions   90
        Tables   94

7   Racism at work   106
        Managing Asian workers   106
        'Economic men'   110
        Who discriminates?   116
        Black Britons   121
        Conclusions   123

8   Black workers in the labour market   126
     Employment trends   127
     Case studies   130
     Unemployment   136
     Conclusions   138
     Tables   143

9   Beliefs and reality   147
     An inclination towards cheap labour   147
     Limitations on the employment of
       Black workers   151
     The legitimation of racist beliefs   153
     Conclusions   155

10   The advantages of discrimination   157
     Labour supply and labour demand   157
     Discrimination   160
     The labour market and the labour
       process   162
     The future   164
     Conclusions   166

Appendix: wool textile processes   169

Bibliography   171

Tables

1.1   Direct production workers in wool textiles in
the UK 1955-79: all workers and Asian workers   8

1.2   Direct production workers in wool textiles in
Bradford 1965-79: all migrants and Asian
workers   8

1.3   Direct production workers in wool textiles in
the UK 1953-80: men and women   9

1.4   Direct production workers in wool textiles in
Bradford 1965-80: men and women   9

1.5   Employment in wool textiles in Bradford
1965-80: workers in direct production and
administration   10

5.1   Selected direct production departments in
wool textiles in Bradford 1965-79: all
workers and women   66

5.2   Direct production workers in wool textiles in
Bradford 1967-79: Asians and women   67

6.1   Asian workers and trends in employment and
wages in responding firms 1972-6   94

6.2   Composition of the labour force in responding
firms 1978   95

6.3   Wages and salaries as a percentage of total
value added in selected wool textile firms
1973-7   96

6.4   Total value added as a percentage of capital
employed in selected wool textile firms
1973-7   97

6.5   Total value added (£s) per employee in
selected wool textile firms 1973-7   98

6.6   Average employee remuneration (£s per
annum) in selected wool textile firms
1972-7   99

6.7   Employment in selected wool textile firms
1972-7   100

6.8   Employment in selected direct production
departments in three Bradford woolcombing
firms 1971-7: all workers and Asian
workers   101

6.9   Direct production workers in three Bradford
woolcombing firms 1971-7: all workers and
Asian workers   102

6.10   Direct production workers on day shift in
three Bradford woolcombing firms 1971-7:
all workers and Asian workers   103

6.11   Direct production workers on night shift
in three Bradford woolcombing firms 1971-7:
all workers and Asian workers   104

6.12   Percentage of workers who were Asian in
three Bradford woolcombing firms 1971-7   105

8.1   Unemployment in Bradford by 'ethnic group'
(quarterly) 1977-82   143

8.2   Unemployment in Bradford by ethnic origin
(quarterly) 1977-82   144

8.3   Black unemployment in Bradford by sex
(quarterly) 1977-82   146

Preface

For those with eyes to see, it has long been obvious that
Blacks living in the UK suffer racial discrimination. Those
who require documentation will find that the evidence has
been available for more than fifteen years (Daniel 1967).
Subsequent research (Smith 1974, 1976) showed that discrimination
remained in spite of legislation which some thought might
prevent it. This later research (see also Runneymede Trust
and Radical Statistics Group 1980) gave prominence to a
particular symptom of discrimination, the 'disadvantaged'
position of Blacks at work. There has been a fair amount of
empirical research on this problem, but little on its corollary:
perhaps somebody, somewhere, is gaining? This book is
concerned with the relationship between advantage and disadvantage.
Who wins when Blacks lose?

Since there seems to be little point in reproducing the findings
of other researchers, the existence of racial discrimination
will be assumed throughout. We will also take the existence of
racial categorisation for granted since this book is not
concerned with first causes. While we may be able to make some
observations on the way in which racism is reproduced, the roots
of racism cannot be found in the relationship between advantage
and disadvantage where Blacks are employed. Nor will we spend
much time discussing Black workers themselves since we will be
more interested in their employers. Research on this topic
cannot easily pretend to be value free, and it is probably best
to point out at this early stage that this book is intended to
contribute something to the struggle against racism. With
this intention it would be indefensible for a White researcher to
turn 'the Blacks' into an object of study. Instead, we will be
concerned with the firms which employ them, in particular those
wool textile (1) firms in and around Bradford which employ
(or employed) large numbers of Asian workers. Some readers may
complain that Asians are not Black workers. Certainly research
in this area is plagued by confusing language. 'Asians', for
example, do not look like people born in Saigon or Tokyo. Nor
are 'Whites' the colour of this page nor 'Blacks' the colour of
print, but these terms have some use. They emphasise that to be
recognised as non White in Britain is to be treated differently
to those with White skin. But, more than this, they indicate
that the differences you receive if your skin is light brown
rather than dark brown amount to rather less than the difference
between your treatment and that of someone with White skin.

The key theoretical discussions of the book are contained in
Chapters Nine and Ten.   Working backwards from these chapters,
Chapters Eight, Seven and Six present conclusions drawn from
the author's fieldwork;   Chapters Five, Four and Three
consider the wool textile industry;   Chapter Two is concerned
with history.   The book has been organised to provide the
minimum of interruption to the text.   The reader will find
that tables are included at the end of the chapter to which
they refer and are numbered according to the order in which
they are mentioned in the text.   The tables in Chapter One
are numbered 1.1, 1.2 and so on.

There is little discussion of the intricacies of wool textile
processing in the main text and readers who are interested in
this subject should refer to the short appendix.   Other readers
may like to use the appendix as a glossary of technical terms.

This book could not have been written without financial support
from the Social Science Research Council and the EEC/DES
Transition to Work Project.   While any mistakes are my own,
I would like to thank all those in Aberdeen, Bradford and Swansea
who gave their help and ideas.   Special mention should be made
of Robert Moore, Huw Beynon and Sheila Allen, and of Michael
Banton for his comments on the last chapter.   I would also
like to thank Phil Brown and Terry Davies of Bradford Metropolitan
District Council, the staff of the Wool Industry Bureau of
Statistics, and Bob Parr for their help in providing much of
the statistical information presented here.   Finally, mention
should be made of two people who are as closely acquainted with
the contents of this book as its author.   Wendy Fevre coped
with the crises which arose throughout its preparation.
Sheila Goodall coped with the manuscript and produced the camera-
ready copy.

University College Swansea
1983

(1)   At the beginning of the 70s, wool textiles had the largest
      concentration of Black workers of any industry in the UK.

1 Asians in wool textiles

Over fifty thousand Black people live in the Bradford Metropolitan District. Most of the fifty thousand, but excluding those born in the UK, migrated to Bradford in the 1960s from Pakistan, including the area which was to become Bangladesh, and India. These Asian migrants had been small farmers and peasants in their countries of origin but had moved to the UK in search of work. From the 1950s they found jobs in the wool textile industry in West Yorkshire, and particularly Bradford.

Wool textiles has two distinct sections: woollen and worsted (1). There are woollen firms in Bradford but the majority of its wool textile workers are employed in <u>worsted</u> mills, indeed Bradford has been the centre of UK worsted production since the last century. Asian wool textile workers are even more concentrated in Bradford than are all wool textile workers. According to the Wool Industry Bureau of Statistics, Bradford had rather less than thirty per cent of the UK wool textile workforce at the end of the 1970s but more than a third of the Asian wool textile workers in the UK.

The textile industry is important to Black workers, much more so than it is to Whites: in 1971 one in twenty male New Commonwealth immigrants worked in textiles as against one in a 100 of all male workers (Department of Employment 1977, Tables E9-11; E14-16). The dependence of Blacks on textiles in Bradford was even greater: Allen and her colleagues estimated that sixty five per cent of the city's 'coloured labour force' worked in wool textiles in the late 1960s (Allen et al., 1977, p.37). By the end of the 1970s probably one in four of Bradford's Asian workers, as against one in ten of all workers, was employed in wool textiles. Despite this decline in the proportion of Asians working in textiles, perhaps fifty per cent of the city's Asian men still worked in that industry (Bradford Metropolitan District Council 1981; Campbell and Jones 1981, p.24).

It is also clear that Black workers are important to textiles. In 1971 only 2.4 per cent of all male workers, but 7.9 per cent of all male textile workers were New Commonwealth immigrants (see Department of Employment 1977, Tables E9-11; E14-16). In Bradford in 1979 only 8 per cent of the total workforce was Asian but 20 per cent of textile workers were Asian (Bradford Metropolitan District Council 1981). Tables 1.1 and 1.2 show how the proportion of all wool textile workers who were Asian grew from the 1950s (as did the proportion of all <u>immigrants</u> working in wool textiles who were Asian).

These tables show that the number of Asian workers in wool textiles continued to increase after Cohen and Jenner's pioneering study of the industry (Cohen and Jenner 1968). In 1978, the year in which I began the research for this book, Asian migrants made up 13 per cent of all direct production workers in the UK wool textile industry and 25 per cent of all direct production workers in wool textiles in Bradford. The comparable figures for 1967, when Cohen and Jenner conducted their fieldwork, were 8 per cent and 15 per cent. Nevertheless, these Asians had been recruited into a shrinking industry. The proportion of wool textile workers who were Asian increased in the 60s and 70s but the absolute numbers of Asian wool textile workers only increased in the 1960s. By 1971 in Bradford, and 1974 in the UK, there were actually fewer Asian migrants in the industry than in 1967. But while the numbers of Asian workers fell they did not fall as quickly as did the numbers of White workers, in particular White women (see Tables 1.3 and 1.4). Table 1.4, for example, shows that in Bradford the proportion of women wool textile workers fell from 45.3 per cent to 34.7 per cent between 1967 and 1978.

There were important variations within these aggregated figures. Firstly, Asians made up an increasing proportion of direct production workers while the numbers of all direct production workers fell faster than did those of all employees (see Table 1.5). Secondly, the size of the proportional increase varied between sectors, between firms and within firms.

Certainly there are fewer Asians in the industry now than there were in 1967 but this does not necessarily entail a reduction in the proportion of Asians. In 1979, however, there was a fall in Asian participation: from 25.1 per cent of direct production workers in Bradford in the previous year to 23.8 per cent. Unfortunately, the Wool Industry Bureau of Statistics (WIBS), which produced these figures, ceased to collect information on the numbers of 'foreign and Commonwealth' workers in the industry in 1980 (2). There is, however, evidence to suggest that the trend was both representative and permanent. The WIBS figures nominally refer to migrants and not to all Black workers but the possibility of undercounting can be ruled out by comparison of WIBS to Census and Careers Office figures (also see ASRP, p.23). According to the local careers office the proportion of Black school leavers going into textiles fell much more quickly than the proportion of White school leavers entering textiles. In consequence the proportion of all school leavers entering textiles who were Black fell from 41.1 per cent to 16.6 per cent between 1974 and 1978 as against a smaller fall from 11.5 per cent to 6.6 per cent of all school leavers entering any employment (Bradford Metropolitan District Council, Directorate of Educational Services. School Leaver Statistics). WIBS themselves were unwilling to state whether they thought the fall in the percentage of Asians had continued after 1979.

Some time has passed since the last research on Asians in wool textiles (3) or indeed since any research on the employment of Blacks in a particular British industry was conducted (4) and it is not clear what we should infer from the trend in Asian participation in wool textiles, i.e., does it suggest that their position is improving or deteriorating? In order to answer this question we may have to tackle a more difficult one: why did Asians come to be concentrated in wool textiles in the first place? This is a particularly pertinent question in regard to wool textiles because most of Britain's Black immigrants went to work in the South East and the West Midlands (see, for example, Collard 1970, p.27) and West Yorkshire - together with some other textile areas in Lancashire and the East Midlands - seems to be something of an exception to the rule. The question has been asked in a number of different ways before, but the answers given so far are only partial:

> When did you first employ immigrants? 'Since the firm was founded 130 years ago'. (Wool textile employer in the 60s, quoted by Cohen and Jenner 1968, p.44).

> 'So they put up ads in Karachi and did the workers down. If management had not been able to import labour, they'd have improved conditions'. (Bradford 'union stalwart' quoted by Gerda Cohen 1971).

> 'I wouldn't think of starting a night-shift without thirty or forty Pakistanis'. (Manager of a Bradford textile firm quoted by Allen 1970, p.125).

> Since the mid fifties new machinery with greater productive capacity was available to the /wool textile/ industry but to be economic it needed to be extensively worked, and this meant shift working. As much of older machinery was worked by women, who are precluded by law from working night shift, the availability of an all-male pool of low-paid labour was a gift to the employers...

> As the investment slowed down, the advantages of Asian labour were established and they were increasingly recruited for general labouring and other unskilled jobs. Many employers admitted that it was otherwise difficult to recruit labour for dead-end and low-paid jobs. (CIS n.d, p.28).

> The Government's decision to cut the number of Commonwealth immigrants by half could have fairly serious short term effects on industry which will be felt to a much greater extent in those areas where immigrants form a very considerable proportion of the labour force, such as the Midlands and the Bradford - Leeds area ... they are more dependent on immigrant labour than anywhere else in Britain. In the hot and heavy industries such as foundries - never popular in times of full-employment to the home labour force - they frequently constitute the only available pool of labour so well have they adapted themselves to the work and conditions, that some firms when seeking to fill vacancies through the local offices of the Ministry of Labour, express a preference for immigrants....

> By far the largest immigrant community in the north is centered on Bradford and the wool-textile industry. This is almost exclusively Pakistani. Large numbers of them man nightshifts. So many in fact that it has been claimed that nightshifts would be forced to close down entirely without them.

3

> In those cases where immigrants have settled down with
> the same firm for a lapse of time their letters home
> attract others to join them and are a source of
> valuable recruits. If the proposed cuts hit this
> type of bespoke immigrant it would seriously effect
> 'topping up' plans of firms already under severe
> pressure for additional labour. (Editorial, _Times_
> 4 August 1965).

The commonsense conclusion to the foregoing is that Asian wool textile
workers in Bradford have constituted <u>cheap labour</u>. This interpretation
was vigorously debated in letters to the local press in the 1960s (see
also Allen et al., 1977, p.63-4).

> No doubt as persons immigrants are very worthy people,
> but their very availability and need have made them
> easily exploited by employers of cheap labour in
> Bradford and in the process lowered what little status
> and bargaining power unskilled men have in the area.

> I do not think this letter will be refuted by any man
> who labours for a living in local factories or mills.
> (<u>Telegraph and Argus</u> 18 February 1966).

> I have employed immigrant labour and far from being
> cheap labour, they know their value and their position
> equally as well as we do. Believe me, they are not
> long in this country before they know how many beans
> make five. (<u>Telegraph and Argus</u> 25 February 1966).

> There is a minimum wage rate in operation which is
> identical to white and coloured alike. Also as
> immigrants are in most cases duplicating women's tasks
> at a man's rate of pay there is an entirely reverse
> picture of cheap labour. (<u>Telegraph and Argus</u>
> 19 March 1966).

This dispute (in which employers took the side of union leaders against
a local vicar!) turned on the confused definition of the term 'cheap
labour'. The commonsense notion that cheap labour equals undercutting
prevailing wage rates leads to difficulties in establishing its
existence and to confused moral and political implications. I have
found no evidence of Asians taking jobs in Bradford's mills at a lower
rate of pay than the workers who preceded them, nevertheless I believe
that they have provided cheap labour.

   Undercutting is an uncommon and rather special case of a more general
phenomenon which should properly be called 'cheap labour'. <u>The term
describes the labour of workers employed at a rate of pay which their
employer would normally expect to leave him (5) short of labour or
with no labour at all</u>. But for the availability of the workers who
undercut, any attempt by their employer to lower wages would produce a
labour shortage. More often, however, the employer of cheap labour
does not reduce wages but rather refuses to increase them. Thus cheap
labour may be employed where an employer's demand for labour is
satisfied at the same wage rate which had previously produced a
shortfall in labour supply. In this case 'cheap labour' describes the
workers recruited in response to a labour shortage when the employer
does not raise wages in order to attract them. The labour shortage
may follow changes which are outside the employer's control, for

example increased demand for labour elsewhere, or it may follow changes which he has initiated, for example where he has made working conditions less attractive. In this case the labour shortage, as in the case of undercutting, is more likely to be <u>potential</u> than actual. It is worth noting that however the actual or potential labour shortage arises, it is ultimately the <u>employer's</u> creation since he does not increase wages so that labour supply matches demand. Of course it is unlikely that any employer will be able <u>entirely</u> to eliminate the potential for labour shortages when he employs cheap labour. The use of cheap labour may suppress this potential which then becomes evident indirectly, for example in high rates of labour turnover. The picture may also be obscured by the simultaneous adoption of additional strategies by the employer of cheap labour, for example where he reduces total demand for labour without reducing output. Where he accomplishes this solely by installing labour saving machinery this strategy represents a real alternative to cheap labour. Yet where he resolves to maintain output by making the existing workforce work harder he may actually reinforce his need for cheap labour since the jobs he now offers may be less attractive.

It is clear that an employer who creates a potential labour shortage, in any of the ways described above, must take some steps to find the cheap labour that he requires. Chapter Two will indicate some of the ways in which employers have got hold of cheap labour by considering examples from the <u>history</u> of the wool textile industry. These examples will also allow us to add detail to the description of cheap labour given above.

Chapter Two will demonstrate that Asians were not the first group of wool textile workers who provided cheap labour. Indeed it should be noted that they were not the only example of cheap labour in the industry when the research for this book was conducted. Many of the features of Asian employment discussed in subsequent chapters were also present in women's employment (6), however this topic deserves a seperate study.

Further research is also required on the role of organised labour in the wool textile industry. Textile workers are not a 'naturally' backward section of the working class: they played a leading role in the Chartist movement, the emancipation of women, and the founding of the Independent Labour Party and the TUC. Furthermore, the West Riding wool textile workers were first in the field in the run up to the General Strike. But the UK wool textile unions' power has declined throughout this century: for example, even the elite (dyeing and finishing) craftsmen were in a stronger position in 1906 (Clapham 1907, p.210) and during the Great War (Goodrich 1975, p.80) than at any time since. The national wool textile union - the National Union of Dyers, Bleachers and Textile Workers (NUDBTW) - was formed in the early 30s out of the largest craft unions following the collapse of collective bargaining in the industry. In the late 30s collective bargaining was re-established but with the employers in a dominant position. Throughout the succeeding years the industry periodically congratulated itself and the unions on its excellent industrial relations record. The only blot was a long recognition dispute in the sixties which was won by the employers, William Denby's of Baildon, after they had locked out the workforce and refused to negotiate.

The NUDBTW and the other textile unions express interesting attitudes towards Black workers. Some of these attitudes may be inferred from some of the comments made by trade union respondents and quoted in later chapters. Nevertheless, the relationship of the unions to Black workers is too complex to be dealt with here. Further research might begin with the events which preceded the occupation of NUDBTW headquarters in Bradford in 1975 by workers involved in a dispute at Intex Yarns or, indeed, with the Commission for Racial Equality's investigation of the NUDBTW's part in an allegedly discriminatory labour supply agreement with the textile firm Bondina.

At the time of writing there are signs that Asian workers are receiving more support from their union. In 1982 the NUDBTW became part of the Transport and General Workers' Union's Textile Trades group although it retained its seperate organisation and conference. In the following year the TGWU gave support to 20 Asian workers at Aire Valley Yarns, Farsley, who struck for four months in order to enforce their right to join the union. The strike was carried out with widespread support from Bradford's Asians and most of the strikers' demands were conceded, although the employer refused to reinstate the strike leader.

Finally, if organised labour in wool textiles receives insufficient attention in subsequent chapters, there is less neglect of other aspects of 'worker resistance'. Capitalism can develop without creating <u>organised</u> resistance if its internal contradictions are manifested in other ways, for example workers may show their resistance to management initiatives by quitting. Such manifestations are clearly relevant to the use of cheap labour and their inter connection will become clear below. For the moment, we need only to know that recent developments in wool textiles may have been conditioned by the <u>absence</u> rather than the presence of organised resistance.

NOTES

(1) The distinction between woollen and worsted processing originally arose from differences in the raw materials used by the two sections. The woollen section processed wool sheared from sheep whose fleeces provided a short fibre or 'staple'. The worsted system used wool with a long fibre or staple. These differences in the character of the raw material led to differences in processing technique and in the end products of the two systems. Although technological change and the introduction of new materials have made fibre length less important, these differences have remained. A full description of processing under the two systems is given in the Appendix.

(2) For an explanation of this change in policy see the author's PhD thesis, <u>Ascription and Racial Relations of Production</u>, University of Aberdeen, 1982, pp. 9-10. In subsequent references this work will be abbreviated as <u>ASRP</u>.

(3) Most of the relevant material in Allen et al., (1977) was collected in the 1960s.

(4) Brooks (1975) suffered from a similar delay to Allen and her colleagues in publishing research findings. The Unit for Manpower Studies at the Department of Employment (1977) largely relied on existing research which was already somewhat dated.

(5) As in the substantive case, the hypothetical employer of cheap
    labour is male, although it should be noted that women do appear
    on the boards of wool textile companies and that some personnel
    managers in the industry are women.
(6) Compare to the letter quoted above, Telegraph and Argus 19 March
    1966. Note that few women wool textile workers are Asian
    although some are European immigrants.

Table 1.1
Direct production workers in wool textiles in the
UK 1955-1979: all workers and Asian workers

Year	All direct production workers	'Indians and Pakistanis'	Asian percentage of total
1955	169,104	840	0.5
1960	160,004	4,541	2.8
1965	133,233	9,299	7.0
1970	96,190	10,373	10.8
1975	59,917	7,727	12.9
1979	48,957	6,709	13.7

SOURCE: Wool Industry Bureau of Statistics.

Table 1.2
Direct production workers in wool textiles
in Bradford 1965 - 1979: all workers, all
migrants and Asian workers

Year	All direct production workers	All Migrants	'Indians and Pakistanis'	Asian percentage of all migrants	Asian percentage of all direct production workers
1965	28,790	5,709	3,635	63.6	12.6
1967	24,005	5,417	3,651	67.4	15.2
1969	22,668	5,836	4,209	72.1	18.6
1970	19,385	4,989	3,445	69.1	17.8
1971	15,849	4,496	3,090	68.7	19.5
1972	16,171	4,835	3,491	72.2	21.6
1973	14,715	4,428	3,228	72.9	21.9
1974	12,462	3,851	2,788	72.4	22.4
1975	10,940	3,456	2,438	70.5	22.3
1976	11,472	3,655	2,688	73.5	23.4
1977	10,830	3,550	2,726	76.7	25.1
1978	10,406	3,404	2,613	76.7	25.1
1979	9,087	2,843	2,164	76.1	23.8

SOURCE: Wool Industry Bureau of Statistics.

Table 1.3
Direct production workers in wool textiles
in the UK 1953 - 1980: men and women

Year	Men	Women	Total	Women as % of all production workers
1953	71,999	102,017	174,016	58.6
1958	67,711	85,131	152,842	55.7
1963	66,606	78,467	145,073	54.1
1968	57,670	57,014	114,684	49.7
1973	43,067	35,871	78,938	45.4
1978	32,080	24,759	56,839	43.6
1979	27,747	21,210	48,957	43.3
1980	21,951	16,044	37,995	42.2

SOURCE: Wool Industry Bureau of Statistics.

Table 1.4
Direct production workers - wool textiles -
Bradford 1965-1980: men and women

Year	Men	Women	Total	Women as % of all production workers
1965	15,284	13,506	28,790	46.9
1967	13,120	10,885	24,005	45.3
1969	12,813	9,855	22,668	43.5
1970	10,911	8,474	19,385	43.7
1971	9,115	6,734	15,849	42.5
1972	9,378	6,793	16,171	42.0
1973	8,708	6,007	14,715	40.8
1974	7,180	5,282	12,462	42.4
1975	6,678	4,264	10,940	39.0
1976	7,157	4,315	11,472	37.6
1977	7,062	3,768	10,830	34.8
1978	6,792	3,614	10,406	34.7
1979	5,997	3,090	9,087	34.0
1980	4,527	2,435	6,962	35.0

SOURCE: Wool Industry Bureau of Statistics.

Table 1.5
Employment in wool textiles in Bradford
1965-1980: workers in direct production
and administration *

Year	Total in Direct Prod	Total in Administration	Total Employees	Workers in Direct Prod as % of all Employees
1965	28,790	9,474	38,264	75.2
1967	24,005	8,649	32,654	73.5
1969	22,668	8,243	30,911	73.3
1970	19,385	7,242	26,627	72.8
1971	15,849	6,279	22,128	71.6
1972	16,171	5,925	22,096	73.2
1973	14,715	5,508	20,223	72.8
1974	12,462	5,194	17,656	70.6
1975	10,940	4,808	15,748	69.5
1976	11,472	4,687	16,159	71.0
1977	10,830	4,497	15,327	70.7
1978	10,406	4,314	14,720	70.7
1979	9,087	3,677	12,764	71.2
1980	6,962	2,936	9,898	70.3

*Including proprietors, partners, active directors, administration, clerical, maintenance, transport, etc.

SOURCE: Wool Industry Bureau of Statistics.

2 Cheap labour in the first capitalist industry

In this chapter we will consider some historical examples which satisfy the definition of cheap labour given in Chapter One. Firstly, however, it is necessary to outline the turning points of wool textile history since the author's interpretation of that history is rather unconventional (for more detailed discussion see ASRP, pp.26-210).

Petty commodity production had been introduced to the industry by the fourteenth century but it was the relationship between _rural_ petty commodity producers and merchants which provided the preconditions for the development of the capitalist mode of production in wool textiles. _Capitalist outwork_ was the dominant form of capitalist production in the period of Manufacture which lasted from the 1550s to the 1770s. This, rather than the growth of hand powered 'manufactories', was the seed bed of Industrial Capitalism but the development of capitalist outwork was arrested in those areas where it had been most widespread, the West Country and East Anglia. Competition from producers in the West Riding led to the relocation of the industry in Yorkshire, where capitalist outwork was not stagnating. Of course it was in Yorkshire that the Factory System in wool textile production was most successful, but the development of Industrial Capitalism in the West Riding from 1770 did not involve an immediate decline in outwork. For decades outwork was as much an essential component of Industrial Capitalism as the Factory System.

Instances of _undercutting_ were rare in both Manufacture and Industrial Capitalism. Some migrant workers were made to work for lower wages than incumbents and some of the latter resented the recruitment of migrants, but examples of cheap labour on our wider definition were much more numerous. Take, for example, the outworking spinners who were paid much less than weavers despite the existence of labour shortages in spinning (for examples of yarn shortages see Pinchbeck 1930, pp.136-138); or the wool textile workers who migrated into an area of outmigration, an absurdity noted by Oastler:

> He had occasion to go to Liverpool docks where he had seen two ships drawn up at the quayside. At the gangway of the one, emigrants from Yorkshire and Lancashire were taking a tearful farewell of their relatives, while from the other were disembarking unemployed Irish come to look for jobs! (Driver 1970, p.297).

Conventional explanations of migration after 1770 see it either as a once and for all event made necessary by the difficulty of recruiting the first generation of factory workers (Marglin 1974, p.100; Redford 1926, p.18) or simply as a response to a shortfall in labour supply in the absence of a sufficiently rapid natural increase in population in

the industrialising regions (Dobb 1975, p.273). Neither explanation
is of much help in understanding this scene on a Liverpool quayside.

The incoming migrants observed by Oastler were Irish. This was
representative of the textile industry for most of the nineteenth
century, although towards the end of the century Jewish immigrations
grew in importance. In wool textiles Irish immigration (mostly to the
West Riding) probably began with the migration of skilled craftsmen who
were directly recruited from the 1820s. At a later date migrants
without textile experience arrived but not until the 1840s did peasants
make up the majority. Irish workers with textile experience migrated
after the destruction of their indigenous industry by the English
colonisers, and the English wool textile industry may have been also
(indirectly) responsible for the later migrations which followed the
switch to sheep farming in Ireland. All of these groups were
represented in wool textile outwork and eventually in wool textile
factories.

The history of the association between Irish immigration and the wool
textile industry can conveniently be dealt with by examining the
experience of one town, Bradford, where textiles occupied the bulk of
the migrants. Most Irish immigrants to Bradford arrived between 1835
and 1851, and most of these came before the Famine, nevertheless the
majority were peasants. In the 1850s Bradford had a larger proportion
of Irish immigrants in its population than any other textile town in the
West Riding and had over 9,000 Irish born inhabitants, i.e., over
9 per cent of the total population, possibly 25 per cent of the Bradford
working class and 21 per cent of all the Irish born in the Riding
(Sigsworth 1958, p.66). In 1861, however, Bradford had less Irish
born than it had a decade earlier and the percentage fell for the rest
of the century. But in 1871 and 1881 Irish born immigrants still
outnumbered those from any other area outside Yorkshire and the Irish
communities themselves remained beseiged and isolated for decades thus
perpetuating some of the characteristics of the original migration.

Towards the end of the nineteenth century a shift occurred in the sex
ratio of Irish immigrants to Bradford. A reversal occurred whereby
later migrants were more likely to be female. At the same time, Irish
women were increasingly employed in woolcombing in Bradford. This
perhaps confirms the observed relationship between the demands of the
worsted industry and Irish immigration (Sigsworth 1958, p.66).

The emigrants seen by Oastler at Liverpool included a few who were
leaving to seek their fortune but most were escaping from the textile
industry in Britain. While immigrants flocked into the textile
districts others left, especially from the West Riding. In the case
of Lancashire emigrants it might be argued that some of them were
encouraged to leave by trade unions concerned with countering labour
dilution. In Yorkshire, however, the rule was for the workers who
were no longer required by indigenous wool textiles to be recruited by
the agents of overseas competitors, mostly from the United States.

The textile industry in the United States, including the woollen and
worsted branches, was dependent upon large scale immigration.
Immigrants who had latterly worked in English textile outwork and
factories (Berthoff 1953, p.31) made up the majority of early immigrant
workers in the US textile industry and the majority of later immigrants
working there as skilled operatives. Many of these migrants came to
America from textile towns like Bradford. In the 1880s the recruitment

of workers in Bradford was expedited by the American consul there.
By the late nineteenth century, however, technical change and the
organisation of English born workers led to a preference for immigrants
from less developed European countries in American mills (Berthoff 1953,
p.39).   Nevertheless, US textiles remained dependent on immigration.
In 1920 wool textiles had the highest percentage, seventy six, of
workers who were born abroad or were of foreign parentage amongst the
US textile industries.   Furthermore, the majority of these, over forty
per cent of the total workforce, were foreign born (Dunn and Hardy 1931,
p.101).

It has been suggested that employers in the US preferred immigrants to
indigenous workers (Berthoff 1953, p.32).   Indeed, it is also contended
that English factory owners preferred Irish migrants to English workers
(Pollard 1965, pp.172-3).   In part these 'preferences' might be
explained by undercutting by migrants - some Irish workers did undercut
prevailing wage rates - but this was only a minor aspect of their role
as cheap labour.   Bradfordians found work in the worsted mills no
longer satisfactory and thought that emigration offered a better
alternative (1).   For the incoming Irish it was work in the mills of
Bradford which seemed to offer the better alternative (to starvation
perhaps) and thus the potential for a labour shortage was transformed
into a labour glut, a glut which actually produced unemployment amongst
both migrants and indigenous workers.   This glut was all the more
remarkable given the increasing demands made of wool textile workers.
As in other cases of cheap labour, scarce work for the labour force as
a whole was combined with the excessive labour of individuals.

In the nineteenth century cheap labour was identified in the
'dishonourable' or 'sweated' trades but classical political economy,
like neoclassical economics, assumed that cheap labour was employed
on relatively low efficiency or labour intensive processes.   Thus the
handloom weavers' problems, for example, were (and are: Bythell 1969)
seen as a temporary aberration arising from the immobility of labour.
But cheap labour is not a matter of low pay for unproductive work, and
it may be more, rather than less, productive.   Indeed, it has
frequently coincided with an increase in the intensity of exploitation.

Some care must be taken in specifying the conditions which are necessary
for an increase in the intensity of exploitation to take place.   The
term has no direct counterpart in neoclassical theory.   For example, it
does not always amount to increased productivity (2).   The intensity of
exploitation will rise where real wages fall without a reduction in
output as well as where output per head rises without a proportionate
increase in wages.   Thus, in Marxist terms, increased intensity of
exploitation need not involve more intense labour or a longer working
day.   Nevertheless, there have been many examples in wool textile
history of increased production amongst the workers who employ cheap
labour.   In several cases output has been varied in inverse relation
to wages: the lower the wages, the higher the output.

Urban petty commodity production imposed restrictions on the quantity
and quality of its output: for example the existence of the Guilds
ensured the exact nature of the final product and the techniques to be
used were specified, hence the merchants' preference for goods produced
in the countryside.   Other restrictions had the same effect:
limitations on the work which could be done by apprentices and journeymen,
restrictions on competition (i.e. the notion of a 'fair price'), hours

of work and numbers of new producers.   Merchants were attracted to rural industry because it was not subject to the same limitations on output: rural producers increased production when prices fell.

In later years weavers cut prices and wages (c.f. Lipson 1953, p.157) and increased output in response to both handloom and powerloom competition.   Employers of both hand and power were, therefore, able to increase output without paying more.   Similarly, as the Factory System developed rural outwork wages continued to fall, but not because of mechanised competition.   Growing numbers of country dwellers submitted to wage reductions: they had reduced production - thus leaving space for new competitors - in the boom, but increased it in the slump therefore depressing wages still further.

Women wool textile workers suffered particular problems.   Part time spinners accepted lower wages and so full time spinners were forced to increase production and wages were further depressed.   Similarly with children, one child after another was put to work yet textile families succeeded only in reducing wages.   In the factories the supposedly low productivity of female and child labour was used to justify their low wages, but this was far from the truth:

'... those that do the most labour are the worst paid'
(evidence to Sadler 1832 in Wing 1967, p.3).

In this respect it is worth noting that cheap labour may not always lead to increased volume of output.   There are instances of cheap labour producing better quality goods.   Take, for example,

... the small Yorkshire clothier who employed little labour
outside his family to improve the quality of the product
and at the same time effect some price reduction....
(Wilson 1973, p.243).

In the latter half of the nineteenth century West Riding producers maintained lower prices but improved the quality of the cheaper grades of wool textile goods they manufactured.

The West Riding industry took an increasing share of a secular expansion of total output on the basis of cheap labour.   This was not simply a matter of more producers since in this and other examples individuals worked harder and longer.   It is clear that rural petty commodity producers and peasant outworking families endured worse hours and conditions of labour than urban petty commodity producers.   In the early Factory System hours of work were extended and parish apprentices were forced to work at night.   But while the working day was extended, labour was also degraded.

Although they are by no means necessary conditions of an increase in the intensity of exploitation, a number of features have tended to coincide with such an increase: labour dilution, deskilling and the degradation of labour, i.e. workers' loss of control over the labour process.   It can also be related to technical change, although increased output per head is not a necessary condition for more intense exploitation and can, in any case, be increased by way of change in the organisation of work alone (3).   Some examples of these tendencies are given below.

Cheap labour has frequently been expended in a transformed labour process.   For example, production amongst the peasantry was not a service to the community but a necessary compliment to agriculture:

neither the terms of sale nor the methods of work were considered inviolable and peasant producers were more amenable to merchants' demands for increased or more regular production, goods made to specifications, or reductions in price. Indeed there was no barrier to prevent the producers from taking merchants' goods on credit and becoming outworkers, and the final degradation of outwork made possible the rise of the Factory System. At this time of greatest degradation capitalist organisers cum millowners decided to introduce machinery and thus the degradation of peasant outworkers did not delay the development of Industrial Capitalism but was part of it. The hardships of peasant outworkers financed, by way of exploitation below the level of subsistence, the rise of the Factory System.

In the peasant outworking family the cheap labour of spinning was integrated into the making of cloth, thus making rural cloth cheaper and helping to establish the relation between merchants and rural petty commodity producers. The development of the manufacturing division of labour denied outworkers all round training but gave them the chance to transfer the traditional rights of apprenticeship to a new 'craft'. For others this specialisation promoted degradation: the genesis of the unskilled worker and extension of the division of labour was accomplished in wool textiles by the employment of unapprenticed women and children. The breakdown of weaving apprenticeships paralleled the increasing entry of women in the trade. Degradation was partly a consequence of the redistribution of ancillary tasks - in fact the major part of the old weaving craft - to nonweavers: hence the epithet 'shuttle-thrower' applied to, especially, women weavers (4). Deskilling and degradation of labour were easier in the West Riding and at least partly explain the shift of the wool textile industry away from East Anglia and the West Country. By the end of the eighteenth century only those who intended to become masters took worsted apprenticeships. In both worsted and woollen, the numbers of women and children increased and they continued to be recruited into hitherto male dominated (outwork) processes as weaving followed spinning into the factories.

As the Factory System expanded so so did the sphere of 'women's work': women were classified, long before men were, as 'minders' or 'tenters'. Their occupations were relative growth areas: technical change increased the proportion of factory work which was allocated to women. This was particularly evident in the latter half of the nineteenth century as the proportion of spinners to weavers began to rise once more. In addition, the number of different tasks to which women were allocated increased throughout the century. While islands of male employment were created in the non mechanised departments of warehousing, woolsorting, warping and dressing, it was women who performed cheap labour in the jobs the men found unattractive. Where women entered skilled jobs (like weaving) these were not defined as craft occupations. The basis of women and childrens' employment was that factory labour was cheap labour. Their work created the Factory System we recognise in terms of steam power and mechanisation. Employers planned their investment in machines in the knowledge that these would be worked by women or children. For example, the proportion of children at work in worsted increased with the spread of the power loom. The Factory System generalised the need to install powered machinery, and to work child labour intensely. Their employment was made obligatory while competition was augmented by, and caused, technical change.

15

All of this is very far from the popular conception of cheap labour as the recourse of employers in labour intensive production. The historical evidence suggests that cheap labour was often employed where capitalists wished to transform the labour process on the basis of new production techniques. Indeed, there is evidence that cheap labour can be seen as the employers' response to the wider requirements of industrial change and capital accumulation. This confirms

> ... the obvious proclivity of capital at all stages of its evolution and development, but particularly in crises, to seek out cheap labour. (Hudson 1981, p.52).

New forms of cheap labour seem to have been introduced at 'moments' - some spanning several decades - of crisis in capitalist development: the shift of wool textile production to the countryside, the development of the capitalist mode of production, the relocation of the industry in the West Riding of Yorkshire, and the development of Industrial Capitalism and the Factory System. Each of these moments represented a quantitative and qualitative break in the process of capital accumulation. The former established the industry on a more productive basis with more and/or cheaper output. The latter transformed significant aspects of the industry's social relations and, frequently, of the forces of production.

These moments may be crises in other senses, for example in a more specific sense of 'crisis of capital accumulation'. Thus the capitalist organisers and millowners, many of whom failed, tried to establish their enterprises on the new basis, and to find the money to do it. Workers in general - not just, or even perhaps mainly, the workers who constituted the new form of cheap labour - found that at such moments their working lives had been changed. The workers who provided cheap labour found that their work was insecure. This insecurity was part of the employers' response to problems of capital accumulation: cheap labour was sometimes absorbed, and on other occasions rejected, when industrial change occurred. While this need not be technical change, the insecurity of cheap labour is confirmed by the nature of the work it performs, i.e. its place in the labour process.

In summary, since it became the first capitalist industry wool textiles in the UK has exhibited a tendency to resort to cheap labour. Cheap labour has been most often used where industrial change has occurred in the course of employers' attempts to raise the level of exploitation.

NOTES

(1) Of course, as with most labour migrations, the migrants' expectations were rarely fulfilled: Berthoff 1953, pp.34-5.
(2) Nor is increased productivity a sufficient condition: it does not lead to an increase in the intensity of exploitation if wages rise in proportion to output.
(3) Nor is technical change a sufficient condition for increased intensity of exploitation since wages may rise in proportion to output.
(4) 'Weaver' was already a narrower term than 'manufacturer' which implied a greater variety of skills.

3 The postwar crisis

At the end of Chapter Two it was suggested that the use of cheap labour represented capital's response to a <u>crisis</u>.   It is therefore of some interest that the UK wool textile industry entered a crisis in the postwar period.

In the postwar period the industry faced a series of threats to its markets and, therefore, to its profitability.   Nevertheless, I would suggest that the effect of these threats was cumulative and that their individual significance was frequently overemphasised in the interests of special pleading for aid for the industry.   Furthermore, I contend that the crisis was less a matter of lost markets than of the adaptions which were necessary to retain those markets.

The production of synthetics provided the first postwar challenge to wool textiles but the challenge turned out to be one of adaption to the use of the new fibres as complements rather than as substitutes.   After a period of transition it was the producers of man made fibres who faced the more significant problems of overcapacity (Cable 1979, p.13). Nevertheless, this period was a painful one for the wool textile industry. It involved changes in the labour process so that wool textile techniques could be used with the new fibres, furthermore the capital requirements of these modifications led to significant changes in industrial structure and ownership (Moor and Waddington 1980, p.10).   The 'synthetic revolution' also had more indirect effects.   It provides at least part of the explanation for the declining importance of speculation in the movement of raw material prices in the industry.   The prices of man made fibres varied to a much smaller degree than those of natural fibres, particularly wool.   Thus the greater the proportion of raw material stocks which were taken up by synthetics, the less opportunity existed for speculation.   Furthermore, there is evidence that competition from synthetics was at least partially responsible for stabilising raw wool prices and stabilising them at a lower level (Hirsh and Ellis 1974, p.73).   Whereas employers had thought to gain from successful speculation they were now forced to look more closely at the profit they earned from production.

In the 1960s new knitting techniques provided direct competition for some sectors of the wool textile industry.   The growth of (circular) knitting was in part a consequence of its suitability for synthetics (Parsonage 1973, p.61-9, 198) and we have seen that wool textile firms were able to adapt techniques in order to make use of synthetics themselves.   Furthermore, those producers who had previously supplied the weavers in the wool textile section now supplied yarn to the knitters.   This was especially true of the woolcombers and worsted

spinners who turned their attention to the production of hosiery yarn.
Weavers were however faced with direct competition, but they were able
to adapt their technology in order to compete successfully (Cable 1979,
p.25).   Both of these groups - suppliers of semimanufactures to knitting
and competitors with knitting - undertook significant programmes of
modernisation in order to adapt to the new conditions.

The growth of synthetics and (circular) knitting was related to a third
factor, changes in fashion (Parsonage 1973, p.213).   The switch to
casual clothing in the 1960s and 70s would seem to have been disastrous
for wool textiles but the industry was used to accommodating such changes
(Rainnie 1965, p.54) and was perhaps better placed than any other
textile section to do so (Parsonage 1973, p.248-9).   Worsted spinners,
for example, turned to the production of hosiery yarn and hand knitting
yarn.   Moreover fashion swung back to more traditional fabrics in the
later 70s and it was the knitters who were left with overcapacity.

Rather more serious for the wool textile producers was the permanent
loss of UK markets which followed changes in the structure and buying
policies of the UK clothing manufacture and clothing retail industries
(Hird, Herman and Taylor 1980, p.12).   Part of the problem was increased
imports, yet while imports may have had a significant impact on UK
textiles as a whole the importance of international competition varied
greatly between textile sectors.   The pro controls lobby was certainly
right to point out that wool textile imports had increased and to note
the poor competitive position of UK producers.   On the other hand, the
anti controls literature (for example, Harris and Hallas 1981;   Kenyon
1972;   see also Hird, Herman and Taylor 1980) emphasised three main
points: controls would not save jobs, increased imports did not
necessarily lead to a negative trade balance, and increased imports did
not necessarily imply a 'new international division of labour.'

On the first point it needs to be emphasised that controls on textile
imports already existed and that only a small proportion of job losses
could be attributed to rising imports (Guardian 20th May 1981, Sunday
Times 10th February 1980).   The vast majority of job losses in
textiles resulted from the employers' response to the crisis, i.e. the
adaptations aimed at improving their competitive standing.

That we cannot infer a negative trade balance from increased imports
is clear from recent figures.   For example, in the first quarter of
1982 exports of tops from the UK were more than three times the volume
and value of imports.   Exports of yarn were nearly two times the volume
and value of yarn imports.   Exports of fabrics were of roughly the same
volume as imports but more than twice their value (Confederation of
British Wool Textiles and National Wool Textile Export Corporation 1982,
p.2, see also Guardian 20 May 1981).   These comparisons suggest that the
UK wool textile industry reaped considerable benefit from the absence
of restrictions on trade and this is confirmed by statistics on the
industry's share of the world market for wool textiles.   It is also
clear that the industry did not fit neatly into the scheme of the 'new
international division of labour.'

In 'The New International Division of Labour' Frobel, Heinrichs and
Kreye admit that increased imports may not lead to a negative trade
balance (1980, p.56, 59, 74).   They also realise that imports were not
directly responsible for the majority of job losses in European textiles
(1980, p.3, 66-8, 70).   Nevertheless, they do argue that these losses
can be seen as the effects of changes in the international division of

labour (1980, p.47n). They describe the increased fragmentation of manufacturing operations, their relocation in (low cost) less developed countries and the export of goods from these countries to the developed nations. In fact UK wool textiles exhibited quite different trends: it relied on the development of foreign wool textile industries to provide it with markets (for semimanufactures) and was traditionally very reluctant to relocate abroad. Indeed foreign subsidiaries were often the first plants to be cut when rationalisation took place. Instead there is ample evidence of increased foreign ownership of wool textile firms in the UK! Finally, the majority of foreign competitors were to be found not in the less developed countries but in the United States, Italy and West Germany. (For more general criticism of Frobel et al., see Castles et al., 1977).

In sum, wool textile imports have not originated - as is popularly imagined - in less developed countries. Secondly, the major impact of international competition on UK wool textiles was felt in foreign markets. The industry relied on the existence of foreign wool textile industries for most of its exports, i.e. of semimanufactures. Its major problem was one of adjustment to the latest shifts in the market for these goods. Nevertheless, this problem - together with those caused by synthetics, knitting and fashion - amounted to a crisis similar to those experienced in earlier periods of the industry's history. The difference lay in the character of the employers' response. Earlier crises of capital accumulation led to an <u>increase</u> in production but in the modern industry it was accepted that output was stable or falling. All the same, the employers' response amounted to a crisis <u>for the workers</u> which recalls our historical narrative. The workers' problems began when the wool textile employers resolved to <u>reduce labour costs</u>.

At first sight it is difficult to understand why employers might concentrate their efforts on reducing labour costs. In the late 60s only four per cent of the total production costs of tops were accounted for by labour. Other figures were higher - 11 per cent for worsted yarn, 10 per cent for woollen yarn, 20 per cent for worsted fabrics and 16 per cent for woollen fabrics - but none suggested that employers should have been preoccupied with labour costs. With the calculation of raw material costs, however, a quite different picture emerges: between 87 per cent and 43 per cent of production costs were accounted for by the purchase of raw material (Atkins 1969, pp.111-23). Once these costs are discounted the proportion of costs which can be put down to labour increases - to over a third in top production for example - and at the end of the 70s the proportion of value added paid out in wages in wool textiles exceeded that in all manufacturing industry (NEDC 1980, p.5). On this evidence, wool textile employers would seem to have good reason for attempting to reduce labour costs (1).

It is impossible to tell from the official figures whether this was indeed the employers' response and we must therefore turn to the information provided by my <u>survey of wool textile firms</u>. A detailed description of the survey and of fieldwork methods is provided elsewhere (ASRP, pp.14-21). Here it will suffice to say that the survey covered 17 firms: 4 woolcombers, 10 worsted spinners, 2 vertically integrated worsted firms and 1 mixed worsted and woollen producer (all but the latter were located in the Bradford Metropolitan District). The woolcombers were Joseph Dawson Ltd.; G.R. Herron and Son Ltd.; Tyersal Combing Co. Ltd.; and Yorkshire Combers Ltd.,. The worsted spinners were J. Baines and Son (Bradford) Ltd.; Bancroft and Sunderland Ltd.;

19

Benson, Turner and Sons Ltd.; Bingley Mills Ltd.; Samuel Cockroft Ltd.;
J. and H. Fisher Ltd.; John Haggas Ltd.; The Multiple Fabric Co. Ltd.;
Salts Spinning Co. Ltd.; and one other firm which would not allow
unqualified use of its name (this firm also undertook recombing). The
vertically integrated firms were Hield Brothers Ltd., and Lister and Co.
Ltd.; and the 'mixed' firm was A. W. Hainsworth and Sons Ltd. The
majority of respondents were interviewed in the summer of 1978 (2).
The survey was supplemented by interviews with senior executives from
other companies - including the largest firms in the industry - and with
representatives of employers' organisations and other bodies which
serviced the industry. In addition, representatives of three wool
textile unions were interviewed together with some informants (3)
outside wool textiles.

Evidence from the survey confirms that employers made a concerted
attack on labour costs in the postwar period. The attempt to reduce
labour costs even provided the most common rationale for capital
investment in wool textiles.

One respondent told me that labour costs had always been the biggest
element in production costs and that the quickest way to cut costs was
to dispense with labour. But he added that this had been done more
frequently because, in contrast to the 1950s, knife edge profits were
now the rule (4). Another respondent thought that capital investment
might explain the preoccupation with labour costs. While labour had
always been the most important cost it began to look larger with
re-equipping, even (by demonstration) for those firms which had not
re-equipped. Yet the more usual case appears to have been where
capital investment was undertaken as part of the attack on labour costs.
For example, all the woolcombing respondents told me that French combs
produced the same volume of output as Noble combs but French combs were
bought because they required less labour. Probably only one survey
firm had re-equipped simply in order to produce more output with the
same number of workers. Most respondents confirmed the view expressed
by this senior executive:

> In the last five years there has been a very quick move
> from recruiting to dispending with labour.

To summarise, all my respondents reported that labour costs had always
been important to wool textile firms but added that they began to look
increasingly important in the 1950s. Efforts to reduce labour costs
began shortly after and this led to demanning which was to become
widespread in the 1970s. This description did not, however, cover
employers' responses to the falling demand which signalled the onset of
recession at the end of the 70s. Labour costs loomed large in the
employers' minds: one senior respondent complained that five years
earlier his firm had paid £18 a week, now they paid £40 and 'we can't
afford to have them doing nothing': most firms were contemplating a
reduction in labour costs as a first step in dealing with reduced demand.
The result was accelerated demanning: one informant had talked of a
'very quick move - to dispensing with labour' in the decade before 1978
but in the four years after 1978 his company had reduced its workforce
by half, from 10,000 to 5,000.

Wool textile employers concentrated on keeping unit labour costs down
by introducing labour saving technology and by remanning even without
re-equipping. Few wool textile firms took the alternative route, even
when re-equipping of increasing output. The majority reduced their

demand for labour and the wool textile industry has been an example of what Jordan (1982, p.114) calls 'automation', i.e. more or less stable output with reduced employment.

THE WORKERS' CRISIS

Did the employers' attempt to reduce labour costs meet with success? One managing director calculated that wage costs in his firm increased by sixty three per cent in four years. On the other hand, this was less than two thirds the rate of inflation over the period and roughly half the rate of increase in other costs. Most of the more advanced firms in my survey reduced the proportion of costs stemming from labour to levels below those indicated by the Wool Textile Economic Development Committee (EDC). It could be argued, however, that a fall in the proportion of total costs stemming from labour might be explained by the inflation of overheads by depreciation allowances for new machinery (e.g. Briscoe 1971, p.70; Miles 1968, p.33; Textile Council 1969, p.119). It is therefore obvious that more detailed evidence is required, for one thing it is clear that there are several different ways of measuring employers' success in reducing labour costs.

Employers are ultimately interested in reducing unit labour costs, i.e. the total cost of employing labour divided by the number of units of output produced. It is through unit costs that labour costs affect competitivity and profitability. The term average labour costs refers to the weekly or hourly rate paid by an employer in wages and the other expenses of employing labour, for example national insurance contributions. The total cost of employing labour is calculated by taking into account both average labour costs and the numbers employed. Thus in wool textiles employers tried to reduce unit labour costs by reducing employment - this affected both the wage and nonwage elements of total labour costs - while not allowing output to drop by the same proportion as employment, and preventing average labour costs from rising in line with increased output per head. In controlling average labour costs they had no direct influence on nonwage costs and therefore tried to prevent wages from rising. We will now examine the employers' achievement in more detail, beginning with employment.

Lipson notes the 'remarkable steadiness of employment' in wool textiles from the mid nineteenth century to the mid twentieth century which was accompanied by a more than three fold increase in output. He also remarks, however, that production was 'remarkably steady' after World War Two while employment fell by two thirds (Lipson 1953, p.169). In fact employment in wool textiles increased gradually up to the mid 1920s. This was followed by a gentle decline up to World War Two leaving the level of employment in 1939 only slightly below the 1901 figure. At the end of the War employment was less than sixty per cent of the prewar total but then rose quickly and had almost reached prewar levels by 1950. It was from this date, therefore, that the most drastic decline in wool textile employment took place. Between 1951 and 1959 it fell by fourteen per cent (Lipson 1953, p.169, Rainnie 1965, p.44-6), and fell at an accelerating rate throughout the 60s and 70s. By June 1982 employment in the industry was down to almost half of the 1975 total (for details of trends in employment and output, see ASRP, pp.228-53).

This reduction in employment was achieved by a combination of reduced employment within firms and a reduced number of firms. Some firms maintained output with a smaller workforce while others went out of business.   It should be pointed out, however, that these changes in industrial structure did not always favour the larger firms.   Indeed small firms may have been more successful in maintaining output while reducing employment.   This does not, of course, apply to all small firms but there is evidence to suggest that small wool textile firms were the most profitable (ICC 1979).   This may be because smaller companies included those with the fastest growth rates, or because they occupied a secure place in the industry's structure.   It may be that small firms serviced larger companies giving the latter an incentive to keep them viable and not to eliminate them by way of competition or acquisition.   For example, the number of woolcombing firms in the UK in 1978 was 15 per cent of the 1965 figure but many of the casualties were very large companies while small combers remained (indeed one was actually started up!).   Furthermore, even where a small firm was acquired by a large group it was the rule for this firm to continue to operate as an independent organisation and subsidiaries of large diversified groups were generally free to trade with outside competitors.

These peculiarities of industrial structure may well be a consequence of the vulnerability of wool textiles to fluctuations (not just in raw material prices).   These fluctuations could be absorbed by small firms. This was particularly the case in worsted where commission work was common (it was not, of course, confined to small firms).   The system whereby a firm processed a client's product existed in all worsted sectors and where vertical integration had taken place the independence of companies working on commission was preserved.   The commission system allowed large firms to avoid carrying extra workers or stocks through a recession since they could 'put out' work in the case of a sudden, or temporary, increase in demand.

It should not be thought, however, that small wool textile firms operated in the interstices of large scale capital.   Those small firms which relied on holding a corner of the market by way of specialisation were most likely to fail.   In contrast, where there was a tendency for small firms to be squeezed out of a larger market, producers in other sectors (suppliers or customers) acted to restore competition - as did the spinners who helped to establish the small woolcomber referred to above.

Whatever the fate of the smaller firms, total output in the industry has fallen.   According to the Wool Industry Bureau of Statistics, overall employment in production had fallen to a quarter of its 1948 level in 1980 but tops and yarn output was down by less than 50 per cent. Weaving output fell more dramatically but only in woollen weaving was the fall in production commensurate with the fall in employment. Furthermore, in most sections the most severe drop in production occurred in the later 70s whereas employment had been falling for a much longer period.

A more precise guide to the relationship between falling output and employment is provided by comparisons of output per head.   These figures suggest a periodic pattern which can be related to, amongst other variables, the wool textile trade cycle.   In general, output per head increased slowly up to the later 60s.   This gentle improvement came to an end with the creation of overcapacity and a lack of impetus to investment in the 1969-71 slump.   Recovery followed in 1971-2 but lack of demand adversely affected output per head until it began to increase in advance of recovery in 1977.   In both periods worsted spinning seems to have led the industry in improving output per head as demand recovered. Increases in output per head were most marked in the late 60s and particularly in 1971-2 and 1975-6. Decline set in once more in the late 70s with the beginning of another recession.

Nevertheless, the operation of the wool textile trade cycle varies between sectors and so do trends in output per head. For example, 1978-80 seems to have been a 'good' period for worsted weaving but a disastrous one for woolcombing. Furthermore, output per head increased consistently in some sectors but not in others. Woolcombing performed better than most up to the late 70s while worsted spinning showed the best overall performance. Woollen spinning showed little or no trend towards increased output per head throughout the period. By the end of the 70s output per head in this section had fallen back towards the 1968 figure.

Between 1980 and 1981 production of tops increased by 1.2 per cent while production personnel in woolcombing - i.e. the majority of employees in tops production - fell by 28.1 per cent. In worsted spinning, production fell by only 1.7 per cent whereas employment fell by 5.5 per cent. Furthermore, the gains made in worsted output per head 1980-81 continued with an upturn in production in 1982. There was, however, no evidence of improvement in the woollen section.

Inferior performance in woollen production has been a feature of output per head comparisons since at least 1958 and woollen continued to disappoint the employers' representatives and the Wool Textile EDC in subsequent years. Woollen spinning in particular shed personnel more slowly than any other section but nonetheless reduced output. In woollen weaving, on the other hand, there was a greater reduction in employment but a much larger fall in output.

At the beginning of the current decade there seemed to be no signs of change in the performance of the woollen section. Between 1980 and 1981 woollen yarn output fell by 11.8 per cent while employment only fell by 3.2 per cent. These peculiarities of woollen production, especially of woollen spinning, are of considerable importance to later discussion of the characteristics of the wool textile labour force and labour process.

As regards the wool textile industry as a whole, the Atkins Report - commissioned by the Wool EDC - demanded a minimum 5 per cent per annum improvement in output per head by the mid 70s (Atkins 1969, p.225). In spite of the poor performance of woollen spinning and weaving this target was nearly reached. In the middle and later 70s increases in output per head in woolcombing and worsted spinning exceeded the revised Wool Textile EDC targets (NEDC 1979, p.7). This trend continued into the 70s but with some hiccups caused by the recession (including the effects of Temporary Employment Subsidy, see NEDC 1980, p.21).

While the overall tendency was for the rate of increase in output per head to accelerate, there were periods of particularly dramatic change in which this rate exceeded the trend for textiles as a whole. While 1958-63 saw little improvement in wool textile output per head there were significant increases between 1963 and 1968 (Parsonage 1973, p.290; Butterworth 1967, p.19). The period between 1968 and 1973 was better still (Fishwick and Cornu 1975, p.2; NEDC 1977, p.10), but this rate of improvement was not reached again until the later 70s (Census of Production 1978). These periods approximate to those described in the analysis of the performance of individual sectors as regards output per head above. In sum, the increases in output per head achieved in

the postwar period were actually achieved in shorter spans amounting to
no more than ten years.   In these ten years output per head was
increased by an amount equivalent to that achieved by a century of
development before the war.

A reduction in employment does not lead to a fall in <u>unit labour costs</u>
if output falls by the same proportion, holding average labour costs
constant.   Similarly, there will be no reduction in <u>unit</u> labour costs
if average labour costs rise in line with increased output per head, but
UK employers were so successful in preventing average labour costs from
rising that they remained at a lower level than in most competing
countries.

The calculation of average labour costs includes the widest possible
range of benefits which might be expected to accrue to workers from
increased output per head.   In the late 60s average labour costs in
UK wool textiles were lower than those in any EEC country (Atkins 1969,
p.xxvi) and were increasing <u>more slowly</u> than those of competitors
(Atkins 1969, p.105).   Little happened to change this picture in the
succeeding decade and a half.   EEC figures for the early 70s confirmed
that wool had some of the lowest average labour costs amongst UK
industries and (still) the lowest average labour costs of all EEC wool
textile industries (Statistical Office of the EEC 1975, p.307).
Ireland entered the EEC figures at this time with slightly lower wool
textile average labour costs than the UK.   Nevertheless, UK wool
textile average labour costs remained the second lowest in the EEC
while wool textiles had the lowest hourly labour costs of any industry
in the UK except for leather and leather goods, footwear and clothing
(Statistical Office of the EEC 1978, p.116).   As the 70s progressed,
moreover, there was no sign of an increase in the UK's relative average
labour costs.

In 1981 the Department of Industry found, to its surprise, that in a
comparison of European wool textile industries,

> The remarkable factor is in the labour cost -
> the Continentals are paying nearly double the
> combined UK labour rate and social charges...
> (Department of Industry 1981, p.117).

This differential was reflected in lower wages in the UK.   Wool textiles
appears to have been even less inclined than other UK industries to pay
increased wages for increased output per head and it has certainly been
less inclined to reward more productive labour than its EEC competitors.
Yet the greatest proportion of UK average labour costs were wages and
nearly 90 per cent of labour costs - only 70 per cent in Italy - were
direct, indicating very low social security payments by employers
(Statistical Office of the EEC 1978, p.178).   This would suggest that
UK wages and earnings may have been closer to EEC levels than average
labour costs were.   At one time this may indeed have been the case.
In the early 70s the absence of nonwage labour costs in the UK widened
the gap between the UK and France, West Germany and Italy (NEDC 1973,
p.32), however earnings were much closer to the level of average labour
costs once the cost of living was taken into account.   Comparisons of
<u>real</u> earnings showed that the differential between the UK and other
European countries more closely approached the gap exhibited by comparison
of hourly labour costs (NEDC 1973, p.30-1).   Furthermore, in the 1970s
low hourly earnings became a much more important factor in accounting
for low hourly labour costs in the UK.

Wool textile trade union leaders seem to have assumed that decreased employment in the industry would be matched by some increase in rewards to those workers who remained. At one time this assumption may have been based on the widespread use of piecework in the industry: increased output per head necessitates an automatic increase in earnings under piecework. Yet in later years it seems that trade union leaders have expected that wholesale changes in wages structures would follow 'modernisation.' This would seem to be the only possible explanation for these leaders' approval of the Atkins Report and of subsequent plans for 'streamlining' wool textiles:

> Workers need not be unduly alarmed at the predicted trend
> for it does not mean wholesale redundancies ... the
> industry's labour force may be smaller, but it will
> certainly be more highly-paid and working conditions are
> bound to improve ... /Atkins' proposals/ are designed to
> make the industry more efficient and enable the unions to
> negotiate the better wages and conditions which textile
> workers deserve. (Jack Peel, Secretary of the NAUTT,
> Telegraph and Argus 10 June 1966).

It is clear that this faith in the employers was misplaced. Their attempt to prevent average labour costs from rising was concentrated in an effort to hold down wages.

The wool textile industry paid below average weekly earnings for the textile industry as a whole - even though a lower proportion of value added was paid in wages in wool (NEDC 1980, p.5) - and there were no signs of the gap narrowing. Furthermore, comparisons with non textile industries in the UK showed that, although weekly earnings looked more healthy than hourly wool textile earnings (because of long hours of work), there was no sign of relative improvement in either category.

The overall trend was for the gap between hourly earnings in wool and in all manufacturing industry to increase slightly. For example, hourly earnings for men were 18 per cent lower in wool in 1968 and 5 per cent lower for full time women (Atkins 1969, p.25), but by 1978 earnings for women were rather more than 5 per cent lower while earnings for men were nearly 20 per cent lower than the average.

Even these figures concealed the extent of low pay in wool. Fifty per cent, and rising, of full time male manual workers in wool textiles earned less than the average for that group (NEDC 1977, p.60). Furthermore, low pay was especially prevalent in certain regions, particularly in those regions where the industry was concentrated (Parsonage 1973, p.406; Statistical Office of the EEC 1981, p.20). Finally, pay was even lower than the industry or regional average in certain wool textile sections. Worsted spinning jobs were amongst the worst paid and large gaps existed between firms. Worsted weaving firms, for example, paid nearly forty per cent higher wages than integrated worsted firms (Moor and Waddington 1980, p.17).

THE EMPLOYERS' FAILURE

It only remains for us to consider whether the employers' success in reducing unit labour costs brought them success in dealing with the postwar crisis in the industry. Their response to crisis was an attempt to pass on the problems of the industry to its workforce. Employment was reduced but without any reward for the workers who remained and who had increased output. Nevertheless, it could be argued that the employers were less than successful in passing on their problems. While profitability tends to be restored only after an adjustment lag (c.f. the challenge from synthetics and knitting), it may be that the loss of markets to foreign competitors continued to adversely affect profits (for trends in profitability see ICC 1979; NEDC 1978; 1979(a)). The employers' support for import controls (in particular through the Wool and Clothing Action Committee, WOOLTAC) might seem to support this assumption but why, given the changes described above, should they still experience difficulties?

A recent Department of Industry report expressed great consternation that, in spite of the lower level of labour costs in the UK, there was 'no proportionate advantage visible in the UK costings compared with those of European competitors' (Department of Industry 1981, p.17). The Report concluded that

> ... the primary textile products are competitive in relation to direct cost comparison but since the anticipated advantages from lower labour costs are not evident, the differentials are narrow.' (Department of Industry 1981, p.18).

In fact this paradox has fascinated commentators since Atkins (1969, p.27), but why should a decade pass without a solution to the problem? The Department of Industry listed all the explanations which employers usually offered for their poor performance - high interest rates, strong pound, unfair trading practices and subsidies to foreign producers - together with the Wool Textile EDC's particular favourite, poor sales technique (Department of Industry 1981, p.2). Others remarked on the industry's tendency to dissipate resources in distributed dividends and payments on borrowed capital, but the Department of Industry report was not primarily concerned with a scarcity of cash for investment since it noted 'substantial re-equipment in productive capacity' (Department of Industry 1981, p.2). Indeed, capital investment was substantial, but a great deal of this investment was dependent on the existence of government subsidies to the industry.

Increased competition from overseas - more than any other component of the crisis - led commentators to conceptualize the crisis as one of low productivity and profitability. This was, it might be argued, largely because the problems of postwar wool textiles seemed to confirm the popular image of the industry. It was seen as a moribund relic of the nineteenth century which would disappear leaving its workers to find alternative (and better) jobs while their employers found better investment opportunities. It seemed to be accepted that the production of wool textiles should be left to other countries which would enjoy comparative cost advantages in an industry which was 'backward' and 'labour intensive'. In the 1960s at least, wool textiles was counted in the list of 'traditional' industries and only earned attention from the Government to the extent that its relocation within the UK might provide short term regional aid to areas like the North East of England. By the 1970s it was becoming apparent that regional aid might be needed in West Yorkshire as well. As the wool textile recession began - in advance of the general recession - it was realised that many of the people who were losing wool textile jobs weren't finding any alternative jobs, let alone better ones. The operation of comparative costs might seem to involve a considerable amount of self sacrifice if this was the case, and attention was focused on the causes of the decline. It was inevitable that these causes should be found in the 'backward' nature of wool textiles. For example the 'low productivity' which had led

26

successive governments to accept that wool textiles <u>should</u> disappear became the predominant explanation for the industry's problems. How much did government contribute to the attempt to solve these problems?

Government aid for the 'modernisation' of wool textiles was seen to be necessary given the unique financial structure of the industry: wool textile companies traditionally relied on short term borrowing, particularly overdrafts. It is likely that their reluctance to issue shares stemmed from a concern to retain control within the existing ownership structure. Apart from the problem of impatient banks, short term borrowing makes companies more vulnerable to variations in interest rates (but not, of course, in share prices). Most importantly it may place limits on the funding available for long term capital investment plans. At any rate, much of the investment in wool textiles was actually undertaken with other people's money - bank depositors' and taxpayers!

The extent of government funding to improve productivity and profitability has been well documented (for example, see Moor and Waddington 1980) and there is no need to provide a full account here. Nevertheless, it may be that important aspects of the effects of government intervention have been neglected. Whether by accident or design, government aid was unequally distributed across the industry. According to one of the most senior executives in wool textiles, government aid was of little benefit to smaller firms. Small firms did not qualify for assistance in the purchase of the cheaper (i.e. second hand) machinery they could afford. Furthermore, they had difficulty in 'topping up' government grants for new investment. My informant also pointed out that small firms needed to realise the benefits of such investment quickly and could not afford to take the risk of trade being slack at this time. It may be, therefore, that government intervention produced changes in the structure of the wool textile industry (5). In fact the only evidence of substantial assistance to small firms confirms this impression: most aid to small firms was given under those provisions of the Wool Textile Scheme which were intended to help firms to go out of business.

In sum, government aid accounted for nearly 30 per cent of wool textile investment between 1973 and 1977 (NEDC 1976). My informant concluded that, over the same period, government money had tipped the scales in favour of a lot of planned investment programmes and it is possible that aid provided the major inpetus to new investment.

Yet even though government subsidies were generous, it is still possible that capital investment in wool textiles was inadequate and/or misdirected. Problems of low productivity remained. This was the main conclusion of the Department of Industry in its report cited above. The report noted that labour was not being used productively because employers were reluctant to scrap old machinery (Department of Industry 1981, p.40). This would lower the rate of increase in output per head and reduce the beneficial effects of lower average labour costs on unit costs. The report also complained of lost markets creating low capacity utilisation (Department of Industry 1981, p.17). Excess capacity will adversely affect output per machine rather than output per head since the number of machines 'needed' to produce each unit is increased. What is the significance of these two explanations of low productivity?

The Wool Industry Bureau of Statistics produces data on output per machine and these figures suggest that output per head increased at a greater rate than output per machine. This is entirely at variance with the predictions of the Atkins Report. The Report expected that most of the increase in productivity which was planned for the nineteen 70s would come from more productive machinery rather than increased 'manual productivity'. In fact, the ratio between the two was predicted at over 4:1 (Atkins 1969, p.xxxiii). In the event, Atkins underestimated increased 'manual productivity' in worsted spinning, worsted weaving and woollen weaving, while considerably overestimating increased 'machine productivity' in woolcombing (where it actually declined, c.f. Atkins 1969, p.226) (6).

How much of the 'drag' on 'machine productivity' can be put down to lack of capital investment rather than to the effects of excess capacity? Official statistics become useless at this point. Although the Wool Industry Bureau of Statistics does produce information on 'machinery activity' which gives a guide to the extent of overcapacity, there is no equivalent series which would allow us to estimate the contribution of old machinery to low 'machine productivity.' Official computations of capital investment, for example, only measure net spending thus the 'negative investment' of 1963-7 (Atkins 1969, p.73) actually concealed some re-equipping. Information on vintages of machinery would be of more help but no comprehensive series is available (c.f. Atkins 1969, p.11, 78). In sum we are unable to distinguish between the two explanations offered by the Department of Industry (1981, p.17, 40) for low productivity: output per machine may be reduced by the use of old machinery as well as the existence of excess capacity. In fact our difficulties reflect those experienced by the wool textile employers since the two explanations offered by the Department of Industry are not independent. The risk of excess capacity may lead employers to preserve old machinery. Briscoe describes the conflicting pressures which affected their attitudes to 'machine productivity' as

> ... the basic problems of the traditional sectors of the
> textile industry: a loss in market share which had led to
> an under utilisation of capacity and has therefore produced
> a disincentive to investment, at the same time as the
> pressure on margins, together with the availability of
> more productive machinery, has provided an incentive to
> invest. (Briscoe 1971, p.69).

There is clearly no simple explanation for the productivity problems of wool textiles, but our discussion of the postwar crisis and the employers' response may provide the basis for such an explanation.

Where output is increasing unit costs may automatically be reduced, but when employers are anxious to avoid overcapacity they must take positive action to reduce them. As we have seen, wool textile employers took this positive action when they attempted to reduce unit labour costs in order to deal with threats to competivity and profitability. They concentrated on reducing their labour requirements either with or without capital investment. The capital investment they did undertake may have been largely labour saving. They did not buy more productive machines which required the same (or even an enlarged) workforce and it may be that the failure of their strategy can be measured in terms of low productivity. Nevertheless, I do not believe that this failure arose solely, or even perhaps mainly, from the employers' fear of generating overcapacity.

The employers' inability to increase machine (rather than manual) productivity stemmed from their concern with the level of wages (see Chapter Five). Investment in labour saving machinery was the more direct method of reducing their wage bills while an even more direct method was to reduce employment without capital investment of any kind. But the same end could have been achieved with investment in more productive machinery since such investment need not lead to increased output. If existing machinery is replaced by fewer, although more productive, machines output will not be increased. Furthermore, there will also be (indirect) labour savings and a fall in the total wage bill. The crucial difference is that more productive machinery also leads to reductions in other costs (although not raw materials). It is these reductions - in particular reductions in the cost of capital - which lead commentators to put such store on increased machine productivity.

The use to which government subsidies were put gives further proof that employers were ruled by an obsession with wages rather than fear of overcapacity. The existence of subsidies obviated the need to retain old machines (7) yet employers still avoided investing in more productive machinery. It seems that they prefered to invest in machinery which was no more productive but which allowed them to dispense with labour (8). But for the availability of government aid, there would have been much less capital investment and (since up to now we have been dealing in generalities) none of the examples of investment in more productive machinery which did take place (9). Nonetheless, employers would have continued to reduce employment in an effort to reduce labour costs. In sum it was the employers' concern with wages that led to their failure to solve the problems created by the postwar crisis.

While UK wool textile employers' preoccupation with wage bills did little to improve their competitive standing (10), it certainly led to an increase in the intensity of exploitation. Given the conclusions reached in Chapter Two, it would appear that this is the wool textile industry's habitual response to a crisis of capital accumulation. The modern example differs from those given in Chapter Two only in that it appears to have been rather less successful and that output and employment was no longer growing. Modern employers raised the level of exploitation by reducing their labour requirements without increasing the wages of the workers who remained. Trade union leaders acquiesced to the employers' wishes in this as in other respects:

> We're just as good as our inheritance, the Luddites.
> If you're Luddites you loose your jobs. We must
> fight for a future for the industry ... and encourage
> the employers to do that too.

But without the expected recompense:

> The industry got what it wanted under the Industry Act.
> We've lost half the jobs and there has been no relative
> improvement in wages.

In the last chapter we found that (historical) instances of cheap labour were frequently distinguished by an increase in the intensity of exploitation. Yet evidence of the latter need not lead us to conclude that cheap labour is involved. Cheap labour will only be required if work has become less attractive, either as a possible effect of a higher degree of exploitation or following the actions taken by competitors for labour. For example, they might raise wages while wool textile pay is merely maintained.

We know that individual workers have increased output. Indeed the figures are probably misleading in that output per head would have been increased more sharply but for the employers' reluctance to scrap worn out machinery. We also know that in some cases increased output per head was achieved without capital investment. We would therefore expect, given no increase in (relative) wages, that the jobs concerned would have become less attractive. Nevertheless, we require more substantial evidence before confirming that this was indeed the case. The following chapter will therefore describe, in some detail, what has been happening to wool textile work in recent years.

NOTES

(1) Although the proportion of value added paid out in wages was lower than in other textile industries (NEDC, 1980, p.5). Note that all textile industries had low value added totals (see, for example, Cable 1979, p.39).

(2) Although the biggest decline in employment occurred after 1979 there were signs that the <u>wool textile</u> recession - although not the general recession - had begun by the time the fieldwork was completed at the end of 1978. It will become clear in later chapters that the fieldwork was conducted at the end of an era in the history of the industry. Changes in subsequent years were of a very different quality to those experienced before 1978. It may be that this was the last point at which useful research of this kind could have been undertaken.

(3) Here and in subsequent chapters I will make use of the now conventional distinction between <u>informants</u> and <u>respondents</u>. The latter applies solely to the owners and employees of the firms included in the survey of wool textile companies.

(4) It was not simply the general crisis which concentrated the employers' attention on labour costs. Labour costs are more important to some firms than others and so the opportunity for cost cutting in this way varies from firm to firm. For example, labour costs were especially large for those (like the woolcombers) who frequently worked on commission but this was less true of those (like the spinners) who bought expensive raw materials. But changes took place in the postwar period which tended to minimise these differences. Thus one worsted spinning respondent related the increased importance of labour costs to the rise of synthetics: by the late 50s and early 60s it was clear that profits were to be made in the conversion of raw materials rather than in speculation. This focused attention on labour costs.

(5) Although not to the same extent as in the cotton industry. Government aid to cotton (in the 50s and 60s) was on a much larger scale with a greater proportion of investment being funded by grants. Furthermore in cotton, rationalisation was achieved by way of the intervention of the two large fibre producers, ICI and Courtaulds, who were helped by the government to streamline the industry. Government plans for rationalising cotton have a long history, stretching back to the prewar years. Wool has traditionally shown more self reliance. The Woolcombers Mutual Association, for example, helped ailing companies to go out of business from the 1920s. The association also arranged for redundant

machinery to be scrapped lest it be bought by new firms
intending to begin production of tops.

(6) Between 1975 and 1980 - i.e. outside the planning period
covered by Atkins - the pattern was repeated in worsted
spinning, worsted weaving and woollen weaving. However
in combing there was no increase in 'manual productivity'
and both kinds of productivity declined in woollen spinning.

(7) Although it may be that the companies which did not scrap
worn out machinery were those which were not in receipt
of subsidy.

(8) Of course this was not the only explanation employers
gave for capital investment decisions. Many respondents
reported that re-equipping had followed directly from the
need to adapt to new fibres and end uses.

(9) Although it could be argued that scarce funds might actually
make this more likely. Employers would be more concerned
to minimise capital costs and so would ensure that _fewer_
machines were purchased while hoping to maintain output.
In this respect it is worth noting that those companies
which _did_ buy more productive machines with the help of
subsidies tended to _increase_ output.

(10) C.f. Department of Industry 1981, p.39 and Winyard 1980,
p.34 where a rather different point is made. It is argued
that low wages _lead_ to low productivity. This assumption
is not confirmed by the figures on output and wages quoted
above where it is shown that while individual output
increased relative wages did not. I do not wish to suggest
that the industry's productivity problems stemmed from low
wages but rather from the employers' _obsession_ with keeping
wages low. While investing in more productive machinery
makes possible _some_ increase in wages without a proportionate
rise in unit labour costs, this is also the case where labour
saving machinery is bought or where employment is reduced
without capital investment of any kind. I therefore disagree
with the Department of Industry and the trade union leaders
who seemed to think that investment in more productive
machinery would necessarily be accompanied by wage increases.
Rather, employers who undertook this kind of investment were
less likely to see wages as the only element of unit costs
over which they had some control.

4 Working in wool textiles

PAY AND CONDITIONS

For most of 1978 the minimum wage for the majority of manual workers in
my survey was £42 for a forty hour week rising to a £50 minimum for
overlookers.   There was, however, some variation above these minima
since the national negotiations from which they were derived
established different minimum rates for each of several grades.   Other
variations arose from the fact that the negotiations for woolcombing
workers were conducted quite separately, and at a different time of
the year, to those for the majority of wool textile workers.

  Most of the firms in my survey, including all the woolcombers, paid
basic wages at the agreed minimum levels.   Of the remaining firms, one
or two paid a little more but a minority actually paid less and one firm
had no guaranteed minimum wage at all.   According to NUDBTW informants
several firms in the industry paid below the negotiated minimum wage
but all of these firms were nonunion.   My survey showed that this was
not always the case: at least one <u>unionised</u> firm paid below the
minimum rate.   Other sources confirmed the existence of firms with many
union members paying less than the negotiated minimum.   In 1979 one
group of workers reported that their basic wage was £25 for forty hours
(<u>Bradford Black</u> 2, 4 May 1979) when they should have been guaranteed
at least £47 a week.   Subminimal rates were not abolished in succeeding
years.   In 1981, by which time the agreed minimum for operatives had
been raised to £57, another group of workers reported wages varying
between £25 and £35 per week (<u>Telegraph and Argus</u> 2 September 1981) and
reliable sources reported cases of juveniles being paid £15 a week.
But these last examples referred to earnings and not to basic wages.
Before we can describe the earnings of workers in my survey in 1978 we
must look at the other elements which made up their weekly wages.   I
will begin by considering premiums.

  Up to 1978 premiums - whether production linked incentives, overtime
or shift premiums - were calculated on lower rates than the basic wages
quoted above.   In that year these were set at £38 for operatives and
warehousemen and £46 for overlookers and technicians.   In the 1978
negotiations levels of bonus or shift payments were referred to plant
level negotiation but most firms in my survey were paying overtime rates,
if not piecerates, at the level agreed in earlier national negotiations.
These were time and a third for the first two hours overtime (i.e. over
an eight hour day or a forty hour week);   time and a half for all
overtime beyond this until 4.00 p.m. on Saturdays;   and double time
for the rest of the weekend.   The night shift premium - for the hours
between 8 p.m. and 6 a.m. - was 20 per cent but some firms were still
paying the old premium of 16.5 per cent while at least one paid 25 per
cent in addition to a 25 per cent shift allowance for workers on a

rotating or 'continental' shift system.   But there was no such unity
in regard to incentives.

The method of calculating production linked payments at one firm of
worsted spinners gives some idea of the variety of incentives which
were possible in wool textiles: piece rates were paid at so much per
'doff' (1).   Production bonuses, however, were paid on a weight basis (2)
in groups: in drawing by 'set' and in spinning by department.   The
calculation of incentives could become so complicated that, as at
another company, a clerk was required to spend all his time working out
the payments due to each worker.   This small firm paid piecerates to
all its operatives and used a complicated list of rates as the basis for
individual calculation of premiums.

The level of incentives, i.e. their proportional contribution to
earnings, varied as much as the methods used in their calculation.
In some firms they amounted to very little, more like an attendance
allowance.   In others, especially traditional worsted spinners, the
bulk of the wage was production linked.   At one firm piecerates made
up all of the wage.   Similarly, while bonuses were guaranteed at some
firms, at this firm the employer did not guarantee a minimum wage.
My respondent claimed that they had an agreement with the union which
allowed them to pay less than the negotiated minimum if the worker
concerned had not reached the level of output required by the piecelists.

While variations in incentive payments sometimes meant that the agreed
minimum wage bore little relation to average earnings, the most common
explanation for this discrepancy lay in variations in hours of work.
Precisely because of the low hourly rate of pay, few workers were
content with a forty hour week.   While this meant that the relative
contribution of overtime premiums could be high, it also meant that some
workers were working for much longer than the basic week on which
minimum wages were agreed.   In 1978, according to the secretary of one
employers' organisation, the average week worked by wool textile workers
was $44\frac{1}{2}$ hours, 46 hours for woolcombing workers.   I do not know if these
figures included the hours of part time or nonmanual workers but they
certainly bore scant resemblance to the actual weekly hours worked by
employees in my survey.   It must be remembered, in addition, that these
were not the hours worked under normal trading conditions.   Most firms
in the survey had reduced hours in response to slack demand, nevertheless
only a small minority of manual workers were doing forty hours a week
while only part timers were working less than forty hours.   The great
majority worked fifty hours or more while some, including some nightshift
workers, did in excess of seventy hours.   Given that the majority of
firms in the survey were not working weekends, these long weekly hours
meant very long shifts.

The non employer sources I consulted were agreed that overtime was
compulsory in wool textiles and saw two twelve hour shifts for five
days a week as almost universal.   These sources included a report on
one of the woolcombing firms in my survey prepared by the Advisory,
Conciliation and Arbitration Service (ACAS).   The report blamed long
hours as well as low pay for the industry's labour turnover problems.
In my survey only three firms were content to operate an ordinary day
shift of 8 or even 83/4 hours plus perhaps an evening shift (3).   At
least ten firms, including all the woolcombers, were working permanent
night shifts of 12 or more hours, and thirteen firms were working at
least one shift which exceeded 10 hours for 5 days a week.

How did long hours affect earnings?   At one woolcombing firm
operatives were earning £85 on the night shift and £80.2p. on the day
shift, but to get these wages workers put in $62\frac{1}{2}$ and $65\frac{1}{2}$ hours
respectively.   While few firms in my survey could match these hours
in prevailing trading conditions, at other companies (especially spinners)
production linked payments played a larger part (4) although the same
stricture about reduced demand applies here.   In sum, few operatives
in my survey were earning more than the workers employed by the
woolcombing firm and most were earning less than £60 a week.   This
figure does not include occasional timekeeping or attendance bonuses
but neither does it take account of involuntary time off, 'short time'.

How secure were the earnings of the workers in my survey?   For many
years, short time had been the wool textile employers' normal response
to a fall in output (5).   This might even include a fall in output
which was unrelated to demand: more than one firm in my survey had had
a period of short time which coincided with the installation or
reorganisation of machinery.   Short time might consist of a three day
week or possibly of lay offs on alternate weeks.   It might even amount
to reduced overtime: complete loss of overtime might actually cut a
wool textile workers' normal hours and wages by 50 per cent.   Thus,

> Once we get down to 40 hours our biggest competitor is
> the dole.   (Personnel Officer, Worsted Spinning firm).

At least three of the firms in the survey had suspended overtime,
another had recently undergone two periods of short time and one
company was working a three day week (6).   Nevertheless, it was
sometimes suggested that short time was no longer as frequent an
occurrence as it once was: one union informant claimed that three months
short time a year was the rule in the 50s.   But an officer of one of
the employers' organisations still saw short time as the industry's
initial response to recession, and as far as most of the unions were
concerned this was as it should be.   For example, the Managers and
Overlookers (the worsted spinning overlookers' union) kept watch for
firms which closed down one plant while another worked overtime.   An
informant from this union claimed they would never allow overtime if a
company was involved in any kind of cutback and that any redundancies
must be preceded by short time (7).   Other unions, for example the
NUGMW, seemed to be powerless to enforce any period of short time.
One respondent claimed that his company - which employed members of the
General and Municipal's woolcombing section - never reduced hours if a
slump in trade occurred but always reduced the number of employees
instead:

> I've never understood why the unions put up with it.

He explained that the company was never forced to make redundancy
payments since he could easily find a quarter of the workforce with less
than two years' service: they had recently made fifteen men redundant
at no cost (to the company) at all.   At another woolcombing firm the
response was more cautious.   The respondent claimed that they no longer
sacked workers in an ordinary seasonal 'quiet spell'.   During the
miners' strike in 1974 they had sacked the whole night shift and staffed
up again afterwards.   This would be harder to do now but they would
resort to redundancies if they thought the slack period was going to
last longer than a month.   Outside my survey there were numerous
examples of wool textile firms which sacked workers in a minor and
temporary recession and even when re-equipping (Telegraph and Argus

9 January 1968).   In the survey at least two firms had never had short
time but both had sacked workers.   Indeed most of the other firms had
used redundancies as part of their response to reduced demand in the
past.

Redundancies were not the only alternative to short time.   Several
firms in the survey had put some of their machinery under wraps.   This
was as undesirable as short time if you were a pieceworker.   As a
NUDBTW informant pointed out, putting machinery in mothballs reduced the
number of machines operated by each worker and therefore their earnings.
Thus whether management chose to introduce short time, to make some
workers redundant or to put some machines under wraps, the wool textile
workers' income was always insecure.   This must be taken into account
when comparing the weekly earnings quoted above to those in other
industries.

We have seen that the workers in my survey were expected to be at work
for long hours each day and for many hours a week.   But for how much
of this time were they expected to be actually working?   The general
rule was that an operative worked continuously unless he could find
another worker to relieve him:

> At the moment we work twelve hours without a break unless
> someone relieves you but there is no one to provide relief
> where a firm doesn't have 'mobile workers' ... This problem
> will come up at the next set of negotiations but we must
> remember that the machines have to run twenty four hours
> a day.   (union official)

> Each worker only (sic) works eleven and a half hours.
> However he must get himself relieved for his break and
> therefore the machinery never stops running.   (Personnel
> manager, worsted spinning firm)

It must be remembered that this was the rule for meals as well as
any other kind of break: most workers in my survey ate when and if they
could find someone to relieve them.   In most of the mills I visited
ovens were provided on the shop floor.   Where canteens existed they
were used mainly by salaried staff.

If workers were not given any official breaks in their long hours of
work, what opportunity was there for them to take unofficial breaks?
One of the employers' organisations had an agreement with the union
which allowed their members automatically to deduct holiday credits
without warning if employees were absent immediately before or after
a holiday.   This indicated some concern over absenteeism and the
example of one worsted spinning company shows the lengths to which
employers would go to reduce it.   In the 1960s this employer gave
'loyalty prizes' of £100 or more to long-serving employees with perfect
attendance records.   These rewards had been discontinued but the
personnel department kept exhaustive weekly records on absenteeism and
the personnel manager said she would prefer daily information.   In the
company's medical centre the sister took pride in her affect on these
attendance records:

> We think we get them back to work earlier or maybe keep
> them at work longer or more often than if we weren't here.

The sister decided if workers were to be allowed to visit their own GP
for a medical certificate.   This kind of 'concern' put the industry's
sick pay agreements in proper perspective. (8)

Whereas absentees could rarely stop a plant running, a few workers turning up several minutes late in the morning could disrupt the change over between shifts and could, if not stop the machinery, stop the flow of material from one department to another (9). At any rate management in my survey was very concerned about timekeeping:

> ... punctuality is very important ... its the characteristic of a good worker. (Assistant managing director, woolcombing firm)

Sanctions against bad timekeepers were similar to those used against absentees. Dismissals for bad timekeeping were frequent. A glance at the 'leavers' journal' kept by one respondent showed that 'timekeeping' figured prominently amongst the reasons given for dismissals. At another company I was told that the easiest way to get sacked was by being a bad timekeeper and at a worsted spinning firm I actually witnessed the dismissal of a young Asian worker for bad timekeeping. Furthermore, promotion was impossible for a worker with any record of unpunctuality:

> ... an overlooker must be a good timekeeper. (Woolcombing overlooker)

On top of these sanctions management frequently operated a system of fines for bad timekeeping which differed only in degree from those imposed in the nineteenth century. Such fines were disguised as timekeeping 'bonuses' - i.e. the fixed bonus was earned as long as the worker was punctual - but they operated, nonetheless, as fines. A worker had his wage docked for turning up five minutes late but earned no bonus for arriving at work half an hour early. Several of the firms interviewed said they operated timekeeping 'bonus' systems and an employers' representative claimed that they were particularly popular amongst woolcombers. One worsted spinner had recently abandoned a monthly 'draw' for good timekeepers (10) and most firms seemed to be increasingly concerned with the punishment of unpunctuality rather than the provision of rewards for good timekeeping (11).

Finally, we must consider the provision of holidays for wool textile workers. In 1978 their negotiated holiday entitlement was twenty six days a year, this was increased to twenty eight paid days off in 1980. To an extent this 'generosity' was explained by the seasonal nature of the wool textile trade. This also explained the lack of flexibility in the timing of holidays. The main holiday was taken in August: two weeks at 'Bowling Tide' for Bradford firms,

> Holidays can't be made flexible, everybody takes the same holiday year after year. (Personnel manager, woolcombing firm)

Most of the wool textile workers in my survey had to be at work continuously in the time for which they were paid. This produced stress. This stress was compounded by the nature of their labour: continuous repetition of a task (as in weaving); or long periods of 'inactivity', during which the 'minder' patrolled his machine, interspersed with periods of heavy work (as in combing). Spinning had labour of both kinds: repetition and attending/minding. Take, for example, this excerpt from a training manual for ring spinners:

RESPONSIBILITY   Responsible to overlooker, for Ring Spinning Frames.

PHYSICAL NATURE OF JOB   Patrolling and standing by Spinning
                        Frames.
SOCIAL NATURE   Not a very clean job. Requiring you to
                        work with others at times.

As every respondent and informant - including those at the industrial
training board (WJFITB) - admitted, combing was worse than spinning
in these as in other respects.   But even the 'nicer' operatives' jobs
had some aspects of stress as a permanent condition, for example
machine controlled pressure and the mental stress of concentration for
long periods, and most employers admitted that they had lost workers
because they were unable to cope with the stress.

   Boredom was probably the most common aspect of stress in wool textile
labour.   It was perhaps at its worst in the job of French comb minder
but it was universal nonetheless.   One personnel manager told me that
the lack of job satisfaction in wool textiles was

     ... a fact of life, you have to clean your shoes every day,
     this is the same... even supervision is boring.

Other managers agreed:

     The term 'minder' shows you how boring most of the job is,
     even woolsorting is tedious.   (Assistant managing director,
     woolcombing firm)

   These jobs also produced discomfort and isolation, again combing was
the worst.   All operatives in woolcombing mills, except perhaps those
in carding, were isolated from each other and had no opportunity for
conversation (12).   In departments where there was some chance of a
'community atmosphere', for example in the burling and mending shop of
a manufacturing firm, the overlooker ensured that conversation was
kept to a minimum.   In one burling and mending department the
supervisor sat on a dais from which he could survey the room.   This
example illustrated the final aspect of stress I found in my survey:
there was no opportunity for 'ca'canny' in wool textiles.   The
supervisors had the usual sanctions at their disposal: at one firm
about fifty per cent of leavers were dismissed or made redundant.
For those dismissed 'won't work/unsuitable' was one of the three
explanations given in the majority of cases.   In addition to these
normal sanctions, wool textile supervisors also had physical violence
at their disposal.   Two managers said that overlookers should have
the ability to physically intimidate workers and fights between
overlookers and operatives were occasionally reported in the press
(for example, Telegraph and Argus 19 July 1980).   Of course in some
mills physical violence was unknown and there was less stress in general
in traditional spinning mills.   Here workers were allowed to make time
for themselves but they were expected to clean and there was
paternalistic control.

   While stress might be the most important aspect of the physical
conditions of wool textile work, dirt was part of the industry's
reputation.   A respondent at the WJFITB described conditions in some
departments as 'terrible'.   Together with the muck of the mill, workers
endured dust, smell, dampness, heat/cold, humidity and noise.   There
were, in addition, problems which were completely unrelated to technology
or the nature of the industry:

It is appreciated that by its very nature woolcombing creates a relatively dirty atmosphere. It was apparent however from the apologetic explanations of the shift managers and overlookers that better results could be achieved if sufficient attention was paid to general tidiness and housekeeping.

The small 'break' room provided which houses the vending machines some tables and one broken chair, was dirty, noisy and thoroughly unattractive.

The condition of the toilets was also far from satisfactory. At least half were out of order, no toilet paper was available, both sinks and toilets were cracked or chipped and in general need of repair. We were not surprised by the comment of one employee interviewed who said he would never use the toilets 'except in an emergency'.

General tidiness, housekeeping and cleanliness should be developed as a main responsibility of the overlookers and use could be made of the supervisors meeting to discuss and monitor progress. For this to be effective Management must accept and publicise the necessity for cleanliness in parallel with and not secondary to production'. (ACAS woolcombing report).

While the ACAS report found that conditions in the scouring section at this firm were the most unpleasant, it severely criticised general working conditions at the company. This firm was not unique: at a typical woolcombing firm the workers had to wash at least three times a day in order to keep themselves reasonably clean yet few firms issued overalls to operatives and an even smaller number provided showers. The ACAS report was designed to explain a labour turnover problem. As with hours and wages, physical conditions helped to explain high levels of voluntary turnover. In fact one respondent made a point of emphasising the noise of their machinery when advertising a vacancy. Nevertheless, despite the problems of labour turnover, several managers told me that they thought they had gone far enough in improving conditions.

A manager at the firm criticised in the ACAS report claimed that four hours a week was sufficient time for cleaning and that working conditions had improved 'dramatically' with reequipping:

... if you think its bad up there now you should have seen what it was like before!

... people won't realise how much conditions have improved in this industry over the last twenty years. (Mill manager, worsted spinning firm)

Nevertheless, in some cases conditions have actually been made worse by modern technology, in regard to the problem of 'fly' for instance (Telegraph and Argus 19 April 1979). Furthermore, the relatively clean and comfortable conditions which I found in two of the mills I visited showed that discomfort was not a technical necessity even though employers claimed it was a natural characteristic of the work. Other employers had taken severe measures against those that suggested that conditions would be improved:

> A 29 year old textile worker claimed yesterday that he had
> been sacked because of a newspaper cutting...
> The newspaper cutting - taken from the previous night's
> Telegraph and Argus - quoted Mr. Gary Armitage,
> Woolsorters General Secretary, accusing some firms of
> allowing working conditions to deteriorate to 'an appalling
> level' ... conditions ... were similar to conditions
> criticised in Mr. Armitage's report. (Telegraph and Argus
> 26 May 1978)

The final aspect of conditions with which we are concerned is health and
safety.   I will describe the known hazards in the processes operated
by firms in my survey.   I cannot, of course, be sure that each of these
hazards existed in every firm undertaking the relevant process.

In woolcombing, wool sorters and pullers had traditionally risked
anthrax, 'woolsorters' disease, and the disease had not yet been totally
eliminated from the raw wool with which they worked.   Conditions in
scouring were believed to be conducive to the development of arthritis
and inhalation of cardroom dust was thought to cause respiratory problems.
In only one firm did I see (a handful of) operatives wearing guaze masks,
the least efficient form of protection against dust.   The revolving
cards themselves were perhaps an even more serious hazard to operatives:

> The percentage of accidents involving moving machinery in
> the wool textile industry during 1977 was nearly twice the
> national average for manufacturing industry, according to
> a Health and Safety Executive report.
> Carding machines gave the greatest cause for concern and
> there was evidence that about 20 per cent of all accidents
> at moving machines in the industry occurred at cards and
> similar machines.   (Telegraph and Argus 26 January 1979)

Between 1966 and 1975 moving machinery accidents made up 24 per cent
of all reported accidents in the industry (Telegraph and Argus 15 November
1979).   Worsted spinning also had moving machinery hazards and, in
addition, the danger of serious cuts resulting from trimming 'laps'
with a razor blade or Stanley knife.   The major hazard in weaving was
noise but as this affected other processes as well, I will deal with
noise as a general problem (see below).   In dyeing and finishing 'flock'
reproduced the hazards of cardroom dust.   There were also the chemical
hazards of solvents, conditioners and so on.   In particular, much
concern was expressed about the use of carcinogenic dyes.   These were
suspected of causing bladder cancer, of which West Yorkshire had an
excessively high incidence.   Other chemical hazards were more familiar:
in 1981 nine textile workers were taken to hospital after being gassed
by chlorine (Telegraph and Argus 16 October 1981).

In addition to those health and safety risks peculiar to textiles,
workers also suffered from the more common problems of back strain and
unguarded machinery.   The most frequent cause of injury, however, was
escaping hot water or steam.   In fact wool textiles' reported accident
rate was below the average but the reverse may have been true of
occupational illness and disease.   To the dangers of dust and chemicals
must be added the neglected problems of shift work and noise.   The
sister employed by a worsted spinning company found that many workers
sought treatment in her centre for migraines: in that company the noise
limit recommended by the Department of Employment was exceeded in
several departments.   A code of practice recommends a ninety dBA

maximum for an eight hour exposure without ear protection, it is the equivalent of working all day within twenty yards of a pneumatic drill. The noise level in the Boyd twisting room at this firm was up to ten times as loud (96 to 100 dBA) as this recommended limit and workers were exposed to this noise for twelve and not eight hours a day. Furthermore on only one occasion, in all of my company visits, did I see a worker wearing ear protection yet many mills had even worse noise problems and one could rarely make oneself heard without shouting at close distance. Although twisting was noisy, the worst hazards were faced in weaving where noise induced deafness was 'endemic' (Telegraph and Argus 15 November 1979). Nevertheless all workers were probably at risk of permanent damage to their hearing.

As with other aspects of physical conditions, it was often suggested that health and safety were technical problems. The Factory Inspectorate, for example, blamed the age of plant and buildings in the industry for many of the moving machinery accidents (Telegraph and Argus 15 November 1979). Certainly moving machinery risks could be increased by narrow gangways and unguarded machinery and at least one woolcombing firm had reorganised their carding department in order to reduce these risks and comply with the 1974 Health and Safety at Work Act. Indeed firms with carding machinery had been able to produce a fall in the number of moving machinery accidents by reorganising their carding rooms, but does this mean that technical progress eliminated health and safety risks?

While it was claimed that new machinery was less noisy, some problems actually got worse with new techniques and machinery (for example flying dust, Telegraph and Argus 19 April 1979). In fact there was no automatic correlation between improved health and safety and new technology in wool textiles. The ACAS woolcombing report suggested that employers saw cleanliness as an alternative to production. Similarly with health and safety, these were seen as costs which must be balanced against any lost production from injury or disease and against any legal requirements. For example, many hazards were caused by excessive work speeds and others, piecing in woollen mule spinning for instance, by the need to maintain quality. Efforts were made to emphasise the benefits of improved health and safety to employers, for example less time off, but these were balanced by costs, for example the £3,000 required to guard a carding engine. Nevertheless most of the costs were born by the workers, although some were taken up by the community: weavers had recently won the right to claim industrial injury disablement benefit for occupational deafness.

It is clearly very difficult to accept that health and safety risks were purely technical problems. Probably the most conclusive proof that they were not lay in the cleaning of moving machinery. This had been eliminated in some mills and new systems were available to make cleaning relatively safe. Nevertheless, cleaning moving machinery still produced accidents and one can conclude that these were necessitated by profit rather than the state of technology.

One aspect of conditions remains to be considered: workers' prospects, i.e. the acquisition of skills, especially transferable skills, and promotion opportunities. I found little evidence of either in my 1978 survey: little training was being done and there was no career structure.

Unskilled wool textile workers, by definition, received no training.
But the level of training which semiskilled workers received varied
from industry to industry.   According to the industrial training board,
training times for the following operative jobs in 1978 were: 2-4
weeks for french combing; 4-6 weeks for Noble combing; 2-4 weeks for
spinners (apart from mule spinners who received at least 12 months
training and were regarded as skilled); 4-6 weeks for automatic
weaving; 3-4 months for non/semiautomatic and fancy weaving; 4-6
months for menders.   Managers' estimates of training were, however,
generally shorter than these ideal times: 2 weeks was given as the
average for a comb minder, 3-4 weeks for ring spinning (but 6-8 for
winding).   These training times - both the WJFITB's and the managers'
estimates - were not the period of continuous instruction but the time
taken to reach competence (13).   Instruction periods were much shorter,
for example one respondent remarked that 'simple jobs can be taught in
an hour'.   Informants at the WJFITB admitted that, although training
generally took less time in worsted than woollen, combing was by far
the least demanding:

> Combing is at the bottom of the heap as regards training needs.

In my survey few workers in semiskilled jobs received any induction
training and most instruction took the form of demonstration by 'Nellie'.
This was the case even in the more complex jobs like weaving: one
personnel manager said that he preferred this method 'but you need a
good Nellie'.   He avoided, for example, using the best workers to
train new recruits because they would be too busy working to be able
to teach.   But weaving was exceptional and for most jobs the following
description of a mill in the 1960s adequately described semiskilled
training in 1978:

> ... there was an almost total unawareness of the training
> function, although a large number of young people consulted
> were actually being trained at the time.   (Cameron et al.,
> 1968, p.64).

In an effort to improve training methods the WJFITB introduced training
for instructors and guidelines for training manuals.   Only a handful of
firms in the survey had followed the WJFITB's advice and a quote from a
training manual will establish what the more 'advanced' companies saw
as 'best practice':

> All new entrants to the company will spend at least one day
> with the instructor to ensure that they are conversant with
> the expected and required company standards...

The manual also stated that the company's intention was that training
would be given, in the future, by qualified instructors teaching agreed
programmes.   These programmes would include retraining where necessitated
by new work methods or machinery.   If these intentions had been put
into practice the company would have become unique in the industry.
In fact some firms in the survey had no training provision at all!
For example, one respondent claimed that his company had not trained a
weaver 'from scratch' for more than ten years.

Training of skilled workers was, in theory, partly conducted in the
firm by the company's existing skilled employees and in part at formal
courses (City and Guilds or TEC) at technical colleges.   While this
may have been the case amongst electricians or engineering craftsmen in
the mills it did not apply to the skilled workers directly concerned

with textiles. According to the Managers and Overlookers very little training of skilled workers was taking place in 1978. An employers' representative claimed that the ratio of trainees or apprentices to existing overlookers and technicians in woolcombing was about one to ten but this exaggerated the number of trainees who would complete their training. Only one apprentice completed his training as a combing overlooker between 1973 and 1978, furthermore those few apprentices who finished their training acquired fewer skills than their unions, at least, would have liked. A Managers and Overlookers' official told me that training for worsted spinners should 'ideally' last for three years ('but it depends on previous experience') and that the union's leaders

> hope our members are trained to do all the jobs between
> combing and spinning.

The WJFITB considered this a vain hope, and one not to be encouraged. One WJFITB respondent explained that even the training of weaving overlookers and loom tuners was very rarely by a 'proper, indentured apprenticeship.' The degree to which the 'pretence' of apprenticeship was kept up by unions and managers varied by area. The training board's ideal, the best school leavers could hope for, was two years' training including a TEC course.

Lack of adequate training at all levels in wool textiles produced concern for the provision of adequate numbers of employees and a shortage of skills, in particular of skills which could be transferred to other firms or industries. While the WJFITB saw training as a way of improving promotion prospects, the managers and employers in my survey saw training as a cost and a risk. For example, there was an almost universal neglect of training or retraining for flexibility and new technology. WJFITB respondents pointed out that employers only trained when forced to do so by the local labour market. There were in fact better opportunities of training (14) in larger wool firms outside the traditional wool textile areas.

In 1978 I found no evidence of a promotion structure in the industry. Most wool textile workers were recruited into semiskilled work and stayed there. Unskilled and skilled workers did little better. Amongst the unskilled, for example, few were acting as 'spares' who would, in time, become operatives. At two firms, recruits had been taken from schools for 'ESN' children and would not be allowed to mind machines and most labourers at other firms were treated in the same way.

My survey produced very few cases of increased responsibility for unskilled or semiskilled workers with age (15), but what opportunity was there of promotion to skilled work for the semiskilled? The only realistic aspiration for semiskilled workers was to become supervisors or overlookers (earning at least 17 per cent more than operatives). One union official claimed that a shop floor worker in woolcombing had little prospect of becoming an overlooker and that

> you still have to be over forty to stand much of a chance
> of becoming an overlooker in woolcombing.

There was, however, very little chance of advancement in worsted spinning or weaving for older workers unless they already had the appropriate qualifications. Older workers had, at one time, been trained as improvers but there was now a 'shortened traineeship' for workers over eighteen. In fact few overlookers of any age were being trained and

of these a tiny number had been taken from the shop floor: the most
popular method of choosing trainees in my survey firms, both combing
and spinning, was from among the sons of existing overlookers.

Skilled workers had as little chance as the semiskilled of increased
responsibilities without promotion. Most had their 'share' of a
department or part of it - say all the machines of a particular make -
and could not be moved around at the whim of their employer, however
some operatives had this security and it would, in any event, be less
common in the future. In the past overlookers had had some hopes of
setting up on their own if their ambition had been frustrated. While
such opportunities were increasingly unlikely so were those for internal
advancement. Some, very few, production managers in my survey had
been overlookers but the rule for overlookers or supervisors was that

> They don't have any promotion prospects: the old boy
> network and father-and-son tradition of textile ownership
> presents this. (Personnel manager, woolcombing firm)

Where this was not the case employers looked for graduates. One
respondent told me that he would not consider an overlooker since

> They tend to have a chip on their shoulders.

Overlookers' prospects were minimal whether they faced family ownership
or a formal career structure:

> Most employers find a kid revolutionary when, as they are
> showing him round the factory, he asks 'O.k. but what will
> I be doing (if I start here) in five years' time?' The
> kid's been trained in interviewing you see, he knows what
> to ask - when he asks 'what will I be doing in five years'
> time?' the chances are he'll be asking someone who has been
> doing the same job for forty years! (Manpower officer,
> employers' organisation)

To summarise, most manual employees in my survey were working for a
basic wage of a little over £40 a week. Their average earnings could
be 50 per cent greater than this with the addition of premiums and
bonuses but to earn this much workers had to put in at least a ten
hour day (or night) five times a week. Furthermore, these earnings
were liable to interruption: short time (or worse) was certain to
reduce average earnings over the year to a much lower level. When at
work, manual employees were not given breaks and were severely penalised
for taking unofficial time off. Holiday entitlement was reasonable
but inflexible. Physical working conditions included various forms
of stress and a very dirty environment. There were also considerable
risks to health and safety, especially the former. Workers had little
opportunity to acquire skills or of promotion to compensate for these
deplorable conditions. Training methods were archaic and training
provision at all levels was negligible. This was not a consequence
of neglect so much as a deliberate policy designed to minimise training
costs and limit the skills, especially transferable skills, acquired by
the workforce. There was no career structure for shop floor workers
and even those who were classified as skilled had little change of
promotion.

After considering the pay, hours and prospects faced by the manual
workers in my survey, it must be admitted that wool textile work in 1978
was particularly unattractive and had very little to commend it, except
perhaps the 26 days holiday. Furthermore, while the employers claimed

that conditions had improved (16) there were grounds for believing that in some respects wool textile work had actually become _less_ attractive.

CHANGE IN THE LABOUR PROCESS

Before 1960 the woolcombers in my survey bought little new machinery. Their only significant investments in the 50s were in the Raper Autoleveller technique for finishing tops. In the 60s the largest comber in the industry, Woolcombers Ltd, bought an early generation of French combs and new cards but no important acquisitions were made by the firms within the survey. By the end of the 60s, however, these firms were starting to re-equip with new cards and gill boxes and one invested in new technology designed to eliminate costly handling problems. Nevertheless, re-equipping between 1965 and 1970 was negligible when compared to investment in new machinery in the 70s.

Most of the woolcombers began their first major phase of capital investment in fifty years in 1976. One respondent claimed there had been nothing comparable to this period since the firm was founded in 1920. At another comber a four year plan of investment had been introduced covering new machinery in the washroom and ancillary processes, in carding and preparatory gilling; but the most extensive changes were made in the combing department. Twenty of the firm's forty French combs were installed in the twelve months preceding the survey. Since the new machines were French, rather than Noble, combs the company were able entirely to eliminate backwashing. Similar changes were made by competitors. In 1973 most of the machinery at one of these woolcombers had been made before the war but the great bulk of it was replaced in the five succeeding years. Again the fastest changes were made in the combing department and in 1978 this firm was nearly two thirds of the way towards the complete replacement of Noble by French combs. All but one of the woolcombing firms made substantial purchases of new machinery between 1970 and 1978. The exceptional firm had its own engineering department and even in this company French combing had been introduced. More typical, however, was the new entrant to the woolcombing section. When it began trading in 1973 the company was operating new (Italian made) French combs and new cards together with some second hand Noble combs, a modernised second hand scouring set and modern high speed finisher gillboxes. Nevertheless, within five years the firm had replaced half of the combs it operated. The last Noble comb was removed only five years after it had been installed. As well as switching to all French combing, the company also replaced many of their gillboxes and purchased new cards with plans to buy more. I calculate that, at 1978 prices, each woolcomber in my survey spent an average of nearly £1 million on capital investment in the 1970s (17).

In the 50s worsted spinning, like woolcombing, adopted the Raper Autoleveller. By the middle of the decade most firms in this section had installed autolevellers in their drawing department, and Ambler Super Draft in their spinning rooms. By 1958-60 the larger worsted spinning firms in the survey were re-equipping with the next generation of new technology. Smaller firms did not invest until the early 60s when further drawing operations were eliminated and new ring spinning frames - Schlumberger or Boyd, Uniflex or Megaflex - were bought to replace cap spinning frames. Some of the new frames had totally automatic selfdoffing. While some companies installed BKN manual winding others went over to electronic clearing of yarn and new types of automatic winding.

While there was very little investment in new worsted spinning technology in the middle 60s, at the end of the decade activity increased once more. In particular in 1968 when many firms in the survey went over to dry spinning of shorter tops with shorter drawing and double apron spinning frames. Some companies bought Volkman twisting at the same time. While the new spinning frames, for example Rieters, could have replaced either older ring frames, cap, or fly spinning, the new Volkman machines may have replaced ancient dolly twisting frames. In the 1970s Rieter spinning, Volkman twisting and automatic winding were still being installed and for some firms their heaviest capital expenditure fell in the period 1974-8. In fact the final elimination of cap spinning (in any but the most backward firms) was delayed until the later year. In the most technologically advanced firms, however, other innovations were being made and one had installed open end spinning. This technique was limited, like fly spinning, to coarser yarns but promised much faster spinning and the elimination of roving and rewinding operations. In 1977 and 1978 one respondent spent £2 million on reorganisation and re-equipping. Other worsted spinners outside the survey spent comparable amounts: Thomas Ambler, for example, spent between £2.5 and £3m. on new machinery in the latter half of the 70s.

Some spinning re-equipping in the late 60s was prompted by changes in weaving technology. Capital investment by weaving firms before this time seems to have been piecemeal, arising from the gradual replacement of conventional by automatic looms. But between 1970 and 1978 the handful of weavers in my survey had re-equipped, at least in some departments, with high speed shuttleless looms like Somets or Sulzers. Investment was not, however, confined to new looms: pirn/cop winding and warping, for example, were all modernised during the 70s. In most cases investment was undertaken between 1974 and 1975 although one firm in the survey continued to re-equip up to the end of the decade. At another investment had been concentrated in ancillary processes and in finishing but this firm was unique in that they claimed to have brought the first Sulzers to the UK before 1960 and to have replaced all their conventional looms by 1965. At a more typical firm spending on fixed assets increased from £828,000 to £1,388,000 in the twelve months ended 31 March 1978.

We now return to the woolcombers and worsted spinners, i.e. the majority of firms in the survey. At the start of the postwar re-equipping phase most machinery in woolcombing mills in my survey was of prewar vintage, especially in scouring, carding and Noble combing. In worsted spinning most machines had been made in the 1930s: for example drawing, cap/flyer spinning, dolly twisting and manual winding. By the time of the survey most of the combs in use had been installed after 1972. The cards, drawing, twisting and winding frames were installed from the late 60s onwards and the ring frames from 1970. In sum the technology was thirty years old or more when replaced but was generally less than ten years old by the time of the survey. The secretary of the woolcombers' organisation concluded that

> more than £20m. had been invested by leading combing companies and old fashioned, traditional machinery was fast disappearing...

> ... By 1981 the whole of the UK woolcombing sector will have modern, efficient machinery with nothing installed earlier than 1976-1977. (Telegraph and Argus 2 August 1979)

Another employers' representative pointed out in 1978 that more new machinery had been put into wool textile mills in the last five or ten years than in the preceding one hundred. Postwar re-equipping phases were not all, or even mainly, examples of re-equipping with a new vintage of technology where old machinery was worn out. They rather consisted of the complete replacement of existing machines by new technology and techniques. Almost every firm had undergone large scale re-equipping and in every case the new machinery embodied a radical change in technique.

Re-equipping was frequently associated with changes in hours of work. The Atkins report had recommended an increase in shift work (Atkins 1969, p.xxxiv, 227) in order to improve the productivity of capital. It predicted that by the mid 1970s 42 per cent of wool textile workers would be working shifts compared with 20 per cent in 1969 (Atkins 1969, p.228). In fact the report overestimated the amount of rotating shift work which would be adopted by the industry (see below), but there was nonetheless a clear trend to extend working beyond the eight hour day. Indeed this trend had been established before the report was commissioned.

Between 1950 and 1960 two out of five responding firms with combs (18) went on to twenty four hour working with two non rotating (permanent) shifts. One worsted spinner went onto seven day working. In the first half of the 60s four worsted spinners started night shifts and another firm also went onto twenty four hour running. In the late 60s one worsted spinner went onto nights and another extended its day shift. Between 1970 and 1978 attempts were made to introduce three shift working: while these attempts failed amongst firms in the survey, a few firms (outside woolcombing) were running three shifts. Day shifts were increased in length as evening shifts were dropped. Elsewhere shifts were lengthened and one respondent introduced twenty four hour running.

The experience of one integrated company illustrates the more complex changes which took place in weaving. In the 50s this firm switched weaving from twenty two hour running with day, evening and night shifts to two shifts (only the night turn was permanent). In the late 60s weaving shifts were extended to seven days from five days a week. During the same period some spinning sections were transferred from day, evening and night shifts to a seven day continental system. This firm also introduced a unique seven day four shift system for women. Between 1970 and 1978 more shifts were started which involved special dispensations for women and the remainder of the spinning operations were put onto a seven day 'continental' system.

At a more typical firm only one section, combing, of the vertically integrated operation was working nights in the 50s but night shifts were introduced into spinning between 1960 and 1965. In the later 60s three shift working was expected but never adopted. After 1970 the evening shift was ended and weaving put onto double days and permanent nights. In sum, the great majority of the firms in my survey had extended hours and increased the proportion of unsocial hours (night and weekend shifts) that were worked.

This conclusion applies particularly to woolcombing and worsted spinning (19). In general an eight hour day shift - plus perhaps a short evening shift - was replaced by a twelve hour day shift or split shift and a twelve hour night shift. Most often the night shift was

permanent - i.e. individual workers did not alternate between shifts -
and even day working was not unusual. Rotating shifts after the manner
of the 'continental' shift system did not last long where they were
tried. Most of the firms I visited had changed to twenty four hour
running - usually with permanent night shifts - by the mid 60s. Although
this practice continued to spread, the distinctive feature of the 70s
was the failure of three shift working and the lengthening of day shifts
as the so-called 'housewives' evening shifts were dropped. Furthermore,
I found that direct production workers were working longer hours, under
normal conditions, than they had at any time since the war. The
postwar period was a more or less continuous chapter of moves to longer
and more unsocial hours.

If this was not always apparent in the official figures - for example,
it is often contended that the average length of shift fell in the postwar
period - then we must remember the widespread use of compulsory overtime
described at the beginning of this chapter. In any case, it is
interesting to note that, even on the official figures, UK wool textile
workers worked longer hours than workers in other EEC countries.
Indeed, the gap between UK and European hours of work actually widened
and in 1973 the hours worked in UK wool textiles equalled those worked
by West German wool textile workers in 1959! By the mid 1970s only
Irish woollen and worsted workers worked (very slightly) longer hours
than did UK workers. The relative position of UK workers - and
especially of those in Yorkshire and Humberside - was still
deteriorating at the beginning of the 1980s (Statistical Office of the
EEC 1978, p.134; 1981, pp.184-206; 1982, p.5).

It might be argued that these differences simply reflected the fact
that all UK manufacturing industries had long hours of work but again
we encounter some difficulties with the official figures. These
suggest that UK wool textile workers' hours were average for manufacturing
industry but once more ignore the existence of compulsory overtime in
wool. Even in 1975, at the bottom of the cycle, 60 per cent of men in
the industry were working over the standard 40 hours while in 1974
40 per cent were working over 48 hours a week (NEDC 1976, p.5). The
wool textile recession produced no fundamental change in this pattern.
In January 1978 woollen and worsted operatives working overtime
averaged an extra 9.2 hours a week (Department of Employment Gazette
March 1978; see also Winyard 1980, p.26), and

> In June 1979, for example, 23,000 operatives averaged almost
> 10 hours a week overtime, i.e. enough to maintain 5,000
> operatives in full employment if shared out. Flexibility of
> production perhaps requires that overtime should be worked
> when order books are full rather than laying off excess
> labour when orders are lacking but with 42 per cent of the
> workforce engaged in 10 hours per week overtime, there seems
> in principle to be potential for more work sharing to
> alleviate redundancies. (NEDC 1980, p.5)

Wool textiles has seen little of the productivity deals which the rest
of UK industry has experienced and there have been few formal negotiations
and little formal work study. Nevertheless, individual firms in the
survey had made changes in work organisation. Firstly, they had
increased workloads: for example, they had increased the numbers of
machines for which each worker was responsible (20). There was also
the possibility - especially, but not only, with more productive
machinery - of increasing workloads by way of faster running, increased

volume of materials and improved quality of output. Quality was
particularly important in the switch to French combing and in spinning
of hosiery yarn; and most employers I talked to were running their
machines as fast as they would go. As regards volume of materials,
handling systems had been reorganised to deal with packages of the order
of three times larger and heavier. In some cases these changes had
followed the purchase of more productive machinery but this had little to
do with changes in job content, i.e. the amount of time actually spent
performing tasks and the breadth of the individual workers'
responsibilities. Changes in job content involved the creation of a
more flexible workforce, and this was the second way in which firms had
altered work organisation.

Firms in the survey had tried to create a workforce that did not
enforce 'custom and practice'. 'Efficiency' demanded that the rigid
division of labour should be dismantled with the extra tasks being taken
on by the remaining workers who would be flexible about their job content.
For example, under the old division of labour rigid compartmentalisation
of operative jobs was complemented by the use of 'spares' and the
proliferation of 'fielding jobs'. 'Spares' included both young workers
waiting to be given charge of their own machine(s) while being trained
and other workers who could not be given a 'share' but might be needed
as machine minders when demand recovered. Spares sometimes did
'fielding jobs' but these jobs also had permanent occupants. This group
of jobs were, as the name implies, not involved directly with machine
minding but supported the operatives' work. When the responsibilities
of operatives were widened, however, fielding jobs were eliminated.
Similarly, the need for spares was reduced when workloads were increased.
It is precisely because these jobs - like those of the craftsmens'
mates in other industries - could be eliminated by changes in work
organisation alone that they tended to disappear more rapidly than other
aspects of the rigid division of labour which characterised wool
textiles. For example, by 1978 all worsted spinning employers had
transferred the responsibilities of doffers to spinners where no automatic
self doffing devices had been introduced. Even the companies with cap
spinning eliminated doffers and the 'liggers', 'takers off' and others
who were part of the complicated division of labour which serviced the
spinning frames. But increased flexibility was not simply a matter of
spinners taking on the auxillary tasks of spinning. They were also
expected to give up their 'share' and to be prepared to work on any of
the frames in their room. In addition, some firms recruited 'mobile
operatives' or 'star workers' who were expected to work on several
different kinds of machines. Management destroyed the complex mill
hierarchy which had been reflected in the multitude of job titles
(doffer, ligger, taker off, etc.). Increased flexibility demanded that
the detailed, rigid division of labour should be replaced by a small
number of grades within which workers would not be allowed to enforce
'restrictive practices'.

The third sphere of activity was managerial control. The system of
control used by wool textile managers before the war would have been
called paternalist. The workers were called 'the girls' no matter
whether they were fifteen or fifty years old. Each worker was assigned
a 'share' and expected to observe high standards of cleaning and
'housekeeping'. This aspect illustrates the element of autonomy to
complement that of paternalism: the workers were expected to 'take an
interest in the job' and were allowed to keep flexible hours and make
time for themselves if they were fast enough. But while absenteeism

was high so was stability: 'the operatives didn't need control'. Their supervisors were really technicians and, most importantly, all operatives were paid on piece rates.

In the last twenty years however, managers had begun to talk about wanting 'plodders' on their payroll. Paternalism had disappeared together with the concern for 'attitude' and stability. The supervisors no longer spent their time as technicians but now had to enforce the pace of production but often without their traditional right to hire and fire (21). The result of this increased pressure on supervisors was a high rate of dismissals and of physical violence against operatives. But while there was no increase in the number of supervisors, or in the costs of supervision, managers successfully dispensed with piecerates.

In many of the firms in my survey workers were given no option but to work hard and continuously. They were assumed to have little independent intelligence and were treated like machines. In fact the pace and continuity of their work was directly related to the pace and continuity of the machines themselves. Of course some machines - in this case those most recently installed - were better suited to 'control the workers' than others.

Since the operative was <u>forced</u> to work as hard as the machines required, no incentives were needed to bring him/her up to this level. Furthermore s/he was not expected to work <u>harder</u> than the machines required since production would not, therefore, be increased. Several employers summed up their rejection of piecerates in this way: 'the machines control production here'. This case was made most frequently by woolcombers who had rejected production linked payment because

> Your bonus depended on how good the machine was and how little it broke down and not on how hard you worked.
> (Combing manager, woolcombing firm)

Woolcombing operatives had very little control over production since this control was vested in the machines.

The rejection of timerates was not confined to the woolcombers in my survey. A worsted spinning respondent explained that management did not feel they needed production linked payment because 'the machines have taken over' and because they had 'a balanced system' with knowledge of what each machine was capable of producing:

> We don't need, or have room for, piecework. We don't like piecework but we pay well - everything goes like clockwork.

While this firm might have paid a little above average other worsted spinners had introduced timerates with much lower wages. But worsted spinners were in general more reluctant to dispense with piecerates: only five spinners had done so. Indeed even in these firms timerates had been adopted selectively. While <u>all</u> the woolcombers abandoned piecework in <u>all</u> departments outside sorting, at one spinner timerates were reserved for recombing and Volkman twisting; at two others only the spinning departments were paid on timerates; and at another they had been adopted in all departments except winding and reeling. Nevertheless, this was evidence of a move away from piecework, once ubiquitous in worsted spinning. Furthermore, some combing mills had used group bonus payments in addition to timerates and the recent adoption of collective bonus systems in several spinning mills seemed to suggest further evidence of the dilution of production linked payment.

In all, five of the firms in the spinning sample together with one weaver and one woolcomber used group bonuses. In three of these firms the bonus was calculated on a departmental basis, in the others for each __team__ of workers. Of course group bonuses were not entirely new to wool textiles. In the past the industry used arrangements resembling the miners' 'butty' system of payment, a variety of internal subcontract. As late as the 1960s, operatives at one mill divided the 'share money' of an absent workmate amongst themselves (Cameron et al., 1968, p.14). But the new forms of collective bonus were very different: they were not incentive payments since they were not __collectively__ earned (22). One respondent told me that

> Whether a bonus is good or bad is decided by the overlooker.
> The overlooker maintains the level of bonus. If the overlooker
> leaves it to the workforce production falls.

Another told me that his firm paid a fixed bonus in their spinning mill because most of the jobs in yarn production were 'machine controlled'.

Further proof that such bonuses were a transitional stage between piecerates and timerates lay in their selective adaptation. At three firms collective bonuses had replaced piecerates in the __spinning__ departments. In fact this pattern seemed to be related to capital investment. At one spinner for example, the bonus system had been introduced in place of piecerates on each new machine as it was installed and so eventually became general to that department.

At the one worsted spinner no departments were paid by piecerates, while in another the spinning department was already on timerates. These companies were the most advanced in the move away from piecerates to timerates in worsted spinning. They represented half way house between the timerates of combing mills and the piecerates of the weavers. There was even evidence of change amongst the manufacturers: one paid group bonuses in departments outside weaving proper. Nevertheless at another firm the department which was most closely related to combing, the recombing section, was paid on a timerate while spinning was paid by collective bonus and winding and reeling - the sections closest to weaving - by piecerate. Variations in this trend could be accounted for by re-equipping and the resulting redefinition of processes as being 'machine controlled'. Thus __Volkman__ twisting was paid on a timerate whereas the older __dolly__ twisting - in which operatives controlled the number of 'ends' - at a competitor was paid by piecerate. Similarly, drawing had been affected more recently than spinning by technical change and therefore only a few firms paid time or bonus rates in this department. Furthermore, the __type__ of bonus was affected by the level of capital investment. With less advanced technologies bonuses were calculated according to machine speeds rather than weight of production; and at one firm the collective bonus in drawing was paid by 'the set' rather than by department as in spinning.

Both the timerates and the bonuses I found in my survey must be distinguished from methods of payment introduced in other industries in the postwar period. 'Scientific' estimates of performance levels and of appropriate levels of payment (which were agreed with the unions) were rare. While the employers' Management Services Centre had conducted some job evaluation programmes in woolcombing and worsted spinning in the mid 60s, only at one survey firm was the initial level of the fixed bonus (in spinning) related to the work done by the Management Services Centre. This was a disappointment to the trade

unions which were in favour of job evaluation (23) but claimed that
very little had been done over the previous five years:

> because of the cost, if they can get away without it
> they do.   (Official, Managers and Overlookers).

Nevertheless, even though measured day work and the like was rare in
wool textiles, the effect of the changes in methods of payment which had
taken place was the same: workers had lost control to managers.   The
transition to timerates was a symptom of increased managerial control.

The overall effect of increased managerial control was increased worker
accountability.   Firms in my survey found this necessary in view of the
transition they had undergone.   Piecework had been designed to create
incentives for workers to acceed to managers' demands for increased
machine speeds and more continuous labour.   Some bonuses were paid only
at the margin, i.e. precisely where an incentive was needed to encourage
workers to speed up their work.   Thus where bonuses were a function of
machine speeds management reported no difficulties in bringing about
speed ups, but the firms that paid timerates were also able to engineer
speed ups: their workers had become that much more accountable to
management.   But increased managerial control was not confined to
workers' loss of autonomy over work pace.   Managers were increasingly
able to allocate tasks and monitor workers' performance (24).   Of
special interest here was the problem of quality control.   Three
managers pointed out that piecerates were 'bad for quality' while two
respondents added that they had opted for timerates in those sections
where 'quality would suffer if we had piecework'.   In fact increased
concern for quality was a feature of increased workloads.   Timerates
had saved the expense of increased wastage or quality control staff as
the pace of production increased and processing became more complex,
though with fewer operations.   Not only did customers demand better
quality goods but also a greater quantity of these goods could be spoilt
in a shorter time by a worker chasing piecerate earnings.

The final aspect of work organisation in my survey firms which seemed
to have altered was the provision of training.   There was, firstly,
evidence of changes in training methods; compare the following details
of superseded methods to the details of contemporary training given
above.   In weaving, for example, training did not begin at recruitment.
Even in postwar times boys and girls did all the ancillary jobs first:
reaching-in, winding and dollying (threading the stop mechanism for
warp breaks).   On occasion they might have got an increase in pay on
the transition from one job to the other (25) and the learning period
lasted for two or three years before the start of weaving training
proper.   The exact length of the delay depended on the ease with which
the trainee found a weaver ready to take her/him on (26).

An informant from the industrial training board gave another example
of changed training methods in regard to the training of overlookers
(again compare to the contemporary training practices described above).
Recruits had been taken on at 14 or 15 and until the age of 21 they
were classed as apprentice overlookers.   If they were considered to be
competent at 21 they were recognised as journeymen.   If an employer
wished to take on apprentices he was first visited by a union official
who would ask him why he wanted apprentices and who was going to conduct
their training.   The local union branch then decided whether or not
this was possible and then looked over the potential recruits.   In
the 1960s, for example, overlooking and craft apprentices' numbers and

<u>personal character</u> were approved by the appropriate union (Cameron et al., 1968, p.12). The union's involvement continued after an apprentice was accepted. An official visited a group of apprentices accepted by the union to monitor their progress throughout their training. By contrast, any union involvement in overlooker training at firms in 1978 was purely cosmetic. My WJFITB informant claimed that the only relic of the system was the 'pretence' of union involvement in the appendage 'society notified' to newspaper advertisements of job vacancies.

When changes in training methods are considered it is clear that there had not been - as the WJFITB liked to suggest - an improvement in, and regularisation of, training. In fact training standards had been uniformly lowered and this corresponded to the diminishing amount of training being given: fewer and fewer operatives and overlookers were being trained (27). In 1974, according to the WJFITB Annual Reports, 70 per cent of new recruits received some training; in 1976 only 49 per cent of new recruits were trained. Furthermore, training periods had been shortened significantly: take the following comparisons of times taken to reach competence in 1946 and 1979:

<u>Combing</u>   reduced from 4-6 months to 2-4 or 4-6 weeks;

<u>Spinning</u>   reduced from 4-6 months to 2-4 weeks;

<u>Weaving (automatic)</u>   reduced from 3 months to 4-6 weeks;

<u>Weaving (non/semiautomatic</u>   reduced from 12 months to 3-4 months;
    <u>or fancy)</u>

<u>Mending</u>   reduced from 3-4 years to 4-6 months (28).

In summary then: there had been a series of alterations in the wool textile labour process, mostly taking place in the late 70s. There was extensive postwar investment in new machinery and the pace of capital investment was much faster than anything previously seen. My survey also showed that longer and more unsocial hours were being worked: some of the worsted spinners had only made this alteration in the 1970s. The transformation was completed by changes in work organisation: increased workloads, a more flexible workforce, increased managerial control, and much less and poorer training.

CONCLUSIONS

Some of the features of work in wool textiles which I have described in this chapter have been identified by other researchers: for example, low pay and earnings and long and unsocial hours of work. Some studies have even included details like the health and safety consequences of shift work (Leeds TUCRIC 1980, p.12), and the fact that wool textile pay is low despite shift premiums (Fishwick and Cornu 1975, p.24). There have also been surveys of wool textile health and safety and the lack of training prospects. Finally, one can find confirmation of patterns of capital investment (29) and increased hours of work.

Nevertheless, despite the availability of studies which confirm many of the conclusions of my survey of wool textile work, I can find no mention of the changes in work organisation which I have described. Furthermore, none of these studies conceive of the changes described in this chapter as a whole, as the constituent parts of a comprehensive transformation of the wool textile labour process. In my 1978 survey

I found that technology, hours of work and work organisation had been altered to create a new form of work which was usually less attractive to existing and potential employees.

On the definition given in Chapter One, the workers who performed this work were providing cheap labour. In the next chapter we will examine the role played by Asian workers in the wool textile labour process. It must be emphasised, however, that this study is concerned with racial discrimination and cheap labour. It therefore neglects the role played by other groups of workers - in particular white women - who have provided cheap labour. In part this omission may be defensible since I am convinced that the greatest increase in the intensity of exploitation in the post war period occurred where Asian men were employed, but it should not be inferred that I wish to minimise the importance of the labour of women who make up over 40 per cent of the wool textile labour force.

Chapter Five will begin by describing the manner in which employers recruited workers prepared to work in a transformed labour process and to endure the unimproved pay, long hours, conditions and prospects I have described.

NOTES

(1) I.e. at a fraction of a penny for each completed yarn package. In weaving firms piecerates were linked to the frequency of 'picks' of the shuttle.
(2) Other firms linked bonuses to machine speeds.
(3) Nine firms - including the great majority of worsted spinners but no woolcombers - worked an evening shift of between 4 and $4\frac{1}{2}$ hours for 5 days a week.
(4) Outside the survey I found an example of guaranteed 'incentives' which increased the basic wage by 30 per cent (Bradford Black 2,4, May 1979). We have already encountered the survey firm in which all pay was production linked.
(5) In 1978 few of the employers in my survey thought that the fall in demand would warrant more severe measures.
(6) But this was one of the two firms visited at the end of 1978.
(7) Nevertheless, it seemed that the Managers and Overlookers did not object when a company decided to dispense with one shift.
(8) In 1978 woolcombing employers were paying £1.50 a day for a maximum of twenty days a year. This was improved in 1979.
(9) One suspects, however, that the historical concern of management for timekeeping - heavy fines predate any continuous production systems - is also a matter of principle in the shop floor struggle over labour time.
(10) And the loyalty prizes the firm gave in the 1960s took into account timekeeping and length of service as well as attendance.
(11) There may be grounds for believing that the situation had changed in other respects. The traditional evening shift worked in wool textile mills was, at least in part, tailored to improve the timekeeping (and attendance) of the female workforce. Male workers were assumed to have none of the timekeeping problems resulting from household demands. A union informant told me of a small, traditional (and paternalistic) firm which had run old machinery with an all female workforce and had allowed the 'girls' flexible timekeeping. It may be that the technology at this firm, for example the absence of continuous

processes, helped to make this flexibility acceptable.   It
was, however, no longer the case that wool textile employers
accepted any form of unpunctuality as normal.

(12) Even if they were able to make themselves heard above the noise
of the machinery.   Of course noise eliminates most opportunities
for conversation in spinning and weaving as we will discover
below.

(13) Except in mending where 12 months experience was needed for a
trainee to be competent, according to the training board.

(14) But not, according to the unions, of apprenticeships.

(15) Although they might expect some increased earnings at eighteen.

(16) In respect of dirt, health and safety they were (surprisingly)
correct.

(17) In 1978 a PB28 Schlumberger French Comb could be bought for
£17,500 while a 2 metre - 96" card would cost £70,000 -
£80,000 and a new washbowl £300,000.   Note that a full
estimate of re-equipping costs would include the cost of new
conveyor belt systems and other handling innovations.

(18) Including the one firm which had a recombing department.

(19) My survey possibly underemphasised the increased number of
night shifts operated by woolcombers after the war.

(20) On occasion there has been a superficial resemblance to
productivity deals.   In the early 60s an industry-wide arrangement
increased a Noble comb minder's allotment from two to between
four and seven combs.   French comb minders attended to an even
larger number of machines despite the fact that Noble comb
minders were paid more, their work being considered rather
more skilled.

(21) A consequence of employment protection legislation.   As one
personnel officer put it,
        I wouldn't go to a tribunal on that basis

(22) Carter L. Goodrich reported that the Bradford Dyers' Association
had agreed a collective bonus in 1913 which seemed to offer the
union some opportunity of workers' control.   But Goodrich
also pointed out that this form of bonus made 'ca' canny'
difficult unless one was to be seen to let down one's workmates
(Goodrich 1975, p.172-3).

(23) Possibly because collective bargaining is removed from the shop
floor and placed under their control.   This is not a new idea,
see reference to Bradford Dyers' Association agreement above.

(24) To an extent this change has already been implied in the
discussion of increased workloads and flexibility.

(25) In the 1960s at one mill 15 year old boys got 50 per cent of the
wage received by 20 year olds, and 15 year old girls got two thirds
of the wage of 18 year olds (Cameron et al., 1968, Appendix I).

(26) In fact this delay became less of a problem after the War as the
practice of the trainee paying the weaver a premium (from his/
her wage) for instruction was phased out and the employer paid
the weaver a supplement to compensate for loss of piecework
earnings.

(27) See the details of training given at the beginning of this
chapter.

(28) But menders took up to 12 months to reach full competence.

(29)   ... virtually the whole woolcombing sector has
        introduced new machinery since 1976.   (Winyard 1980, p.49).

5 Labour supply and Asian recruitment

The UK wool textile industry was short of labour for much of the postwar period.   Several commentators saw a direct relationship between the industry's labour shortages and attempts to recruit workers from further afield.   Such attempts were many and varied: my respondents pointed out that the industry had relied on workers from Eastern Europe, the Mediterranean countries, and displaced persons as well as on Asian migrants.   They also mentioned recruitment of Irish women and of women elsewhere in the UK, particularly from the coalfields of the North East and South Yorkshire.   Many of these attempts to widen the area of recruitment involved advertising, personal visits to other areas, and the provision of hostels or free transport.   All these alternatives had been tried by some responding firms, yet none seemed to have considered a more obvious response to labour shortages: wage increases.

We have seen something of the employers' attitude to wage increases in preceding chapters, but it may be worth emphasising here that my respondents took low wages for granted.   They unanimously agreed that the industry's (low) wage level was given, however low wages were not simply an article of faith.   As one respondent explained, wage levels were a question of common practice.   His firm did not want to be the first woolcomber to initiate a round of competitive wage increases. In any case, they could not afford to raise wages unilaterally because labour was such an important cost and they would be forced to raise prices.   This would finish them in such a cutthroat market.   Such constraints have traditionally provided the industry's working rules with the effect that employers did not simply try to keep wage increases to a minimum but regarded low wages as the basic, immutable condition of wool textile production.   This assumption frequently seemed to make it difficult for employers to make a connection between labour shortages and wage levels, an aberration which has also been noted in cotton textiles:

> Alistair Sutherland, discussing the case of the Yarn Spinners'
> Agreement in the Restrictive Practices Court, comments on
> 'the odd treatment of a labour shortage as determined by
> something quite other than wage rates and working conditions'
> by industry witnesses, and quotes the President of the Yarn
> Spinners Association as saying 'there would be no excess
> capacity if it were not for labour problems.'   (Miles 1968, p.83)

Wool textile employers' reluctance to increase wages or improve conditions was not, however, shared by non textile employers.   This explains, in part, the creation of labour shortages in the postwar years:

> At one time Woolworths couldn't get counterhands, then the
> shop wages were improved. (Overlooker, worsted spinning firm).

In consequence, young women could no longer be recruited for millwork.
Or, as one union official put it:

> The women used to work to supplement the family wage,
> especially if their husbands worked in textiles. They
> had to because their husbands' pay was so low. Therefore,
> later on, they priced themselves out of the market I suppose.

Wool textile employers found they could no longer consider their
traditional labour force of White, English women as a source of labour
supply. There was also nonwage competition for labour. This was
particularly damaging in woolcombing - the women 'had cleaner, nicer
jobs to go to' - but employers in other sections were also affected.
This had been painfully brought home to respondents in one worsted
spinning firm largely because their company was located in a suburb of
the city. The managing director of this firm complained that the mill's
reputation had sunk so low in the postwar period that local - i.e. White,
English (1) - labour simply would not come forward. This company had
also suffered from the creation of new employment opportunities for women.
Thus the personnel manager recounted the difficulties of enticing women
back into textiles from munitions work after 1945. She also explained
that light industry had moved into the area and several factories had
been established within walking distance of the mill. There was also the
particular problem of competition from 'Government' employers including
contractors working indirectly for the state. Such employers were
thought to have paid 'unfairly' high wages.

Other wool textile employers were also affected by increased (wage and
nonwage) competition for labour. As a result, worsted spinning firms
in particular had had difficulty in keeping old machines running because
of a shortage of female labour. There had been similar problems
elsewhere:

> We actually had looms standing idle because we couldn't get
> labour. We had seventy six looms then but we couldn't get
> the thirty plus weavers to work them.

This respondent's machines already demanded a high workload of their
minders, in part a consequence of labour shortage, and they did not allow
any margin for operative error. Workers could get the same money for
less work elsewhere even though they were minding more looms. An
industrial tribunal apparently agreed with this judgement when it
awarded redundancy pay to two ex-employees in the mid 60s. These
employees, both women in their forties, claimed they could not make a
living wage working as weavers for this firm.

Much of the discussion of labour shortages so far has been concerned
with female labour but employers faced even more severe difficulties in
recruiting (White, English) men. For example, the personnel manager
of a worsted spinning firm complained that while he could rely on a
stable supply of women there was 'no supply of local male workers'.
The majority of responding firms had faced competition for male labour
from the local authority, other state employment and from carpet weavers
and engineers. Again respondents were reluctant to see this as wage
competition. Many complained that the industry had had a bad image.
Part of this image was the 'impression that the industry was dying'
but some respondents admitted that this 'impression' was very real to

individual workers.   One of the main reasons for their difficulties in
recruiting and, especially, _retaining_ men lay in the lack of secure
employment in the industry (this was also applied, but to a lesser degree,
to women).   I was frequently told that workers had taken just so many
job changes in slumps that they no longer returned when demand picked up.

Cohen and Jenner suggested that the recruitment of Asian _men_ may have
followed increased competition for _female_ labour elsewhere in the labour
market (1968, p.42).   This was commonly accepted in the industry: for
example, one overlooker claimed to have been one of the first in the
industry to have charge of Asian workers ('They said it was an experiment
but I knew it wasn't).   At first they had come in ones and twos, he
explained, usually getting turned away because their English wasn't good
enough.   But the 'experiment' had begun in earnest with the creation of
labour shortages in the mid 50s when non textile employers increased
their wages _for women_.

There is statistical evidence to support Cohen and Jenner's tentative
conclusion.   In Chapter One we established that Asian recruitment into
the UK wool textile industry had been _in some way_ related to a decline
in the proportion of women direct production workers and Table 5.1 shows
how the proportion of direct production workers who were women fell in
individual sections of the industry.   Of the four sections listed in
the table, all except woolcombing had proportions of women workers in
excess of the industry average but in all four the proportion of direct
production workers who were women fell throughout the 60s and for most
of the 70s (2).   It is likely that these falling proportions were
matched by increased proportions of Asian men: Table 5.2 shows that
between 1965 and 1977 the proportions of women and Asian men varied
inversely, while from 1977 there was less variation in either proportion.
At this point it should be noted that some women workers in wool textiles
were Asian.   WIBS statistics show that women made up a small but stable
percentage of Asian wool textile workers from the mid 60s.   Asians
therefore made up an increasing proportion of women working in wool
textiles nevertheless their numbers remained quite small.   The presence
of some Asian women in the mills did not disturb the relationship
between the recruitment of Asian men and falling numbers of women workers.

So close was this relationship that if the numbers of women workers and
of Asian workers are added together the resulting proportion seems to be
fairly stable for the whole of the period between 1965 and 1979.
Asians and women tended to form a fairly consistent proportion (roughly
sixty per cent) of wool textile workers in direct production despite
considerable variations in their respective proportions.   It is,
however, very doubtful whether all Asian recruitment in this period was
due to shortages of women workers caused by increased competition from
non textile employers.   Certainly this _does_ seem to have been the case
in the first half of the postwar period.   In the 50s the association of
Asian recruitment with falling proportions of female workers clearly
followed increased competition for women workers.   Competition, in both
wage and nonwage forms, led to increasing difficulties in recruiting
workers to the least attractive jobs.   Apart from some labouring jobs
in combing and worsted spinning (see below), these jobs were most
likely to have been held by women.   In the 1960s, however, the regeneration
of labour shortages was accomplished by the wool textile employers
themselves.

We have already noted that one firm at least exacerbated its problems of labour supply by increasing its employees' workloads. In the 1960s the actions of many other employers undoubtedly produced labour shortages which led to the recruitment of Asian workers. Thus a representative of the woolcombing employers reported that the reorganisation of the section in the 1960s which had increased workloads and hours of work, had driven women out of combing. For one thing, he thought they were not physically capable of taking on the extra work. Similar problems arose in subsequent re-equipping since the new machines produced larger and heavier packages.

While not all respondents agreed that women had been disbarred because of the sheer physical strength required, there was some agreement that women left the industry because they could now earn their money more easily elsewhere. Re-equipping did not simply increase package sizes. Together with the changes in work organisation which accompanied it (3) re-equipping made work in the mills less attractive to White, English women. It brought increased workloads and isolation but less variety and autonomy. The degradation of wool textile work has already been described in Chapter Four. Here it will suffice to say that the transformation of the labour process (from the 1960s onwards) discouraged potential recruits while encouraging resistance amongst women already in the industry. Thus one woolcombing manager had found women 'unreliable' and unsuitable for the form of work organisation which was now required. That this view was commonly held was confirmed by others, including a union official. In worsted spinning, respondents were more likely to say that women were reluctant to retrain on the new machinery. Most often this resistance was expressed by quitting; women either left the industry for good or, especially if they were middle aged, moved to a firm where the labour process had not (yet) been transformed.

In Chapter Four we discovered that changes in hours of work had featured in the transformation of the labour process in wool textiles. Something of this was noted by Cohen and Jenner. They found it difficult to establish to what extent White, English women left the industry and to what extent they were pushed out. They found that in the 1960s wool textiles no longer had the same need for female labour (Cohen and Jenner 1968, p.44). Employers had bought new machinery which necessitated shift work and women were not permitted, by law, to work these shifts. This was certainly an important restriction and my respondents also complained that their traditional workforce was prevented from working the new shifts they had instituted. Nevertheless, they also thought that women did not want to work the longer hours which were now required even when they were legally allowed to do so. Cohen and Jenner reached the ambiguous conclusion that female labour was only a 'partial substitute' in a labour shortage. Unfortunately, subsequent use of these findings has tended to ignore the ambiguity of this finding. In fact, the industry's demand for female labour was only reduced in the special case of hours of work which actually disqualified rather than discouraged women workers. More often the transformation of the labour process created labour shortages by reducing the numbers of workers prepared to work in wool textiles rather than the numbers of workers who were allowed to do so.

To recapitulate, in the 1960s increased competition for labour was increasingly accompanied, even replaced, by pressures originating with the employers themselves. It was no longer outside competition which made it difficult for them to recruit in the least attractive jobs since they were making every effort to ensure that these jobs would be even less attractive than in the past.   Ironically, policies which we might have interpreted as efforts to reduce labour demand actually made the labour shortage worse.   The transformation of the labour process which they initiated actually made their problems of labour supply more acute. It discouraged yet more workers and made it difficult for those who were not discouraged to remain.   We have already observed the consequences of this in tables 5.1 and 5.2 which describe the relationship between a rising proportion of Asians and a falling proportion of women workers. Nevertheless, labour shortages were not always followed by Asian recruitment.

Most of our discussion so far has been concerned with shortages of female labour.   All respondents reported difficulties in recruiting White, English men to do the jobs from which women were excluded and the impossibility of getting them to do the jobs the women had rejected. Most union informants thought that the problem was the low level of premiums paid for long or unsocial hours but, once again, the employers were reluctant to see such problems in terms of wage rates:

It's the hours that put the locals off wool textiles.
(Personnel manager, worsted spinning firm).

We couldn't work girls on the night shift and men,
White men, wouldn't work nights at any wage.
(Consultant, worsted spinning firm).

In any event, where the labour process was transformed so that women were excluded it was Asian men rather than White, English men who replaced them.   This does not, however, mean that White English men were replaced by Asians.   In worsted spinning for example, where many Asians found work, night shifts were a new innovation.   If employment on day shifts was reduced in consequence this only affected women workers. Furthermore, Asians were rarely recruited into jobs which had previously been held by White men.(4)

The jobs in which White, English men were traditionally recruited were unlikely to have been affected by the transformation of the labour process described in Chapter Four.   Many of these jobs were still untouched by mechanisation, for example, in the late 70s.   It would therefore seem to be the case that a labour shortage which resulted from outside competition alone, i.e. which was not exacerbated by the employers, did not lead to Asian recruitment.   Employers did face difficulties in finding White, English men: we have already noted that the shortage of men in the 1950s was probably more severe than the shortage of women workers.   Nevertheless, any recruitment of Asians to replace White, English men was very limited.   Such recruitment was largely confined to jobs which were clearly unpopular on nonwage as well as wage grounds such as the dirty jobs in woolcombing.   This is almost certainly the explanation of Asian recruitment into combing in the 50s in the absence of large numbers of women workers (see table 5.1).

In fact, while the shortage of White, English men was more severe than the shortage of women workers, there was no general move to replace them with Asians.   Nor did this situation change in the 60s when more and more Asians were joining the industry.   For example, Asians were not recruited into skilled and/or supervisory positions despite increased competition for labour and, according to Union informants, some reduction in differentials.   In most cases responding firms were able to muddle through.   While some lost skilled and supervisory workers there was

also a general increase in the supply of ready trained personnel because
of the contraction of total employment in the industry. For example,
one of my respondents could recall requiring four overlookers for
specific departments with little apparent hope of finding the men he
needed. This problem was solved overnight when another firm closed
down releasing its skilled workers. New recruits were scarce but
employers were led to believe that this kind of labour was in infinite
supply. They therefore behaved as if they occupied a favoured position
in the labour market (5). In consequence many firms stopped training
skilled workers: an officer of an employers' organisation complained
that 'they just don't recruit enough people in total'. Even some
respondents admitted that they had been 'lazy about training technicians'.
They had not perceived a need for training because they were reducing
their overall requirements and, if they should need any, there was
trained labour already available because of reduced demand amongst their
competitors. Thus, when skilled or supervisory workers left, or, as
was increasingly the case, retired, then companies could advertise for
trained workers or redeploy existing personnel. Asians were not
employed except in some night shift jobs where the employers'
overconfidence in the continued availability of trained workers had
created problems.

  According to one employers' representative, by 1978

> The big reservoir was nearly empty, or, at least, it no
> longer had the skills the industry needed.

For the firms with the worst pay levels this was beginning to cause
problems. Now that most firms were relying on poaching labour from
each other, those with the worst pay levels were bound to suffer and
responded by lowering their standards. One respondent admitted that
they could not tempt workers from other firms because they 'don't pay
the top rates' so they advertised and got:

> blokes who you know aren't the best overlookers in Bradford.

This strategy frequently coincided with increased workloads. This was
sometimes an adjunct to redeployment but not necessarily: at one firm,
for example, the number of overlookers had been reduced from thirty to
fifteen between 1973 and 1978:

> We were overstaffed and therefore did not recruit or train
> but got rid of overlookers and increased the spread of each
> overlooker's responsibility. (Personnel manager,
> woolcombing firm).

  By the late 70s most firms found that they were once more required to
consider training skilled workers. Some were unsure as to how this
policy should be implemented. For example, a personnel manager at a
woolcombing firm thought that the 'sensible thing to do' was to keep the
standard of recruits down and increase their workloads. Others
followed the advice of the industry's manpower officer by beginning to
introduce career structures for supervisory staff but these innovations
were not always successful. Union informants thought the only sure
solution to the employers' problems was increased pay:

> The employers say they won't increase wages until they get
> good men but they won't get the good men until they pay.

It is clear that problems of labour supply remained, even though in a
suppressed form, in those occupations where Asians were not recruited.
This was also the case in particular firms which did not recruit Asians
in significant numbers. Not all employers responded to the postwar
crisis by transforming the labour process. Some, including smaller
worsted spinners, simply kept on as before and, in consequence, few
Asians were recruited. White, English women could be found to do the
work and thus the absence of Asians in operative jobs in such firms was
analagous to the retention of White, English men in skilled and supervisory
occupations. These were the jobs in which employers had experienced
the least problems of labour supply because they were simply facing an
authentic labour shortage which had not been exacerbated by their own
actions. Nevertheless, the threat of labour shortage did not disappear.

In large part, firms which relied on the traditional workforce, like
employers with vacancies for skilled or supervisory workers, made do
with workers displaced from other firms. In this case these were women
who had resisted the transformation of the wool textile labour process
and who sought out employers who had not made changes. Nevertheless, as
with skilled and supervisory labour, such workers were a nonrenewable
resource. By 1978 it was becoming more difficult for employers to find
women workers who had been displaced from other firms and many of the
women still in the industry were nearing retirement age. The labour
shortage became evident when employers tried to recruit young women in
competition with non textile employers:

> We take what we can get ... they can get more on the dole.

> The training board tell us to pick our recruits more
> carefully but we have to take the first one that comes.
> You can't have frames standing idle. (Managing director,
> worsted spinning firm).

While this respondent was aware that low wages might be the root of the
problem, other employers were, as always, reluctant to blame low pay.
One managing director blamed his problems on the firm's location:
'women for the mill don't come out of the semis, and they can't walk
from Bradford'. This respondent stubbornly resisted pressure to
increase wages, seeming to trust in paternalism:

> I send them flowers if they are ill ... flowers say more
> than money. I know their names, and their husbands' and
> kids' names.

Nevertheless, despite these remaining difficulties where Asians were not
employed in significant numbers, there is evidence that the wool textile
industry's labour supply problems eased throughout the late 60s and 70s.
It is, however, unclear whether this can be put down to recruitment
outside the traditional labour force.

In 1966 the Wool Industry Training Board declared that 'it is clear
that the industry is very short of labour' (Wool ITB Annual Report 1966),
but this difficulty receded as the 60s advanced. WJFITB reports show
that while the numbers of vacancies in the industry increased between
1967 and 1969, they did not return to the high levels of 1966.
Furthermore, there was an overall fall in the ratio of vacancies to
numbers employed. Even after 1966, however, problems remained in
certain sectors of wool textiles. Firms in Yorkshire and Humberside
generally faced more difficulties in recruitment than firms elsewhere in
the UK and in 1968 the training board reported particular problems in

worsted weaving (WJFITB Annual Report 1968). By 1969 dyeing and finishing were also short of labour but spinning had replaced weaving as the worsted 'bottleneck' (WJFITB Annual Report 1969). Both worsted spinning and worsted weaving continued to give some cause for concern in the early 70s (WJFITB Annual Report 1973) and, although the ratio of vacancies to total employment in the industry never rose above three to 100, this aggregate may have concealed the difficulties of individual companies operating at less than full capacity. The training board's worries about the number of wool textile vacancies were to some degree replaced in the 70s by concern over the high level of labour turnover in the industry, i.e. difficulties in retaining rather than recruiting labour (for example, see WJFITB Annual Report 1975). WIBS surveys of the age structure of the industry did not indicate severe problems in operative recruitment, but the fact that so many workers felt able to quit suggests that (immanent) labour shortages persisted (6).

While the easing of labour supply difficulties coincided with large scale Asian recruitment, it also coincided with demanning (something of a misnomer given that most of the jobs lost had been held by women). Furthermore, we have seen that labour shortages remained in Yorkshire - where the great bulk of Asians were recruited - and in worsted spinning, a section with a high proportion of Asian workers. It may be that these shortages were only experienced in firms which did not employ Asians but we have no way of testing this proposition. Similarly with labour turnover in the 70s: high turnover may have affected all workers or it may have reflected the continued resistance of White, English employees to the transformation of the labour process. In sum, we cannot be sure that the recruitment of Asians solved problems of labour supply, however it should be pointed out that the responding firms with the largest numbers of Asian employees were those where respondents were least likely to complain of current shortages of (operative) labour. This contrasts with the findings of earlier studies but we should note that it was never clear in these studies whether employers and managers considered the very act of recruiting Black workers to be prima facie evidence of a labour shortage (c.f. Allen et al., 1977, p.44-8). They may have had no vacancies for operatives but still considered themselves short of labour because the vacancies had been filled by Black workers.

To conclude, we have found evidence to support the findings of earlier studies which suggested that wool textile employers turned to new sources of labour when they experienced labour shortages in the postwar period. They certainly did not respond by increasing wages or improving conditions even though their competitors for labour were offering more attractive alternatives. They therefore suffered shortages of White, English workers of both sexes. There is evidence that the shortage of women workers led to the recruitment of Asians, but in the 1960s labour shortages were regenerated by the employers themselves when they disbarred and discouraged female recruits by transforming the labour process.

Yet labour shortages were not always followed by Asian recruitment. For example, only in the very worst jobs did Asians replace White English men even though employers faced very stiff competition for male labour. Most of the jobs which had been traditionally occupied by men had not been affected by the transformation of the labour process and hadn't been made less attractive. Furthermore, Asians weren't taken on in operative jobs where the labour process had not been transformed even though these had been occupied by women. In both cases employers managed on windfalls of experienced (generally older) workers who had left other firms, but immanent labour shortages remained. Elsewhere, however, labour supply problems subsided and on balance we can conclude that this was, at least in part, due to the recruitment of Asians. But, to an extent, the effect of Asian recruitment on labour shortages is immaterial. It is rather more important to have discovered why they were recruited. In particular, we have discovered that the recruitment of Asians was crucially dependent on the employers' attitude towards wage levels and on their White, English employees' attitudes towards change in the labour process which made their jobs less attractive.

Whatever the initial cause of the employers' labour supply problems, they did not attempt to solve them by increasing wages. We have consistently found that employers were reluctant to increase wages and that many were not even aware of, or denied, the relationship between labour shortages and low pay. This is faintly surprising when competitors elsewhere were offering better wages, but thoroughly astounding given that wool textile employers were making their own jobs even less attractive. Both White, English men and White, English women left the industry because of low pay yet wages were never increased in order to retain them, indeed those that remained were expected to work harder for the same pay. There is no need (c.f. Allen et al., 1977, p.64-5) to speculate on the size of wage increases required to persuade White, English workers to stay in wool textiles since it is clear that the recruitment of Asians allowed employers to proceed with the transformation of the labour process in the industry with no worse, and probably fewer, problems of labour supply than they experienced where work had not been transformed.

Of course Asians did not always replace incumbent workers where employers made changes in technology, hours of work, or work organisation. For example, there was some re-equipping in work dominated by White, English men. Nor were incumbent women workers replaced by Asians in every case of change. For instance, one respondent thought that there had never been any difficulty in the recruitment of worsted weavers yet a large number of weavers were women (see table 5.1 above) and most weaving firms had re-equipped. Many of these companies had installed new Sulzer looms and therefore, because of increased output per head, 'there was a glut of weavers'. He added that there had always been

> A ready market of experienced weavers willing to retrain onto Sulzer. We have never in the last ten years trained a Sulzer weaver from scratch. (Personnel manager, integrated worsted firm).

Where White, English women were replaced in weaving, they were replaced by White, English men. Asian worsted weavers were much fewer in number than Asian worsted spinners. Why should this be the case?

Change in the labour process occurred in both sections and both reduced their overall demand for labour, however in weaving this change was not resisted. Unlike the traditional spinning workforce, the weavers did not leave en masse. It is unlikely that weavers had fewer alternatives than their sisters in spinning and much more likely that the changes which took place had differing effects in each section. Weaving has always been better regarded than spinning and in 1978 most weavers worked shorter hours than spinners for better wages. The transformation of the labour process in worsted weaving had not yet succeeded in making weaving less attractive than alternative employment opportunities (7).

In summary, Asians were recruited into wool textiles when either or both of two sets of conditions held. Firstly, they were recruited where non textile opportunities were improved, leading to outright rejection by the traditional workforce of the least attractive jobs, for example the dirty labouring jobs in woolcombing in the 1950s. Asians were not employed in jobs which were thought (by the workforce) to be slightly more attractive, such as operative jobs in unmodernised worsted spinning mills in the 60s and 70s. While young women could not be found to train as spinners, these firms survived by employing older workers with an 'investment' in the industry who did not find alternative opportunities so attractive. Secondly, Asians were recruited into already unpopular jobs which were <u>made</u> (by employers) so unattractive to incumbent workers, let alone new recruits, that they were renounced. These were the conditions under which most Asian workers were recruited into wool textiles. Where incumbents did not resist the changes made by their employers by quitting, Asians were not recruited.

Of course any worker's capacity for resistance of the kind discussed above is limited by the availability of alternatives. It is clear that the number of alternatives may shrink if expansion in employment is halted or even reversed. Furthermore, it has been implied throughout this chapter that Asian workers did not have the same number of alternative employment opportunities available to them as did White, English workers. Both of these questions will be considered in Chapter Eight but before we discuss the local labour market we must learn more of the distribution of Asian workers in wool textiles.

NOTES

(1)   It is necessary to specify that these workers were <u>English</u>. We noted at the beginning of this chapter that wool textile employers recruited numbers of Europeans in the period after 1945. These men and women - most of the former were Eastern Europeans, many of the latter were Italians - were recruited into the jobs left vacant by non textile competition even before the recruitment of Asians. Nevertheless the supply of European workers was soon exhausted: in contrast to the Asians' experience, there was no protracted migration to the UK and the sons and daughters of Europeans were not recruited into wool textiles.

(2)   Indeed 'weaving and turning' was relegated from fourth to fifth place amongst those sections which employed the largest number of women.

(3)   Indeed changes in work organisation alone were often all that was required.

(4)   European migrants were not able to resist the transformation of the labour process in the same way as English workers. This implies that the range of alternatives open to Europeans was more limited. In any event they frequently constituted the rump of White operatives who remained in mills where the labour process had been transformed and Asians had been recruited. Nevertheless, their numbers declined thereafter: by the mid 60s two thirds of the 'foreign and commonwealth' workers in the industry were Asians. Some Europeans had retired after twenty years employment in wool textiles, others had given up paid employment on marriage, still others may have eventually found suitable alternatives to wool textile work. They were replaced by Asians. It is therefore clear that Asians did replace men in some cases, in particular East European operatives, but they did not replace <u>English</u> men.

(5) For further discussion of the idea of a (local) labour market see Chapter Eight.

(6) As always, employers were reluctant to respond by increasing wages, even where they knew pay was the root of the problem. Thus one personnel officer admitted that low wages had led to high turnover in a particular process but went on to explain that the problem had not been solved by increasing wages but by substituting machinery for men.

(7) Something similar happened in dyeing and finishing although here the picture was complicated by the existence of labour supply agreements between employers and unions (see Chapter One).

TABLE 5.1

SELECTED DIRECT PRODUCTION DEPARTMENTS IN WOOL TEXTILES IN BRADFORD 1965-1979 : WOMEN

YEAR	WOOLCOMBING INCLUDING CARDING AND/OR RECOMBING			WORSTED SPINNING: OPERATIONS UP TO AND INCLUDING FOLDING			WORSTED SPINNING: WINDING REELING AND WARPING			MANUFACTURING: WEAVING. TUNING, ETC.		
	ALL WORKERS	WOMEN	WOMEN % ALL WORKERS	ALL WORKERS	WOMEN	WOMEN % ALL WORKERS	ALL WORKERS	WOMEN	WOMEN % ALL WORKERS	ALL WORKERS	WOMEN	WOMEN % ALL WORKERS
1965	3948	341	8.6	7566	5098	67.4	2151	1743	81.0	2871	1603	55.8
1967	3112	264	8.5	5942	3681	61.9	1917	1503	78.4	2393	1193	49.9
1969	2981	262	8.8	5536	3297	59.6	1818	1381	76.0	2196	908	41.3
1970	2216	127	5.7	4598	2650	57.6	1633	1242	76.1	1957	804	41.1
1971	1703	90	5.3	4086	2287	56.0	1461	1086	74.3	1338	533	39.8
1972	1753	93	5.3	4298	2369	55.1	1370	1049	76.6	1425	546	38.3
1973	1786	77	4.3	3691	2038	55.2	1240	928	74.8	1352	520	38.5
1974	1127	37	3.3	3085	1710	55.4	1088	805	74.0	1156	468	40.5
1975	1234	51	4.1	2615	1344	51.4	937	661	70.5	844	308	36.5
1976	1438	40	2.8	2770	1449	52.3	999	706	70.7	900	296	32.9
1977	1398	39	2.8	2543	1187	46.7	863	598	69.3	879	235	26.8
1978	1414	40	2.8	2340	1053	45.0	761	528	69.4	805	223	27.7
1979	1198	36	3.0	2176	1113	51.1	674	469	69.6	708	177	25.0

SOURCE: Wool Industry Bureau of Statistics.

TABLE 5.2

DIRECT PRODUCTION WORKERS IN WOOL TEXTILES
IN BRADFORD 1967-1979: ASIANS AND WOMEN

YEAR	ASIAN % OF ALL DIRECT PROD WORKERS	WOMEN AS % OF ALL DIRECT PROD WORKERS	ASIANS & WOMEN AS % OF ALL DIRECT PROD WORKERS
1965	12.6	46.9	59.5
1967	15.2	45.3	60.5
1969	18.6	43.5	62.1
1971	19.5	42.5	62.0
1973	21.9	40.8	62.7
1975	22.3	39.0	61.3
1977	25.1	34.8	59.9
1978	25.1	34.7	59.8
1979	23.8	34.0	57.8

SOURCE: Wool Industry Bureau of Statistics.

6 The division of labour

THE DISTRIBUTION OF ASIAN WORKERS BETWEEN FIRMS.

Sheila Allen and her colleagues note, in respect of Peter Wright's work, that it is difficult to explain why some firms do, and some do not, employ Black workers, where the research sample has been biased towards those firms in the first category (Allen et al., 1977, p.43). They also remark on the difficulties involved in getting any information from wool textile employers (Allen et al., 1977, p.21). This is especially true of figures on Black workers:

'Ethnic registers are being resisted all over the place.'
(Personnel officer, large textile group)

'We haven't done it because of the cost.' (Industrial training board official)

Nevertheless, while being fully aware of these problems, we must make some attempt to relate the characteristics of different firms to the varying percentages of Asians they employed. Table 6.1 shows, for those firms who were able to supply information, the proportion of all employees in 1978 who were male Asians. As we might expect from the built in bias of the sample, almost all firms had a higher percentage than the average for Bradford - less than twenty per cent (1) - in 1978. There were, however, considerable variations between firms which did employ Asian men. Some 'bunching' emerges at 55, 45, 25 and 15 per cent; however it is very difficult to find common characteristics in the firms bunched in this way. For example, the distribution of Asian men was not obviously related to product (tops, yarn or cloth). The companies with very high Asian percentages, for instance, included one woolcomber, one worsted spinner and one integrated producer. Furthermore, worsted spinners were distributed throughout the range: from 0 to 55 per cent Asian. Similarly, Asian employment was not obviously related to the size of firm. Table 6.1 shows that the companies with the highest Asian percentages included very small and very large firms. This does not modify Allen's conclusion that Asians worked for the largest firms in Bradford (Allen et al., 1977, pp.42-4) since we are concerned with a single industry. Nevertheless, within wool textiles smaller firms were as likely to have high as low percentages of Asian employees.

Table 6.1 also includes information on trends in employment and wages since we might expect Asians to be concentrated in firms with expanding employment and low wages (indicating a potential labour shortage). Unfortunately this information was not available for all responding firms. Furthermore, the details for firms K and L refer to their parent, topmaking companies. Employment trends in these two firms partly reflected trends amongst white collar staff and woolsorters employed

by the topmaker but not by the woolcombing subsidiary.   Furthermore,
average remunerations in these firms was inflated by the relatively
high wages paid to woolsorters.   Nevertheless, despite these problems
of availability and comparability (2) of information, we can make some
suggestions about the relationship between Asian employment and trends
in employment and wages.   Firstly, it is possible that the companies
with low Asian percentages were more likely to have increased employment.
Secondly, it is possible that the firms with the highest Asian percentages
numbered amongst those with higher wage levels.   Support for this
contention can be found in supplementary information (ICC 1979; NEDC
1978, 1979) not supplied in the table.   This shows that, while none
of the responding firms were particularly high payers for the industry
as a whole, the firms with no, or very low, Asian employees paid the
lowest wages of all.   It is clear that we have no evidence that Asians
undercut prevailing wage rates.   Nevertheless, I do not dispute Allen's
conclusion that Asians received less than the average wage for the
industry (cf. Allen 1972, p.45).   Interestingly, the firms with higher
wages (and high Asian percentages) were not necessarily those with the
highest rate of growth in wages, however there was no evidence of a
correlation between low wages growth and Asian employment.   In any
event, Table 6.1 does not fulfill our expectation that Asian workers
would be concentrated in firms with expanding employment and low wages.

It is clear that this initial attempt to relate levels of Asian
employment to the more obvious characteristics of firms is inadequate.
The problem is complex and depends, in the first instance, on a useful
classification of firms.   Criteria other than the percentage of employees
who were Asian should be used as the basis for this classification.
We can then investigate any relationship between the groups we have
identified and the employment of Asian workers.   Our first task is,
therefore, to discover a basis for useful classification: we can be sure
that simple grouping according to product, size or wage levels will not
do.

Moor and Waddington's research in the Batley area led them to classify
wool textile firms into four groups based largely on the level of technology
employed in each enterprise (1980, pp.20-1).   Unfortunately, on this
classification my sample included none of the firms Moor and Waddington
considered most advanced and none of those they considered most backward.
The bulk of my sample fell into their type two, 'centralised labour-
intensive firms'.   This is unsatisfactory since there were significant
differences between firms in this category; and a new classification
based on calculations of firms' assets, profits, sales and costs (3),
as well as on levels of technology, was devised.

There were firstly the most profitable firms, group one.   These
included small as well as large concerns although not the very small or
very large.   In Moor and Waddington's classification these were all
type two firms although one company probably aspired to type one.   They
had spent money on re-equipping but there was no clear relationship
between the size of assets and the level of capital investment.   Most
importantly, this capital investment had been successful despite
relatively slow sales growth.   The outstanding firm in this class,
'firm A', was essentially a worsted spinning company which had undergone
some diversification during its (considerable) growth in recent years.
Together with another firm in group one (firm D) this company had proved
an attractive take over proposition in the 70s.   In the late 70s firm
A's assets were only exceeded by a handful of wool textile firms and

only one of these companies figured in the response to the survey.
Firm A performed even better on measures of profitability.   Capital
intensity was above average but capital investment was not especially
high although there was some significant expenditure in 1977-8.   There
were no signs of excess capacity.

Firm B in group one was a much smaller (worsted spinning) firm but
was notably even more ambitious than firm A.   Throughout the 70s this
company's profits, capital employed and capital investment rose.   Firm
C, a worsted spinner, and firm D, an integrated worsted producer, were
rather more marginal to group one.   Firm D's classification was
particularly problematic but its performance may have been affected by
the expense of completing a programme of centralisation in the 70s.
This company was also something of an exception amongst the more
profitable firms in that it invested proportionally less in capital and
in this respect firm D had more in common with group two.

Group two consisted of firms which had had obvious difficulties in
increasing (or even maintaining) profitability, despite their large
assets.   Firm E was a woolcomber.   Firms G and H were both worsted
spinners and both subsidiaries of a large wool textile group.
Financial details were not available for these firms and therefore I
have included those of the parent company, firm I, where necessary.
This is not entirely satisfactory since the group included many other
firms and because firm G was a rather more profitable company than
firm H.   Firm F engaged in integrated production and was the only
company in the group which did not sell a relatively high proportion of
its product abroad.   Profitability in all cases was about average with
occasional signs of recovery throughout the 70s but with little sign of
this inspiring the confidence required for injections of new capital.
In some cases capital investment fell significantly indicating contraction,
and this was usually associated with losses.   Where no contraction was
evident there were indications of excess capacity although firm J, also
an integrated producer, made a significant recovery with increased sales
after 1976.

Firm J was a smaller firm than the others in group two and this,
together with its performance after 1976, made it marginal to group
three: smaller companies with limited resources.   This group included
three woolcombers: firms K, L and M.   Both K and L had undertaken a
proportionally large amount of capital investment, but both found
difficulties in maintaining profits where sales were falling.   The two
remaining companies in group three, firms N and O, were both small worsted
spinners who had spent very little money on re-equipping.   Nevertheless,
firm N seemed to be the most successful in the group.   In contrast, one
topmaker-comber, firm L, seemed to have done especially badly and had
almost as poor a record as the fourth group.

Group four consisted of small, traditional firms which had spent very
little money on capital investment (usually even less than the worsted
spinners in group three).   It approximated to Moor and Waddington's
type three, independent firms which were increasingly marginal to the
industry.   All three firms, P, Q and R, in group four were worsted
spinners.   Firm R was the most successful but all three had had little
success in reducing costs and maintaining profits.   Unfortunately, we
are unable to document the full extent of this failure since financial
information was not always available for group four firms.

Table 6.2 shows the concentration of Asian workers in the sample firms classified into these four groups, and confirms the inverse relationship between Asian and female employment (see Chapter One), however it is not of immediate help since the classification does not take sufficient account of product or size.   Although these characteristics had no obvious relation to a firm's propensity to employ Asian workers, they did set limits on its chances of achieving profitability.   Size (of assets as well as employment) was of relevance because some firms were simply too small to make far reaching changes in the labour process. This was the case amongst some worsted spinners.   Product was of relevance since it helped to determine firms' chances of increasing sales.   In the 1950s a short lived boom persuaded many firms throughout the industry to increase output (4) but in later years only those with the opportunity of increasing sales in new markets did so.   These firms did not include companies in woolcombing (5) since the conversion to french combing was universal.   But worsted spinners were able to increase sales by picking up a share of the substitute (non weaving) market for yarn.   Where they were large enough to do so, worsted spinning firms were able to shift to the production of yarn for machine knitting (see Chapter Three).   Integrated producers, on the other hand, seemed to fare best where a large share of their production and marketing effort was committed to exports, however further research is needed before we can be sure that this was a general rule.

Since product is clearly of some importance, we will analyse the relationship between type of firm and Asian recruitment for each wool textile section in turn.   We will begin with worsted spinning.   Three worsted spinners were classified in group one, i.e. as the most profitable of the responding firms.   Unfortunately, full information was not available for firm C although we can safely assume that it was a less successful version of firms A and B.   Data on total value added in production (tables 6.3-6.5) shows why they were so successful.   The proportion of value added which could be attributed to wages and salaries in these two firms was lower than in any other firm for which details were available.   Indeed, it was lower than the industry average, and this was unique amongst the responding firms.   Furthermore, the proportion of value added resulting from wages and salaries was falling more quickly in firm B than in any other responding firm.   Both firms had incurred considerable expense with re-equipping which was still underway in the period covered by tables 6.3-6.5, yet in most years total value added formed a higher percentage of capital employed than in almost all other responding firms.   Finally, firms A and B had the highest value added figures per employee and firm B had the fastest rate of growth in total value added per employee.

Now the most important point, one which cannot be over emphasised, is that firms A and B achieved success with Asian proportions which were amongst the lowest in responding firms.   In fact the proportion of firm B's employees who were Asian was lower than the average for the industry.   These two firms had solved the riddle of increased 'machine productivity' which so puzzled the NEDC, and were able to take advantage of low labour costs by competing successfully in new markets.   Their rising sales confirm our judgement (see Chapter Three) of the most successful solution to the postwar crisis.   These were the only responding firms which could clearly be classed as companies which responded by buying the most advanced and productive machinery, and did so without recruiting large numbers of Asian workers.   Nevertheless, small numbers of Asian workers did not always signify success.

71

Group four consisted of the least profitable firms, all of which were small worsted spinners (firms P, Q and R). However, as we have already noted, there was little financial data on these companies. Nevertheless, we know that they had attempted little capital investment, or few other changes come to that. We also know that they employed very few Asians: firm R employed only two, firms P and Q none at all. These were not employers who responded in a more, or less, successful way to the postwar crisis; they did not respond at all. At least one of these companies closed soon after fieldwork had been completed.

Other worsted spinning firms did respond, but in a less successful way than those in group one. The most fortunate of these were firms N and O in group three. Although they had only slightly greater resources than group four firms, they were able to make a minimal response. Unfortunately, value added information was only available for firm O (firm N was probably more profitable). In this company the proportion of value added arising from wages and salaries was slightly above average for responding firms but was stable. But what little capital the firm had at its disposal was put to very good use: value added as a proportion of capital employed was higher than in any other firm. In consequence, value added per employee was exceeded in only two other firms and its rate of growth was only exceeded by one other firm.

Both firms N and O had large numbers of Asian employees. In both cases Asians made up more than fifty per cent of all employees. These companies had responded to the crisis by introducing shift work with little re-equipping (and that being in second hand machinery). This was why they were able to force high productivity from little investment. They were nowhere near as profitable as firms A and B but had made some response, and had done so without burdening themselves with new machinery which they could not afford and would find difficult to run profitably. The final group of worsted spinners suffered from exactly these problems.

Group two included two worsted spinners, firms G and H, which had large assets but obvious difficulties in maintaining profitability. Since both firms were part of a large, integrated group seperate financial details were not available. Nevertheless, the figures of the parent company, firm I, show that the group had very low added value per employee. The resources of firms G and H were at least as extensive as those of the spinners in group one, and were far superior to those of group three spinners, yet they did not invest in more productive machinery since they were constrained by the fear of over capacity. Instead, they adopted the 'classic' solution described in Chapter Three: re-equipping was only undertaken in order to reduce labour costs, although some shift work was introduced in an effort to use this machinery more productively. In consequence, they employed large numbers of Asians: in both cases the Asian proportion of employees was well above the average for responding firms.

We will now consider woolcombing. Information is only available for firms K and L (indeed details for these firms apply to their parent, topmaking companies) but it is clear that these combers faced rather more problems than worsted spinners in the same group, group three. Value added made up an exceedingly low proportion of capital employed in both firms while value added per employee was only average with little sign of growth. These woolcombers had adopted the 'classic' solution: they had invested in machinery which was no more productive but was more costly than they could afford. As in other sections, this response had relied upon large scale Asian recruitment: <u>47.4 per cent of firm</u> <u>L's employees were Asian while firm K had the highest Asian proportion,</u> <u>56.2 per cent, of all responding firms (6)</u>.

Finally, what of the integrated producers? The most successful of these was classified as marginal to <u>group one</u>, firm D. As the statistics on value added per employee demonstrate, firm D was not as successful as the worsted spinners in group one. It did not adopt the same strategy as other firms in that group but rather adopted the 'classic' response with capital investment which demanded Asian recruitment: <u>54 per cent</u> <u>of its employees were Asian</u>. In fact, firm D had clearly made efforts to work its (labour saving) machinery as intensively as possible in order to boost 'machine productivity'. It is possible that firm D was able to succeed with this strategy because of its varied product. Certainly a worsted spinner with this policy would have been rather less fortunate.

The remaining integrated firms were classified in <u>group two</u>. The least successful of these, firm F, was the only integrated firm which did not sell a large proportion of its product abroad and it had the worst record of all responding firms in terms of value added per employee. This firm had extensive assets yet behaved rather like a group four firm with no resources at all. Its main response to increased pressure on profitability had been extensive rationalisation <u>and less than fifteen</u> <u>per cent of its employees were Asian</u>. The third integrated company, firm J, responded to the crisis rather more positively in spite of its more limited resources. Although wages and salaries accounted for a high proportion of value added, productivity was high and value added per employee was almost as high as in firm D. <u>Firm J employed</u> <u>proportionately more Asians (24.3 per cent) than firm F</u>.

Chapter Three was largely concerned with trends which were general to the industry as a whole, however one did note that it was possible that our <u>general</u> conclusions on the employers' response to the postwar crisis may have concealed variations in response between sections or even between firms in the same section of the industry. Indeed, these differences were only to be expected since, at the end of Chapter Three, we concluded that the general response had been less than successful in solving the employers' problems. UK firms had not been able to make the most of lower labour costs because of slow increases in 'machine productivity'. Their 'classic' response had concentrated on reducing labour costs - even when re-equipping - and did not invest in more productive machinery.

Like all abstractions, this view must be modified to take account of empirical data (some of which has already been presented in Chapter Four). Firstly, we know that some responding firms did re-equip with more productive machinery. Secondly, we know that some firms made other efforts to increase machine productivity by putting labour saving machinery onto shifts. Thirdly we know that some firms actually introduced shift work without re-equipping. Fourthly, we know that some firms did nothing at all. It is clear from the preceding pages that firms which adopted the first and fourth varieties of response employed fewer Asians. The highly profitable worsted spinners in group one re-equipped with more productive machinery while the least profitable spinners in group four and one integrated producer in group three made no response at all. Neither category of response required large scale Asian recruitment.

By way of contrast, large numbers of Asians were employed by firms which introduced labour saving machinery and shift work. This proved a profitable strategy for integrated firms and the largest of these was actually classed as marginal to group one. It proved much less successful for some worsted spinners, who were classed in group two, and disastrous for woolcombers, who were classed in group three. Both spinners and combers were unable to achieve high productivity in spite of considerable capital investment: total value added as a percentage of capital employed and value added per employee were chronically low. Ironically, their attempt to reduce <u>total</u> labour costs made it almost impossible for these firms to reduce <u>unit</u> labour costs, hence wages and salaries accounted for a much higher proportion of value added than in the most profitable firms. (Indeed, <u>average</u> labour costs may also have been higher in these firms, see below).

Firms which had introduced shift work <u>without</u> re-equipping also suffered from high unit labour costs, however these firms - worsted spinners in group three and one integrated producer in group two - were generally more successful than other firms of the same size. Shiftwork allowed them to increase productivity but they did not suffer pressure on unit costs arising from the costs of capital. Of course the extension of shiftwork was dependent on large scale Asian recruitment.

We are now in a position to reconsider the (unexpected) relationship we discovered between Asian employment and wage levels and employment trends (see tables 6.6 and 6.7). Firstly, we have seen that firms which introduced labour saving machinery generally extended hours of work in order to increase productivity. Other firms introduced shift work in order to make old machinery more productive. <u>Both sets of firms were therefore paying shift premia which inflated average wages and of course both sets of firms employed large numbers of Asians</u>. Secondly, we have seen that the <u>most</u> successful firms were those which employed few Asian workers: these companies could be expected to maintain or even increase employment. By way of contrast, their less successful competitors in groups two and three, with proportionately more Asian employees, were concerned to reduce their labour requirements.

To summarise, the relationship between the proportion of a firm's employees who were Asian and its product, size, employment trends and wage levels was complex. Nor was there an obvious relation between Asian employment and profitability since product and size affected firms' chances of achieving success. Once product and size were controlled, however, a relationship did emerge. Asians formed the highest proportion of employees in firms of the middling kind, neither the most profitable nor the least successful. These companies had made some sort of response, albeit flawed, to the postwar crisis.

In numerical terms these firms were typical of the worsted section of the wool textile industry. In contrast, firms in the <u>woollen</u> section (which has not been considered here) made no response (see Chapter Three). They resembled the unprofitable worsted spinners we classified in group four, and employed fewer Asian workers than worsted firms.

THE DISTRIBUTION OF ASIAN WORKERS WITHIN FIRMS

In the preceding section we were able to take a broad view of the distribution of Asian workers in wool textiles and to draw some conclusions as to why particular sections of the industry, and particular firms within those sections, should have proportionately more Asian employees. We now wish to discover whether these conclusions can also be applied to the distribution of Asian workers within these firms. We are therefore primarily interested in companies with large numbers of Asian employees and not in those firms which invested in highly productive machinery or made no changes at all. We wish to know how Asian workers were distributed within companies which favoured Asian recruitment, and to discover how this distribution came about.

All respondents were asked to explain how their company had initially recruited Asian workers. While many were unable to reply, a number of those who did answer said that Asians had first been recruited as labourers. In the 50s Asians had been most numerous in the dirtiest labouring jobs in combing mills (although few wool textile jobs could be described as 'clean') but there had also been some Asian general labourers in worsted spinning. One respondent reported, however, that his company began to recruit Asians into their spinning operation at the end of the 50s. There is some evidence that firms in my sample saw this company as a pacesetter in this and other respects. Certainly my respondent there regarded his employer as particularly advanced: he claimed that the company had been the first to introduce Uniflex spinning frames to the UK. Other firms followed their lead, and with the new frames recruited Asian workers. For example, the spinning manager at a firm in the same district as the pacesetter told me that his company bought Uniflex machinery in 1964 knowing that their neighbour already had this machinery and employed Asians to operate it. They contacted this firm when the new frames were installed and were 'sent down' some Asians to work the new machinery. Before re-equipping their machines had been worked by White women on the usual worsted spinning system of day and evening shift. In every case where re-equipping occurred they immediately introduced twelve hour night shifts worked by Asians. Were these accounts typical?

While Cohen and Jenner recognised that Asian workers had been recruited to work new shifts (especially night shifts) on new machines, they admitted that they had been unable to 'pinpoint the crucial steps within the decision-making process' (1968, p.49). By this they did not mean the process whereby Asians were recruited. As the example given above illustrates, chance often played a part in this. Several respondents described how recruitment of Eastern European, Italian or Asian workers had been determined by fortuitous personal contacts or those of an employee. Furthermore, companies which were closely related in some way - for example, as subsidiaries of a large group - had often exhibited similar recruitment patterns: they recruited workers from the same source, at the same time, to do the same kind of work. But while they are undoubtedly of interest, such processes are not our primary concern. Rather, like Cohen and Jenner, we wish to discover how employers created the situation described in Chapter Five. We want to know how they experienced the transformation of the labour process, and their consequent need for Asian workers. Not surprisingly, there was some variation in their accounts.

We will begin with worsted spinning, where one respondent provided a most comprehensive account of events. According to this employer, the first industry wide phase of re-equipping occurred in the late 50s but at this time few employers contemplated introducing longer hours or shifts (7). With time, however, they saw that the cost of new machinery was rising (cf. Cohen and Jenner 1968, p.44) and concluded that if they were going to re-equip they would have to buy a smaller number of machines. Since these machines did not have high productivity they would therefore have to work shifts with any new machines they bought even if they only intended to maintain production (8). By the 1960s most firms could see 'the say forward': they knew that they were going to work shifts and they knew, <u>before they re-equipped</u> that Asian workers would be available to work on the new machines. The Asians enabled employers to re-equip on the cheap.

Nevertheless, this respondent admitted that some firms did not pass through all the stages of decision making he described. He thought that in the 60s a lot of old plant was transferred to shift work once employers discovered that the (Asian) labour was available. This was confirmed by other respondents but in such cases I found the initial impetus to Asian recruitment had been a desire to <u>increase production</u>. For example, one small worsted spinning firm had first employed Asians in 1957 but only recruited large numbers of Asians in the 60s when they introduced night work for the first time. This firm wanted to increase production but had few resources and started a night shift <u>in advance</u> of any re-equipping. Only after night work had begun did management realise they had an 'opportunity' for re-equipping, 'but we couldn't have run night shifts with the old cap frames although some people did.' The local press gives an example of 'some people':

> Taylors, once a world famous profit sharing firm, was taken over by Kagan Textiles Ltd. of Elland in February ...
>
> Immediately a coachload of coloured workers from Elland started arriving daily at the Batley Blakeridge Mill. This is continuing. Within six weeks of the takeover the firm announced that for the first time in twenty years the carding and spinning department were to work a night shift. Mr. Kagan said that in the short time since the takeover production had increased by more than 100 per cent and was still rising. (<u>Telegraph and Argus</u> 18 September 1967).

In other respondents' accounts employers had been concerned with <u>a change</u> in product rather than <u>increased</u> production. Thus, at one worsted spinner management began to look for the type of machinery they were going to buy in 1964 while making sure they had a new market to supply. They decided that this market would sustain, and the machines would require, twenty four hour running. They installed the machines and established the 'system' they were going to run on the day shift and then introduced a night shift. From the beginning they had known, from the experience of other firms, that labour for this night shift would be available and that the operatives on it would be Asians.

This was the more usual case: where shifts were introduced after re-equipping or at the same time. In most cases shift work followed from the desire to make new machinery pay for itself as quickly as possible rather than to boost output. Thus a mill manager explained that the decision to introduce two twelve hour shifts was necessitated by the need to make their new (large package) ring frames profitable. Nevertheless, management was already aware that Asians would be recruited to work on the new machines before twenty four hour running was introduced. But the company installed ring frames in 1959-60 and for most of the firms in my sample the first large scale recruitment of Asians came later.

By the time the majority of sample firms were making decisions about
re-equipping, introducing shifts and employing Asians, they were able to
copy the pattern already established elsewhere.

It is clear from the foregoing that some firms in the sample
introduced new machines, and Asian workers, earlier than others. For
example this seems to have happened at an earlier date in the larger
worsted spinners, yet even some of the larger concerns were still
'catching up' in later years. Thus changes in shifts and technology
further increased the Asian percentage (and decreased the female
percentage) of workers employed in spinning and associated departments
at one integrated firm in 1969-70. Similarly, a large increase in the
proportion of one worsted spinner's workforce who were Asian followed
re-equipping and reorganisation in spinning at the beginning of the 70s
when a mill was closed and operations centralised. Indeed the
proportion of another worsted spinner's employees who were female fell
throughout the 70s (by fifty per cent between 1968 and 1978) as changes
in technology and hours increased the proportion of Asians employed.
In 1975, for example, thirty jobs disappeared when the cap spinning
department was finally closed. All of these jobs had been held by women.
Similar changes were made at a competitor in the same period.
Furthermore, at a smaller worsted spinner the changes associated with
Asian employment had been initiated in the 60s but were still being
completed in 1978 when I conducted my fieldwork. Women were still
employed on 'short' day and evening shifts in some departments where it
had always been intended to have twelve hour day shifts. Nevertheless,
no matter how and when new machinery and shifts were introduced, all the
employers were aware that they could recruit Asians to work in the new
'system'.

While the timing of large scale Asian recruitment varied between firms,
it also varied between departments. In worsted spinning, most firms
had begun to employ Asians on new ring frames in their spinning
departments by the mid 60s but the majority did not employ large numbers
of Asians in their twisting and winding departments until later, when
they introduced Volkman twisting and automatic winding (9). Even after
this had been accomplished, subsequent changes might still increase the
proportion of Asians employed; this happened at one firm in the late
70s with further re-equipping. Other firms had not been able to make
changes in twisting and winding even by 1978. There was still some
manual winding at one firm and this department was run on a 'short'
day shift and without Asian workers (10). Other firms had similar
patterns of Asian employment. At one there were few Asian men in
drawing where only day shifts were run and most employees were White
women. Spinning and twisting had been re-equipped with Boyd and Volkman
machinery respectively and almost all workers in these departments were
Asian (including some Asian women). Both departments were on twenty
four running with twelve hour, permanent nights. In winding, however,
there was a mixed system. The newest (Schlafhorst) machines were run
by White women on the day shift and by Asian men on twelve hour,
permanent nights. Older machines were run only on days and by White
women (some of whom were European). At another spinner Asian workers
were over-represented in recombing, spinning, twisting (11) and winding
but the winding department had been completely re-equipped and was run
on the same two shift, twenty four hour system as the other departments
in which Asians were concentrated. Even one of the most advanced
worsted spinners had a high proportion of White women in winding while
Asian workers were concentrated in spinning and Volkman twisting.

In woolcombing the association of the transformation of the labour process and Asian recruitment was even more recent than in worsted spinning. While Asians made up between ten and twenty per cent of direct production workers in the sample woolcombers in the 50s, they were largely employed in 'dirty jobs' and the largest increase in the proportion of employees who were Asian occurred in subsequent years. In the 60s there was some evidence of a fall in the numbers of Asians employed but an increase in the proportion of Asians although this was associated with changes in work organisation rather than re-equipping. Dramatic increases in the proportion of Asians with re-equipping - such as those described in worsted spinning - did not occur until the 1970s in my sample firms (12).

Two woolcombers were of less interest in this respect since one relied largely on a speciality trade while another was newly established. Nevertheless, the Asian proportion of employees in lambswool combing at the former company increased with re-equipping in the late 70s. At the other combers, however, the relationship between re-equipping and the proportion of employees who were Asian was rather more pronounced. Between 1972 and 1977 the proportion of Asians in the carding and combing departments at one increased in line with re-equipping which began in 1973-4. Indeed the proportion of Asians at the end of this period was greatest in the combing department where the most extensive re-equipping had taken place with conversion to French combing. At the other, the proportion of Asians in carding increased a little between 1975 and 1977 but substantially increased between 1977 and 1978 when this department was re-equipped. The proportion of Asians in other departments also increased in line with re-equipping and again this was especially the case where French combing was introduced. Fortunately, three of the woolcombing firms were able to provide personnel details which allow us to examine trends in the employment of Asians in more detail.

Table 6.8 confirms that, like Asians in worsted spinning, Asian woolcombing workers were distributed unevenly across different departments. The three selected departments all had stable or increasing numbers of direct production workers and in all three the numbers of Asian workers were increased. Yet while in one firm's woolcombing department and another's scouring department this led to all direct production jobs being done by Asians, the proportion of the third firm's carding workforce which was Asian remained below the average for all departments in that company (13).

In other respects, however, woolcombing differed from worsted spinning. We have already remarked that in 1965 woolcombing workers were less likely than those in other sections to be female (and more likely to be Asian). Nevertheless, the Asian proportion of employees in the three woolcombing firms continued to increase in later years. Table 6.9 shows that in all three the proportion of all employees who were Asian in the early 70s was more than twice the proportion for all wool textile firms in Bradford (14). The table also shows that this proportion increased quickly in subsequent years while the proportion of Asians in all wool textile firms in Bradford increased more slowly (see Chapter One above). The exceptional firm reduced their Asian proportion when night working was suspended in 1974 (see Table 6.11). Nevertheless, the numbers of Asians increased in all three firms in the period covered by their personnel figures and this was the reverse of the Bradford trend: the number of Asians employed in all Bradford's wool textile firms fell by a third between 1973 and 1979 (see Chapter One).   There can be no doubt that these differences arose from the re-equipping which took place in woolcombing in the 70s.

Table 6.10 shows that, unlike some worsted spinning companies, combing firms did not completely exclude Asian workers from their day shifts, and that re-equipping increased the proportion of day shift workers who were Asian.   Woolcombing had been worked on twelve hour day shifts for some time whereas they had only recently been introduced into worsted spinning where some firms retained eight hour day shifts.   In all three woolcombing firms the numbers of Asians employed on day shifts increased. The proportion of Asians in all three firms also increased but at differing rates according to the trends in total employment on the day shift.   At one the numbers of all direct production workers on days fell while at another there were some variations but an overall increase and at the third a small increase over the two years for which figures were available.   Thus, although the percentage of all workers on days who were Asian exceeded fifty per cent in all three firms in the early 70s, by 1977 it had reached 66 per cent, 77 per cent and 93 per cent respectively.

Despite the increasing Asian representation of Asians on day shifts they remained over represented (although not to the same degree as in worsted spinning) on night work.   Indeed the proportion of all night workers who were Asian continued to rise in all three combing firms. Table 6.11 illustrates this: the Asian proportion of night workers rose in all three firms: from 59 per cent to 92 per cent, from 93 per cent to 97 per cent, and from 78 per cent to 82 per cent.   In two out of three cases the 1978 percentage exceeded the 1978 proportion of day shift workers who were Asian (15).   Table 6.12 confirms that even in woolcombing Asian workers were more likely to work nights but also describes the occupational distribution of Asian wool textile workers.

Throughout the 70s, Asians remained in the work to which they had originally been recruited: overwhelmingly manual and, within the manual grades, concentrated in machine minding.   They were rarely employed as warehousemen, let alone as overlookers!   At the three woolcombing firms covered by the table only one nonmanual Asian worker had been employed at any one time and there were very few Asian warehouse labourers. Warehousing was of course manual work but not a direct production department and was unaffected by the transformation of the labour process. This also applied to the other ancillary, manual jobs from which Asians were conspicuously absent.   Finally, Table 6.12 shows that the highest number of Asian overlookers in any of the three firms was two.   This means that the best ratio of Asian to White overlookers was one in five.

To summarise, in the 60s and 70s Asians gained access to areas of wool textile work outside those to which they were initially recruited in the 1950s (for example, 'dirty jobs' like woolpulling in the scouring departments of combing mills).   Nevertheless, they only gained access when this work was transformed and rarely found new opportunities in mills or departments working old machinery in the old way.   Throughout the firms in my sample there were very few Asians and no Asian men, to be found in cap or flyer spinning, dolly twisting, manual winding or even conventional weaving.   Most Asians were concentrated in French combing (16), ring spinning, Volkman twisting and automatic winding.   It was the spread of these machines - and of the longer hours and changes in work organisation with which they were associated - which increased the numbers of Asians and the proportion of all employees who were Asians.

In most cases, Asians gained initial access to new areas of work on night shifts.   In worsted spinning, few Asian men were employed on day shifts and those that were usually worked twelve hours if they were eighteen or over.   By way of contrast, Asians often made up all of the permanent night shift and were always over represented in the departments with the longest and most unsocial hours.   In woolcombing, Asians had begun to find work on day shifts at an earlier date, and it was a woolcombing firm which provided the only case where the Asian proportion of day shift employees exceeded - although only by one percentage point - the Asian proportion of the night shift.   This does not, however, suggest a more equitable distribution of employment opportunities for Asians.   While the segregation of White and Asian workers according to shift was less pronounced in woolcombing this was simply a consequence of the high overall proportion of Asians employed (over ninety per cent on both shifts at one firm).   Only in those firms where the vast majority of all direct production workers were Asian was there some similarity between the Asian proportion of the day shift and the Asian proportion of the night shift.   The proportion of all Asians who worked nights in responding firms which employed Asians was only less than fifty per cent in two cases and both of these were woolcombers in which the majority of all employees were Asian.   Furthermore, the proportion of all night workers who were Asian exceeded fifty per cent in all cases.   In most firms at least three quarters of the Asian employees worked nights and at least three quarters of night workers were Asian.

After the initial expansion of Asian employment to include machine minding as well as labouring, Asians were confined to a limited number of occupations.   Few Asians were to be found in non manual jobs or even in ancillary manual work, and they were rarely employed in a supervisory capacity.   There were more opportunities for Asians to become overlookers in woolcombing than in worsted spinning, but even here the best ratio of Asian to White overlookers was one in five.   There were no more than a dozen Asian overlookers amongst all the workers employed in responding firms, with never more than two in any one mill.   Thus, while in most firms more than a quarter of all employees were Asian, less than five per cent of overlookers were Asian.

In terms of promotion to supervisory positions such as overlooker Asian men did rather better than White women.   Nevertheless, there were similarities between the distribution of Asians and of the traditional female workforce.   Although we have established that Asian men were employed in areas where the labour process had been transformed (and women were not), both groups worked as operatives while White men worked as ancillary workers or supervisors.   While some women were employed in non manual work - mostly clerical, although in later years some women found work as laboratory technicians - most worked as machine minders.

Yet Asian workers did not simply 'inherit' the employment distribution of White women.   In many respects the opportunities open to Asians were more limited: throughout the 60s and 70s White women retained better access to the more skilled operative jobs, like weaving, and a monopoly of the relatively well paid occupation of burling and mending.   Burling and mending, together with some processes intermediate between spinning and weaving, provided access to non mechanised work (17).   By way of contrast, where Asians were employed in jobs from which White women were absent their work was of the least desirable kind.   Thus Asians found work as machine minders in combing mills (where very few women were employed) and in the least attractive of the non mechanised occupations, for example woolpulling and general labouring in spinning mills (where no women were employed).

It is therefore clear that the extant, sexual division of labour between White women and White men was not simply replicated in the division of labour between Asian men and White men. Instead, the division of labour was established on a three cornered basis (18) with White men retaining the best jobs but with White women and Asian men working separately in the remainder. While the sexual division of labour remained, an additional element became apparent with the recruitment of Asians: the division of labour now had a racial basis, i.e. the distribution of workers across different elements of the labour process was based on race as well as sex. This racial division of labour was visible in the distribution of Asian workers between firms, between departments within mills, and between shifts of workers employed in the same departments.

CHANGE AND RESISTANCE

In their accounts of the circumstances leading up to Asian recruitment, respondents tended to make a direct connection between this recruitment and the transformation of the labour process. There was no spontaneous mention of the process we have already described, i.e. the process whereby the transformation of the labour process made jobs so unattractive that White workers rejected them. The simple fact is that they thought this too obvious to mention. When asked specifically, none of the respondents said that they had chosen to employ Asians. Instead, they explained that they had known Asian labour was all they would be able to get if they made the changes they desired. For example, in the 60s:

'Yes, we would have preferred locals but local labour only worked four nights.'

Similarly, one respondent explained that he couldn't get 'indigenous' workers in 1978 but would be 'delighted if they did come forward'; and another firm had tried, unsuccessfully, to maintain a deliberately high percentage of White workers. There were no such problems with Asian workers in the 60s since 'immigrants were at the door all the time.'

In the course of my fieldwork I was told several stories which illustrated the ease with which Asians had been recruited in the 1960s. At one responding firm, for example, management had decided to introduce a work study programme and while the day shift workers had accepted after some resistance the night shift had walked out. Management then approached some Asian employees and the following night had a full shift 'of their cousins and neighbours'. I was also told that in a mill not covered by my survey word had got around that jobs were available and when the day shift began the shop floor was full of Asians standing by the machines and demanding work. The police had then been called to remove them. While this last story may be apocryphal - there were in fact many similar stories circulating in Bradford in the sixties (see also Cohen and Jenner 1968, p.53) - it does at least suggest that all managers and employers viewed the supply of Asian workers with a degree of confidence. This was still the case in 1978:

'There is an army of immigrant workers out there who are already trained for most of the jobs we need operatives for'.

This last respondent told me that every Monday morning thirty or forty Asians waited at the gate for work. They were not permitted to pass through the gate to the personnel office, although some managed to get through with friends who were already employed there. Most firms had a waiting list of Asian workers and the general view was that they could 'pick and choose amongst the immigrants' (19).

We already know, in outline, why White workers rejected the work that Asians were only too glad to do. We know that the transformation of the labour process brought long and unsocial hours which White workers found unattractive but it also brought changes in work organisation which Whites resisted. New technology wasn't of itself distasteful but workers rejected the reorganisation of work which came with it. We have briefly referred to these changes already in this section, for example in the accounts of reorganisation of one worsted spinner and in woolcombing in general. In their talk of a new 'system', respondents were in fact describing a change in the character of work. As we discovered in Chapter Four, the transition from piecework to timerate payment can be regarded as a proxy for other changes in work organisation. One worsted spinner's Asian workers were concentrated in recombing, spinning, Volkman twisting and automatic winding. The recombing department at this firm had no night shift whereas the others were run for twenty four hours each day. What was common to these departments, apart from the proportion of Asians employed in each, <u>was the absence of piecerate payment</u>. Similarly at another survey firm where Asians were concentrated in spinning and this was the only department not paid on piecework. Piecework had been abolished on individual frames as cap spinning was slowly displaced by ring spinning and Asians replaced women workers. Finally, even where technology and shifts had been changed <u>but piecework remained</u> there were relatively few Asians employed. This was the case, for example, in the (Sulzer) weaving sheds of the weavers in the survey: there had been no Asian recruitment on a scale comparable to that experienced in woolcombing and worsted spinning. As we might expect, firms with piecework <u>and</u> old technology and 'short' shifts were those with few Asians and predominantly female employment.

My respondents regarded traditional female jobs on the old technology as skilled and a degree of responsibility was attached to this work. Each worker was assigned her own machine and expected to observe high standards of cleaning and 'housekeeping'. While (sexist) ideas of women's work prevailed - note also the significance of the employers' term for all women textile workers, 'the girls' - there was an opportunity for autonomy within managerial paternalism: women employees were expected to 'take an interest in the job' and were allowed to keep flexible hours and make time for themselves if they were fast enough at their work.

By way of contrast, the jobs the Asians were recruited to do were regarded in a different light. Employers wanted a more flexible workforce, one that did not enforce 'custom and practice' - i.e. the old rigid division of labour with its established hierarchy of reward and control. Efficiency demanded that this should be dismantled with the extra tasks being taken on by the remaining workers who should be 'flexible' about their job content. Thus I was told by one personnel officer that it was considered an advantage if operatives were more a adaptable. This applied especially in Volkman twisting, a department almost always staffed by Asians! But if management did not manage to create a completely flexible workforce with Asian recruitment, this was because flexibility tended to conflict with their second aim of

82

deskilling.   For example, the personnel officer referred to above
told me that Volkman twisting could be 'learnt' in two weeks.   In fact
the need for flexibility was really a reflection of the desire to
establish a new division of labour in the mill and was not concerned
with improving the capabilities of the workforce.   While established
'custom and practice' were broken down, the bulk of the jobs which
became 'Asian jobs' were redefined as 'minding' or 'inspection' with the
skilled element of the operatives' work eliminated or simply
unacknowledged (20).   It should be pointed out, however, that it was
the White workforce which was actually deskilled.   The Asian workers
who replaced them performed deskilled work, but their labour had not been
deskilled in the transformation of the labour process which brought them
into employment.   In any event, this change corresponded to the change
in the system of control signified by the transition to timerate payment
and respondents' belief that work was now 'machine controlled' (see
Chapter Four).

The identification of a relationship between the recruitment of certain
groups of workers and change in the labour process is not original
(see for example Erickson 1957, p.132;   cf. Sandberg 1974;   also see
Montgomery 1973, passim).   Indeed some aspects of this relationship
have been identified in respect of Asians in wool textiles (Allen et al.,
1977, pp.51-3, 67;   Moor and Waddington 1980;   pp.20-1) and Cohen and
Jenner found that the numbers of Asians employed tended to increase when
a firm bought new machinery and changed the pattern of shift working
(1968, pp.45-6) (21).   Yet the foregoing pages tell us more than this;
we have found that Asians were initially recruited as labourers into
'dirty jobs' and when employers realised that Asian labour was available,
into jobs in the transformed labour process.   This involved the introduction
of new machinery and hours of work as noted by Cohen and Jenner but the
transformation lasted beyond the period covered by their fieldwork.
Several firms in the sample, 'caught up' throughout the 60s and 70s,
for example there was a large increase in the Asian percentage of worsted
spinning workers after Cohen and Jenner's fieldwork in 1967.   We have
considered many examples of large scale recruitment of Asians together
with changes in technology and shifts in this later period.   Furthermore,
we have found that the employment of Asians was related to the changes in
work organisation described in Chapter Four and this is only hinted at
by Cohen and Jenner (1968, p.54-6).

Cohen and Jenner made some attempt to explain the relationships they
had observed.   They thought that shift work was something of a
technical necessity where new machinery was introduced (22).   They
concluded that, given the statutory exclusion of women from night work
(23), re-equipping naturally led to the increased employment of men
(1968, p.44).   They did, however, suggest that neither shift work nor
re-equipping would have been considered profitable alternatives by
employers if they had been forced to pay the wage increases which White
men would have required to persuade them to work nights (1968, p.44-50).

It is clear that Cohen and Jenner were aware of the industry's problems
although they did not think wool textiles was in crisis.   It was simply
that wages had to be kept down because the industry was so competitive
(1968, p.50).   In fact, my respondents said that they had recruited
Asians because Whites could not be persuaded to work in jobs affected
by the transformation of the labour process.   They were not, however,
referring simply to the jobs on the new night shifts they had created
(24) but to almost all jobs which had been affected by changes in hours

of work, re-equipping, or changes in work organisation. All three factors contributed to the transformation of the labour process in wool textiles and this was less a matter of technical necessity than an indication that all three increased the intensity of exploitation.

In the conclusions to their research, Cohen and Jenner speculated on what might have happened if Asian labour had been unavailable and decided that

> ... some of the less efficient forms in the industry have been allowed time to become more efficient and modernise and an extremely painful and over-rapid concentration of the industry has been avoided. This slowing down of the possible decline of certain firms may have relevance to those companies who used immigrants mainly as labourers and had embarked on a process of modernisation but did not have sufficient resources to do the job in one go.
> (Cohen and Jenner 1968, p.56).

While this may have been the case in particular firms, it cannot stand as a general statement about the wool textile industry. The 'contraction' to which Cohen and Jenner referred was merely postponed, and not for long at that! In the decade after their fieldwork the wool textile workforce was reduced by half. It is more likely that an increase in the proportion of Asian workers was a feature of the contraction of the industry in the 60s and 70s rather than an alternative to it. The observed relationship between the employment of Asian workers and contraction was in fact a consequence of the tendency for the industry as a whole to increase output per head by producing the same, or less, output with fewer workers. Employers' efforts to achieve this aim were largely dependent on an increase in the Asian percentage of the workers who remained.

In view of the unsatisfactory nature of Cohen and Jenner's speculation, I resolved to ask my respondents what their companies would have done without Asian workers. A few reached the same conclusions as Cohen and Jenner, for example,

> The area occupied by immigrants was our source of White labour before they were driven out ... but we would probably have gone bust.

The more usual response, however, was given by a woolcombing manager who said that, if the Asians had not come, wages would have been increased and hours shortened. 'Local' labour would then have been recruited into textiles and not into engineering (although this assumes that the engineers would not increase wages in reply). Another woolcombing respondent thought that wool textiles would have experienced more bankruptcies without Asian workers but the labour would have been found 'somehow'. It is noteworthy that this last respondent, in common with several others, was not only sure that control of the immigration of Black people to the UK had not affected labour supply, but thought controls should be more stringent:

> If we'd known how many were going to come we wouldn't have let them in.

Other respondents speculated that shift working would have been less extensive and shift premiums higher without Asian labour. It was thought that this might have led to rationalisation, to more productive

investment, to relocation of the industry elsewhere in Britain, or even
to less rationalisation as plants were kept open in order to maintain
capacity in the absence of shift work.   One respondent who thought that
rationalisation would have been less likely also suggested that
employers might have invested in different kinds of new machinery in
order to be able to increase wages and therefore attract White workers.

It is clear that there were alternatives to the employment of Asian
workers, indeed we have already concluded that the strategy which
ultimately led to Asian recruitment did not satisfy the employers'
aims.   They adopted this strategy because it was historically available.
As Chapter Two demonstrated, the postwar period was not the first in
which wool textile employers had made changes which led them to employ
cheap labour.   Wool textile employers in other countries did not have
such precedents to shackle their thinking and were able to adopt alternative
solutions to the postwar crisis.   For example, US employers migrated to
the Southern States while West German textile firms extended outward
processing, particularly in East Germany.   Of course some employers
did adopt the same solution as their UK counterparts and it is
interesting to note that the number of foreign workers in West Germany's
textile industry increased from 22,000 in 1961 to 105,000 a decade later.
In 1966 foreign workers made up 14 per cent of the textile workforce in
West Germany and by 1973 22 per cent of West German textile workers were
foreign born (NEDC 1973, p.58).   This was more than double the
proportion in other manufacturing industry (Frobel et al., 1980, p.78).
Nevertheless, it is clear that alternatives to Asian recruitment -
including capital export and outward processing - were theoretically
open to UK employers.   If they had adopted one of these strategies,
instead of the tried and tested solution, they might have been better
placed to deal with the postwar crisis in wool textiles.   Indeed we
have already noted in this chapter that the more successful companies
among the responding firms did not have large numbers of Asians.   It
is possible that this represents a trend which will in time become
general to the industry.

RECENT TRENDS

In Chapter One we discovered that the fall in the number of Asian
workers in wool textiles in Bradford (25) in 1979 was proportionally
greater than the reduction in total employment.   We have also found
that in the late 70s the proportion of (predominantly White) women in
the industry in Bradford (26) had stabilised.   Furthermore, in Chapter
Five we saw that the proportion of workers who were women increased in
some sections of the industry.   Whereas the proportion of workers who
were women had not increased by more than half a percentage point in
any section in any one year before 1977, a rising trend was established
in 1978 and 1979 (27).   Indeed, by 1979 the female proportion in worsted
spinning occupations had been restored to its 1975 level.   By 1980
there was an increase in the proportion of all wool textile workers in
Bradford who were women.   Given that the proportion of wool textile
workers who were women has tended to vary inversely to the proportion
of Asians, this confirms the fall in the proportion of Asians and suggests
that the decline continued after 1979.

There is some evidence that the jobs held by Asian workers were
affected by the reduction in demand which signalled the onset of the
recession in wool textiles in 1978 since companies which wished to
decrease output in the medium to long term dispensed with night shift

workers.   Given the concentration of Asians working at night this led
to a fall in their proportion of the workforce at individual firms.
For example, at one worsted spinner Asians were only employed so long
as the night shift lasted - from 1964 to 1976.   Nevertheless the more
usual method of reducing output was to take some machinery out of
commission, thus reducing work for the day as well as the night shift.
But employers also coped with reduced demand by suspending recruitment.
Labour turnover amongst Asians was high and they were therefore likely
to be disproportionately affected by reductions in employment through
'natural wastage'.   This does not, however, explain why the decline in
wool textile employment amongst Black school leavers was so much greater
than the decline in wool textile jobs found by White school leavers
(see Chapters One and Eight).   Moreover, it might be suggested that the
direct affects of recession actually led to an <u>increase</u> in the
proportion of workers who were Asian since declining demand had most
effect in group four firms which employed few Asian workers.   Thus one
group four firm had no Asian employees when the company closed down in
1980.   The disappearance of group four firms therefore tended to increase
the proportion of workers who were Asian in the industry as a whole, and
it is clear that these companies were indeed the most likely candidates
for closure.   There is, however, another way in which the recession
may have affected Asian wool textile workers.   It may be, for example,
that increased unemployment made Whites more willing to work in the
industry.

If the initial Asian recruitment in the 1950s had followed the
expansion of employment opportunities elsewhere, might not later contraction
in employment have reversed the process?   Yet unemployment in Bradford
increased throughout the 1970s while the Asian proportion of wool textile
workers also rose.   Nevertheless, some respondents thought that some
kind of threshold had been reached in 1978.   For example one worsted
spinning employer told me that labour supply problems had eased at all
levels and that:

> Unemployment does make a difference ... they aren't
> flippant about work now.   At one time they would walk
> out of the door if you asked them to do something they
> didn't like - it was becoming serious.

Rising unemployment may eventually have made it easier for wool textile
employers to <u>retain</u> White workers, thus reducing recruitment, but again
this cannot account for the disproportionate reduction in <u>entry</u> amongst
Blacks.   Furthermore, in 1978 no respondents reported any dramatic
improvement in the standard of White applicants: for example, some were
content to give apprenticeships to Whites <u>with no qualifications</u>.

White workers need not, however, have been persuaded to join, or stay
in, the wool textile industry by rising unemployment.   We might suggest
an alternative hypothesis: that further change in the labour process
in the late 70s made existing jobs more attractive to Whites, but this
once again requires evidence of improvement in the standards of White
applicants.   Furthermore, there were few signs of improvement in the
jobs themselves.   The only likely area of improvement lay in shift work.
Some respondents were keen to introduce three or four shift 'rotating'
or 'continental' systems and to dispense with permanent night shifts.
Asians were disproportionately represented on permanent nights and this
work had always proved particularly unattractive to Whites.   Furthermore,
some respondents were making efforts to get special dispensations for
women workers to be exempted from restrictions on hours of work.   This

may have been related to the move towards rotating shifts: one
integrated firm had employed women on a four shift system for some time.
At any rate, there were signs that the employers' efforts to gain
dispensations were increasingly successful (although the numbers of
women involved remained small).

Nevertheless, attempts to introduce rotating shift systems had been
made over many years but with little success (in the responding firms
at least). They had not proved sufficiently attractive to induce
White workers to come forward in large numbers. Nor were employers
making the basic changes which were necessary to attract White workers:
even after the 1981 pay increases, operatives and warehousemen in
woolcombing were receiving basic wages of £57.50 per week (£68.67 for
overlookers and senior technicians). Indeed, far from making wool
textile work more rewarding or less taxing, the changes being undertaken
by employers were actually leading to further deskilling (28) and
increased workloads. It would therefore seem more likely that Asian
workers were still replacing Whites in existing jobs, as was the case
in responding firms in 1978.

In sum, none of the accounts we have considered so far give a wholly
convincing explanation of the falling proportion of Asian wool textile
workers, and it is as well that we can find a more plausible alternative.
This final explanation again relies on the assumption of further change
in the labour process, but change which eliminated the jobs in which
Asians were over represented rather than making them more attractive.
This would account for a disproportionate fall in the numbers of Asians
recruited and/or any over representation of Asians amongst those leaving
the industry.

Asians were concentrated in unskilled or semiskilled operative and
labouring jobs, and there is no doubt that the number of such jobs was
falling. In some firms, respondents could show me departments in which
a handful of machine 'inspectors' and technicians had replaced two or
three overlookers and numerous operatives. As one manager remarked,

> When you show somebody round ... they ask 'where have all
> the people gone?'

In fact, the number of operative and labouring jobs was falling more
quickly than employment for the industry as a whole. Operatives and
labourers made up the majority of direct production workers and we
have already remarked that employment in direct production was contracting
at a faster rate than total employment (see tables in Chapter One).
But this does not solve our problem since we have identified a fall in
the Asian proportion of direct production workers. It simply means
that we may have underestimated the extent of the decline in Asian
representation in wool textiles. We must rather find an explanation
as to why the jobs held by Asians should disappear more quickly than
other direct production jobs.

The first possibility is that very recent change in the labour process
may have led to the concentration of job losses in those departments
where Asian workers were concentrated. Thus some of the reduction in
Asian employment at one firm followed re-equipping in weaving and related
departments and reorganisation. In one department at least, the company
had seen Asian labour as a short term solution to a problem of labour
demand which was later reduced by re-equipping. But this would not
explain why the proportion of Asians within such departments should
fall, and this seems to be the implication of the most recent figures on

the female proportion of employment analysed by individual section (see Chapter Five). It would seem that Asians were not simply losing jobs because they worked in department Y rather than department Z. They also seemed to be more likely to lose employment than other workers in department Y. We must therefore look for labour process changes which were likely to hit Asians harder than Whites who worked alongside them.

This was certainly the effect of mechanisation in the 'dirty jobs' associated with Asian employment in some scouring and carding departments of woolcombing mills. Thus at one woolcomber the proportion of scouring workers who were Asian fell with re-equipping in the 70s and at another a future fall in the Asian proportion of scouring and carding workers was expected with changes in wool pulling and card feeding. It wasn't that the jobs held by Asians were to be automated - although this was more likely in card feeding - but rather that mechanisation would take them out of the province of Asian workers. Thus auxillaries were being allocated to areas of work previously done by operatives and also by labourers: for example fork lift truck drivers were now doing the work done by woolpullers. This may have been happening for some time in operative jobs in some responding firms. Unfortunately, the relevant (time series) personnel details were not available for the companies most likely to have affected, group one firms with the most advanced and productive technology. At any rate, such changes depressed the Asian proportion of new recruits as well as the Asian proportion of leavers. For instance some employers in the survey had suspended operative recruitment while introducing recruitment of trainees for more skilled jobs for the first time in several years. Rather than making existing jobs more attractive to Whites, recent change in the labour process made it easier for employers to recruit Whites into areas of work which might have been done by Asians.

Finally it is possible for the proportion of workers in a particular section to fall following changes in the distribution of employment between firms as well as within firms. We know that the most successful (group one) companies had proportionately fewer Asian workers than most other firms in the same section, excluding only group four firms. We also know that employment was more likely to increase in group one firms and to contract amongst their competitors. Ceteris paribus, we would therefore expect the Asian proportion of employment in that section to fall. Although we cannot prove it conclusively, it is almost certain that this has happened. Indeed, were it not for the decline of group four firms with no Asian employees, the resulting effect on the Asian proportion of employment would have been even more marked.

A further check on the decline of Asian employment was produced by the recession. Far from explaining the fall in Asian participation, reduced demand after 1978 actually slowed it down since it discouraged new capital investment. Textiles as a whole was amongst the three UK industries with the lowest volume of new investment at the beginning of the 80s. Save for the obvious need to reduce capacity, we can assume that firms in group two, and possibly three (although their resources were less extensive), would have tried to emulate their more successful competitors by finding a lasting solution to the postwar crisis. Such a solution would not have been dependent on the employment of Asian workers in upwards of a quarter of all jobs. Moor and Waddington's typology of wool textile firms included high technology firms without Asian workers as well as unmodernised firms without Asians. Asians were

thought to be concentrated in 'capital-extensive' companies (Moor and
Waddington 1980, p.20-1). But Moor and Waddington's classification,
like our own, was really a snapshot of a process. They did not go on
to suggest that capital extensive firms might be converted to high
technology and the Asian proportion of employees reduced. In fact their
explanation for the observed correlation between type of firm and Asian
representation was in terms of relative wage rates, the high technology
firms paying better wages. We have already dismissed this argument,
indeed the company with the most modern technology in my sample had
lower wage rates than most other firms in the industry.

Nevertheless, Moor and Waddington's research did capture an aspect of
the relationship between Asian workers and the wool textile labour process
that had not been evident to Cohen and Jenner a decade earlier, or to
Sheila Allen at the beginning of the 1970s. Allen suggested that Asians
could not be (disproportionately) removed from wool textile jobs because
whole processes were dependent on them (Allen 1971). By way of contrast
we have concluded that this dependence was quantitative rather than
qualitative and that the concentration of Asian workers may have made
them easier to remove. Just as the Asian proportion of wool textile
employees was increased very quickly in earlier years, so this proportion
could be quickly reduced: a whole shift or process might be reorganised
or eliminated. If Asian workers had not been concentrated in machine
minding in certain processes and on certain shifts but evenly distributed
throughout the industry, it would have been much more difficult to reduce
their proportion of the total workforce.

The conclusions reached in this section are obviously at variance with
existing research. To summarise these conclusions, we expect the fall
in the Asian proportion of wool textile workers to continue but do not
think it results from the direct effects of recession on the industry.
Reduced demand tends to maintain or increase the Asian proportion as
much as, or more than, it tends to reduce it. The indirect effects of
recession may play a part in that rising unemployment may have made wool
textile jobs more attractive to White workers, however it is worth noting
that unemployed textile workers were probably more likely to be Asians
than Whites. Indeed White workers in general were far less likely to
be unemployed than Asians (see Chapter Eight). Disproportionate
increases in the numbers of Asians leaving the industry, and especially,
disproportionate reductions in Asian recruitment, were more likely to
result from further change in the labour process and from changes in the
distribution of employment between firms associated with such changes.
There is no evidence that these changes have made existing jobs more
attractive to Whites but they have reduced employment in areas - jobs,
departments and firms - where Asians have been most likely to find work.

If we are right to conclude that the fall in the Asian proportion of
wool textile workers resulted from further change in the labour process
rather than in product demand or the labour market, then we can identify
a new aspect in the relationship between the employment of Asian workers
and work in wool textiles. It is clear that Asian workers were not
used as an alternative to modernisation by wool textile employers. The
only firms which did not employ Asians were the most backward in the
industry, nevertheless the employment of Asians may have represented a
transitional stage in the industry's development. In the 60s and 70s
wool textile employers were able to remove obstacles to increased output
per head without increasing wages. By the end of this period 'custom
and practice' over workloads and responsibilities had been successfully

challenged and the worker autonomy symbolised by piecework had been
replaced by increased accountability.   Furthermore, the workforce had
in large part been converted to shifts and low premiums and to work on
new machinery.   It may be that these changes prepared the way for a more
lasting solution to the employers' problems.   In other words, the
recruitment of Asian workers allowed employers to overcome worker
resistance and to make changes which would later allow them to dispense
with the need for Asian labour.

CONCLUSIONS

We have established that a racial division of labour was introduced
into wool textiles in the 1950s when Asians were recruited into labouring
and the dirty jobs rejected by other workers.   In the 60s, Asians were
recruited into some operative jobs in woolcombing (following early
attempts at reorganisation) and in worsted spinning, where employers
were attempting to transform the labour process.   In succeeding years
Asians gained access to a wider range of machine minding jobs in both
sections with the continued implementation of combinations of new
technology, hours of work and work organisation.   This even took Asians
into weaving (although in small numbers) and they also found a handful
of jobs in the least attractive ancillary work.   But the racial division
of labour was only modified as the number of jobs which White workers
found unattractive increased, i.e. as employers found that yet more of
their vacancies attracted only Asians (29).

In large part the division of labour in responding firms had been
established for two decades when I visited them in 1978.   In woolcombing,
for example, woolsorting departments were occupied by exclusively White,
skilled workers on nonmechanised work paid by the piece.   On the floors
below the sorters, Asians did unskilled work on two twelve hour shifts
and were paid timerates.   They were concentrated in dirty nonmechanised
jobs or in those like French combing where re-equipping had occurred.
Similarly in worsted spinning where there was a division between White
craft and Asian unskilled workers and between White semiskilled workers
employed on old machinery and working in the old way and Asian workers
operating the new machines, shifts and work design.

There were, however, signs that further change had begun in the late
1970s.   There was no modification of the racial division of labour -
Asians did not, for example, gain access to nonmanual or supervising
occupations - but further change in the labour process threatened to
reduce the proportion of workers who were Asian by disproportionately
reducing employment in those areas of the racial division of labour in
which they were concentrated.

NOTES

(1)   Cf. 25 per cent of direct production employees - see Tables
      1.2 and 1.5 in Chapter One.
(2)   Further problems of comparability result from the inclusion
      of shift premiums, production linked payments and part time
      wages in the data on 'average employee remuneration';   and
      from the inclusion of part time workers in employment data.
(3)   Most of this information was taken from ICC 1979;   NEDC 1978
      and 1979;   company records and press reports.

(4)   It may be useful to bear in mind more recent fluctuations
        in demand when considering the indirect measures of
        profitability (Tables 6.3-6.5) discussed below. Wool
        textile profit margins fell between 1974 and 1976 but
        recovered thereafter; return on capital was increased
        from 1976; and profit per employee was stable between
        1972 and 1975, slumped in 1976, but rose in the following
        year (to greatly exceed the trend for other textile
        sections) (ICC 1979).

(5)   With the exception of one firm, firm E in my survey, which
        had a specialised product.   Firm E is classified in group
        two instead of group three - with the other combers -
        precisely because it had greater latitude in marketing
        and therefore responded to the postwar crisis in a
        different way.

(6)   The third woolcomber in group three, firm K, had a
        notably lower proportion of Asians, amounting to only
        thirty eight per cent of this company's employees.
        Firm K was probably the most successful of the three.
        Although no details were available, it is probable that
        this company remained in profit by curtailing investment
        to match its (smaller) resources.

(7)   This account is of most relevance to worsted spinning since
        woolcombing firms already worked extended hours at this
        time.

(8)   They also bought machinery which was suitable for this
        kind of intensive running.

(9)   Change in winding was particularly slow, hence the slower
        fall in the percentage of workers who were female in
        winding, see Table 5.1 above.

(10)   Note that this firm's spinning department was run on
        'short' hours during the day despite being entirely
        converted to ring spinning.   This day shift was largely
        staffed by White (Italian) women and therefore the department
        had a relatively low percentage of Asian workers.

(11)   But note that some of this firm's twisting machinery was
        not up to date and that their machines were operated by
        Asian women.   There was a similar situation at another
        spinner where Asian women were employed in winding and
        reeling while Asian men were concentrated in the departments
        with newer technology and two shift, twenty four hour
        running: drawing, spinning and twisting.

(12)   It may be that these changes had begun at a slightly earlier
        date in the larger combers which were first to convert to
        French combing.

(13)   The proportion of Asians in one of the other firm's carding
        departments increased with re-equipping in the later 70s.
        In fact the numbers of Asian employees actually fell,
        although not as much as total employment in carding.

(14)   Note that the proportion of all direct production workers
        who were female in each of these three firms was even
        lower than the proportion for woolcombing as a whole and
        was still falling (ASRP, p.324 and Appendix Two).

(15)   Note, however, that there were some variations in trends
        in the 1970s.   Thus the longest series shows that the
        Asian proportion of night workers varied between 76 and 81
        per cent in the middle of the decade.   Furthermore, the

numbers of Asians on night work actually fell in one case.
In fact this reflected the overall trend for all night
shift direct production workers. Similarly at another
comber where the numbers of all direct production workers
on nights and of Asians on nights were more or less stable.
But at the third firm numbers in both categories increased.

(16) One woolcomber's Asian workers were concentrated even within
the combing process, in wool rather than cashmere combing.
Note that within combing mills Asians were concentrated in
combing rather than in the ostensibly similar process of
carding.

(17) Very few Asian women found work in burling and mending.
Like Asian men, they were concentrated in departments
where the labour process had not been transformed.

(18) It might be argued that a full account would refer to a
four cornered division of labour which would therefore
cover the allocation of Eastern European and other White
migrants to certain areas of wool textile work. However,
most of the Europeans who had worked in the industry had
moved elsewhere before fieldwork was conducted in 1978.
Furthermore, those Europeans who remained were no longer
confined to the jobs in which they had originally been
recruited. It is more sensible to conceive of the period
when Europeans were recruited as a transitional stage
between a division of labour based solely on sex and one
in which race was also relevant.

(19) Although one or two worsted spinners thought that the
recruitment of Asians might prove more difficult if they
relocated outside the inner city (where most Asian workers
lived):

>   We wouldn't like to move out of this particular
>   area - its so good for labour. We thought of
>   moving to a purpose built, single storey building
>   but we couldn't find a vacant site in this area.
>   There is a lot of labour here.

(20) For a useful discussion of deskilling, both real and imagined,
in a similar context, see Cockburn 1983, especially Chapter
Four. For further discussion of deskilling in wool textiles
see ASRP, Section One, especially pp.134-9, 206.

(21) It should be no surprise that some of Cohen and Jenner's
conclusions were reproduced above since my fieldwork used
a similar sample and similar methods to those employed by
Cohen and Jenner and indeed to those used by Allen and her
colleagues. The reader might, however, be surprised that
my fieldwork reproduced some of the findings of Cohen and
Jenner even though it was conducted a decade later.

(22) For an alternative view of this kind of process see
Ayattollahi who thinks that capital investment follows
the labour shortage which shiftwork creates. (Ayattollahi
1976, p.248-50).

(23) This emphasis seems to contradict Cohen and Jenner's
suggestion that White workers, and particularly women, did
not want to work in wool textiles if more flexibility was
demanded by employers (1968, p.54-6). However, as noted
above, this suggestion is in fact barely more than a hint.

(24) Note that we must therefore be wary of the importance
Cohen and Jenner attach to statutory limitations on
women's working hours in bringing about an increase in
the proportion of Asian workers.
(25) The UK figures did not reflect the local trend because
of the increased concentration of the industry in Bradford
(where a disproportionately large number of Asians were
employed).
(26) There was, once more, a lag in the UK figures: the proportion
of all wool textile workers who were women fell between 1979
and 1980.
(27) With the exception of the weaving section where the proportion
of workers who were women fell in 1979. It is worth noting
that the proportion of workers in this section who were
Asian was below the average for the industry.
(28) See Chapter Seven for an account of a scheme for training
woolcombing technicians which reflected the employers'
intention to deskill by separating the technical and
supervisory components of overlooking. For an earlier
attempt to deskill technicians in woolcombing see
Telegraph and Argus 22 April 1969.
(29) Note that it is often assumed (see, for example, Bourguignon
1977, p.30-1; for a rare exception see Montgomery 1973,
p.5-6), that employers incur extra costs by recruiting
workers in this way. In fact the Asian workforce proved
to be self renewing and self training and their employers
were able to reduce the costs of advertising, selection,
training and even of dispensing with labour!

TABLE 6.1

ASIAN WORKERS AND TRENDS IN EMPLOYMENT AND WAGES IN RESPONDING FIRMS 1972-1976

Firm	Male Asian % of all Employees 1978a	Total Employment 1978a	% Change in Employment 1972-6(+/-)	Average Employee Remuneration (£s per annum) 1976	% Change in Employee Remuneration 1972-6(+/-)
K	56.2	121	-5[b]	2807[b]	36[b]
O	55.0	100	-9	2824	86
D	54.0	950	+11	2387	96
N	50.0	60	N/A	N/A	N/A
E	47.7	392	N/A	N/A	N/A
L	47.4	154	-28	3350	110
H	45.3	201	N/A	N/A	N/A
G	42.1	328	N/A	N/A	N/A
M	38.0	74	N/A	N/A	N/A
A	24.4[c]	545[c]	+56	2691	82
J	24.3	140	+4	1919	84
B	15.6	225	+9	2004	102
F	14.1	638	-20	2068	108
R	1.3	150	+20	N/A	N/A
P	-	100	N/A	N/A	N/A
Q	-	107	N/A	N/A	N/A

a Figures for some firms are estimates. Figures are for Summer 1978, except for two firms where details are for December.

b 1972-1975.

c Applies to one mill only.

SOURCES: Author's fieldwork, NEDC 1978 and 1979.

TABLE 6.2

COMPOSITION OF THE LABOUR FORCE IN RESPONDING FIRMS, 1978a.

	All Employees	Male Asian Employees	% of all Employees	Female Asian Employees	% of all Employees	Total Female Employees	% of all Employees
Group One firms b							
Firm A c	545	133	24.4	0	-	N/A	N/A
Firm B	225	35	15.6	35	15.6	125	55.6
Firm D	950	513	54.0	N/A	N/A	380	40.0
Group Two firms							
Firm E	392	187	47.7	0	-	N/A	N/A
Firm F	638	90	14.1	60	9.4	N/A	N/A
Firm G	328	138	42.1	26	7.9	91	27.8
Firm H	201	91	45.3	4	2.0	61	30.3
Firm J	140	34	24.3	2	1.4	29	20.7
Group Three firms							
Firm K	121	68	56.2	0	-	N/A	N/A
Firm L	154	73	47.4	0	-	N/A	N/A
Firm M	74	28	38.0	0	-	0	-
Firm N	60	30	50.0	0	-	19	31.7
Firm O	100	55	55.0	15	15.0	20	20.0
Group Four firms							
Firm P	100	0	-	0	-	85	85.0
Firm Q	107	0	-	0	-	91	85.0
Firm R	150	2	1.3	0	-	120	80.0

a   Figures for some firms are estimates. Figures are for summer, 1978, except for two firms where figures are
    for December.

b. Firm C is excluded since figures were only available for one department.

c   Figures apply to employment in one mill only.

SOURCE: Author's fieldwork.

TABLE 6.3

WAGES AND SALARIES AS A PERCENTAGE OF TOTAL VALUE ADDED IN SELECTED WOOL TEXTILE FIRMS 1973-1977

	1973	1974	1975	1976	1977
GROUP ONE FIRMS					
Firm A	36.5	38.1	39.3	40.5	38.4
Firm B	56.3	49.7	60.5	44.6	N/A
Firm C	70.5	76.5	75.1	75.9	N/A
Firm D	71.8	64.2	67.7	83.0	86.0
GROUP TWO FIRMS					
Firm F	77.5	74.0	79.4	94.2	90.5
Firm I	63.4	60.6	73.3	81.5	72.8
Firm J	63.6	67.5	66.6	67.8	63.3
GROUP THREE FIRMS					
Firm K	52.3	54.6	73.0	N/A	N/A
Firm L	67.7	55.2	151.4	76.6	62.6
Firm O	71.2	71.7	71.3	71.4	N/A

SOURCE: NEDC 1979.

96

TABLE 6.4

TOTAL VALUE ADDED AS A PERCENTAGE OF CAPITAL EMPLOYED IN SELECTED WOOL TEXTILE FIRMS 1973-1977

	1973	1974	1975	1976	1977
GROUP ONE FIRMS					
Firm A	70.1	60.2	78.7	63.8	69.0
Firm B	82.2	101.0	53.6	85.3	N/A
Firm C	61.1	61.9	70.5	78.2	N/A
Firm D	68.1	68.0	71.3	68.7	60.0
GROUP TWO FIRMS					
Firm F	54.5	53.3	47.9	51.0	53.5
Firm I	48.5	42.1	43.2	45.0	53.7
Firm J	73.7	55.8	72.2	81.3	69.0
GROUP THREE FIRMS					
Firm K	28.1	27.2	47.4	N/A	N/A
Firm L	39.7	12.7	33.2	40.6	51.7
Firm O	98.3	81.3	78.2	103.9	N/A

SOURCE: NEDC 1979.

TABLE 6.5

TOTAL VALUE ADDED (£s) PER EMPLOYEE IN SELECTED WOOL TEXTILE FIRMS 1973-1977

	1973	1974	1975	1976	1977
GROUP ONE FIRMS					
Firm A	4618.0	4746.9	5433.6	6642.7	7558.6
Firm B	2167.1	2612.6	2846.0	4491.5	N/A
Firm C	2456.5	2607.2	3094.5	3595.5	N/A
Firm D	2030.0	2541.9	2780.6	2876.4	3109.6
GROUP TWO FIRMS					
Firm F	1524.8	1765.2	1958.7	2196.6	2725.6
Firm I	2051.0	2254.6	2271.6	2458.8	3336.7
Firm J	1852.2	2013.2	2277.5	2829.8	3618.2
GROUP THREE FIRMS					
Firm K	3938.9	3829.3	3847.8	N/A	N/A
Firm L	2353.0	3189.5	1225.1	3276.6	5347.8
Firm O	1994.6	2338.2	2592.2	3954.1	N/A

SOURCE: NEDC 1979.

TABLE 6.6

AVERAGE EMPLOYEE REMUNERATION (£s PER ANNUM) IN SELECTED WOOL TEXTILE FIRMS 1972-1977

	1972	1973	1974	1975	1976	1977
GROUP ONE FIRMS						
Firm A	1476	1686	1806	2130	2691	2899
Firm B	991	1220	1298	1722	2004	N/A
Firm C	1409	1732	1993	2324	2730	N/A
Firm D	1218	1457	1631	1881	2387	2674
GROUP TWO FIRMS						
Firm F	992	1181	1306	1554	2068	2467
Firm I	1062	1301	1363	1664	2005	2427
Firm J	1044	1178	1358	1517	1919	2288
GROUP THREE FIRMS						
Firm K	2059	2061	2092	2807	N/A	N/A
Firm L	1592	1762	1855	2510	3350	3754
Firm O	1520	1420	1675	1952	2824	N/A

SOURCE: NEDC 1978 and 1979.

TABLE 6.7

EMPLOYMENT IN SELECTED WOOL TEXTILE FIRMS 1972-1977

	1972	1973	1974	1975	1976	1977
GROUP ONE FIRMS						
Firm A	552	692	756	835	862	888
Firm B	175	154	231	211	191	N/A
Firm C	239	265	253	232	258	N/A
Firm D	979	978	1030	1116	1090	1103
GROUP TWO FIRMS						
Firm F	5371	5291	5293	4792	4320	4048
Firm I	11316	10000	9829	9154	9997	9849
Firm J	384	383	370	416	401	392
GROUP THREE FIRMS						
Firm K	217	221	207	205	N/A	N/A
Firm L	286	271	227	197	206	223
Firm O	109	114	113	96	99	N/A
GROUP FOUR FIRMS						
Firm R	102	111	137	185	123	N/A

These figures are for total employment in a company and may differ from personnel figures given elsewhere which apply to sites or mills.

SOURCE: NEDC 1978 and 1979.

TABLE 6.8

EMPLOYMENT IN SELECTED DIRECT PRODUCTION DEPARTMENTS IN THREE BRADFORD
WOOLCOMBING FIRMS 1971-1977a: ALL WORKERS AND ASIAN WORKERS

YEAR	DIRECT PROD WORKERS	ASIAN DIRECT PROD WORKERS	ASIAN % OF ALL DIRECT PROD WORKERS IN DEPARTMENT
FIRM E – WOOLCOMBING DEPARTMENT			
1973	25	20	80.0
1974b	21	20	95.2
1975	23	22	95.7
1976	52	50	96.1
1977	37	37	100.0
FIRM K – SCOURING DEPARTMENT			
1974	11	10	91.0
1975	19	16	84.2
1976	14	12	85.7
1977	16	16	100.0
FIRM L – CARDING DEPARTMENT			
1971	31	16	51.6
1972	31	15	48.4
1973	28	16	57.1
1974	25	14	56.0
1975	25	13	52.0
1976	28	17	60.7
1977	32	20	62.5

a. Figures for December of each year.
b. This firm suspended night working in 1974.
SOURCE: Author's fieldwork.

101

TABLE 6.9

DIRECT PRODUCTION WORKERS IN THREE BRADFORD WOOLCOMBING FIRMS
1971-1977a: ALL WORKERS AND ASIAN WORKERS

YEAR	ALL DIRECT PROD WORKERS	ASIAN DIRECT PROD WORKERS	ASIAN % OF ALL DIRECT PROD WORKERS
FIRM E			
1973	163	96	58.9
1974b	114	57	50.0
1975	136	90	66.2
1976	180	148	82.2
1977	170	158	92.9
FIRM K			
1974	78	59	75.6
1975	115	89	77.4
1976	102	87	85.3
1977	82	72	87.8
FIRM L			
1971	101	66	65.3
1972	119	78	65.5
1973	91	57	62.6
1974	89	58	65.2
1975	87	54	62.1
1976	101	73	72.3
1977	103	76	73.8

a. Figures for December of each year.
b. This firm suspended night working in 1974.
SOURCE: Author's fieldwork.

TABLE 6.10

DIRECT PRODUCTION WORKERS ON DAY SHIFT IN THREE BRADFORD WOOLCOMBING FIRMS
1971-1977 : ALL WORKERS AND ASIAN WORKERS

YEAR	ALL DIRECT PROD WORKERS ON DAY SHIFT	ALL ASIAN DIRECT PROD WORKERS ON DAY SHIFT	ASIANS % OF ALL DIRECT PROD WORKERS ON DAY SHIFT
FIRM E			
1973	124	73	58.9
1974	114	57	50.0
1975	103	61	59.2
1976	96	70	72.9
1977	93	87	93.5
FIRM K			
1974	N/A	N/A	N/A
1975	N/A	N/A	N/A
1976	56	37	66.1
1977	48	37	77.1
FIRM L			
1971	49	25	51.0
1972	64	33	51.6
1973	48	24	50.0
1974	46	23	50.0
1975	47	22	46.8
1976	53	34	64.2
1977	53	35	66.0

Figures for December of each year.

SOURCE: Author's fieldwork.

TABLE 6.11

DIRECT PRODUCTION WORKERS ON NIGHTSHIFT IN THREE BRADFORD WOOLCOMBING FIRMS 1971-1977a: ALL WORKERS AND ASIAN WORKERS

YEAR	ALL DIRECT PROD WORKERS ON NIGHT SHIFT	ALL ASIAN DIRECT PROD WORKERS ON NIGHT SHIFT	ASIANS % OF ALL DIRECT PROD WORKERS ON NIGHT SHIFT
FIRM E			
1973	39	23	59.0
1974b	—	—	—
1975	33	29	87.9
1976	84	78	92.9
1977	77	71	92.2
FIRM K			
1974	N/A	N/A	N/A
1975	N/A	N/A	N/A
1976	46	43	93.5
1977	35	34	97.1
FIRM L			
1971	52	41	78.9
1972	55	45	81.8
1973	43	33	76.7
1974	43	35	81.4
1975	40	32	80.0
1976	48	39	81.3
1977	50	41	82.0

a Figures for December of each year.
b This firm suspended night work in 1974.
SOURCE: Author's fieldwork.

TABLE 6.12

PERCENTAGE OF WORKERS WHO ARE ASIAN IN THREE BRADFORD
WOOLCOMBING FIRMS 1971-1977a

	1971	1972	1973	1974	1975	1976	1977
FIRM E							
Total direct production			58.9	50	66.2	82.2	92.9
Day shift direct production			58.9	50	59.2	72.9	93.5
Night shift direct production[b]			59	-	87.9	92.9	92.2
Woolcombing department			80	95.2	95.7	96.1	100
Warehouse			29	15	28.6	24.1	24.1
Non-manual			- One or no Asian workers -				
FIRM K							
Total direct production				75.6	77.4	85.3	87.8
Day shift direct production				N/A	N/A	66.1	77.1
Night shift direct production				N/A	N/A	93.5	97.1
Scouring Department				91.0	84.2	85.7	100
Warehouse				0	0	22.7	5
Non-manual				0	0	0	0
FIRM L							
Total direct production	65.3	65.5	62.6	65.2	62.1	72.3	73.8
Day shift direct production	51.0	51.6	50	50	46.8	64.2	66.0
Night shift direct production	78.9	81.8	76.7	81.4	80	81.3	82
Carding department	51.6	48.4	57.1	56	52	60.7	62.5
Warehouse	- One Asian worker only -						
Non-manual	0	0	0	0	0	0	0

a   Figures for December of each year.
b   This firm suspended night working in 1974.

SOURCE: Author's fieldwork.

7 Racism at work

This chapter summarises respondents' opinions of the Asian workers they
employed.   In some cases they were asked directly for their views on
Asian workers, but on other occasions respondents volunteered this
information and made use of racial categorisation while discussing other
topics.   We know from the preceding chapter that Asians were confined
to the least desirable jobs in the mills.   Much of this chapter will be
devoted to respondents' explanations of why this should be the case and
to an assessment of the significance of these explanations (1).   We will
not, however, waste time by establishing the existence of racial
discrimination in recruitment and promotion in wool textile mills.   This
would require us to prove that Asians had the qualifications and capabilities
needed in more attractive jobs, and this has been done quite adequately
in many other studies (for wool textiles see Allen et al., 1977; for
non textile work see Daniel 1967; Smith 1974 and 1976).   We can, however,
briefly make the point that most respondents did not want to employ
Asians in skilled or supervisory occupations.   One worsted spinning
respondent told me that he had once employed an Asian in an unskilled
job who said he had been a manager in India and wanted promotion.   The
respondent had told him, 'Well, you had better get back to India then.'
The worker concerned 'left' - 'we are careful.'   Similarly, one of the
woolcombing firms in my sample had a single Asian training as an
apprentice overlooker.   The respondent explained that 'it's better to
give unemployed local lads the job isn't it?'

   Such examples could be multiplied interminably, but there is little
point in boring the reader in order to establish what is now generally
accepted: that British employers discriminate against Black workers on
the basis of mistaken beliefs about the qualities which can be attached
to skin colour (2).

MANAGING ASIAN WORKERS.

   Several respondents argued that the promotion of Asians might threaten
managerial control.   Typically,

   'You have to be careful about what position of power
   you put them in.'

This seems paradoxical: why should managers worry about control, i.e.
worker resistance, when previous chapters have shown that Asian
recruitment solved the problems caused by the traditional workforce's
resistance to change?   Yet White workers' resistance led them to leave
the industry for better jobs elsewhere.   We cannot assume that Asians
did not resist managers' initiatives simply because they did not follow
Whites out of wool textiles.   In a straw poll of Britain's Asian

workers as early as 1974 it was concluded that two issues occupied them above all: the struggle to work less ... and the reduction of the intensity of actual work (Race Today Vol.6, No.4, 1974). We know why this should have been the case: Asians were only employed where work was, or had been made, hard and working hours were long. But how was their resistance expressed?

We are certainly not concerned in this section with cases of Luddism, or (in the main) of organised resistance, although one exception does come to mind:

> 'We have excellent relations ... virtually no problems
> with the Asians in the mills ... by and large excellent
> relations at every level. Only one small area ...
> Ramadan, where the priests are interfering. No other
> problems.' (Employers' representative).

As this quote indicates, the demand by some Asians for time off at the end of Ramadan to celebrate Eid achieved significance even in the minds of the most complacent observers. Employers and managers did not see this merely as a question of lost labour time. They might, for example, lose only one shift, and that was unpaid. Rather, they saw the demand as a threat to their 'right to manage'. Firstly, Eid was the workers' idea: it was not a bank holiday and it didn't fall in Bowling Tide, the Bradford holiday observed by all the mills. Secondly, Eid was a moveable feast and its date could not be predicted in advance. Thus the workforce told their employers when they would not turn up for work. Employers responded, with the agreement of the unions, by automatically deducting holiday credits. But it is also as well to point out that the meaning of the demand for time off was not lost on the workers who made it. Eid achieved an extraordinary significance amongst Asian wool textile workers which cannot be explained by the assumption (often made by anthropologists) that Asians in Britain strive to be 'more Asian' than those who have not migrated.

In the main, however, the resistance of Asian workers was unorganised. It did not even amount to 'ca' canny'. We know from Chapter Four that much labour was now 'machine controlled' - this was why management could afford to dispense with piecerates - and that the opportunities for 'going slow' were limited. Instead, we are concerned with cases of workers indirectly refusing managers' orders in an effort to make their jobs more bearable. Of course managers did not see it this way, they thought any difficulties in control stemmed from the fact that the workers were Asian. Two issues will be used to illustrate both the managers' view and their response: supervision and 'language problems'.

We have already noted that some respondents thought that the control they exercised over Asian workers might be disturbed if Asians were appointed in more senior positions. Nevertheless, throughout the 60s and 70s, some employers made use of unofficial Asian supervisors. These workers were given no formal recognition but were rather paid a bonus for their additional services in recruitment and control of the Asian workforce.

> 'They only fit in a big factory where you can keep them
> all together and you need a leader.'

Respondents gave examples of 'godfathers' (their term) who had exercised a 'hold' over other Asian employees which could be turned to management's advantage, but they were also aware that this addition to the normal mechanisms of control could prove a two edged sword. Many respondents had abandoned the practice because there was a risk that the 'godfather' might actually appropriate the management function.

It is possible that respondents were making too much of the power available to 'straw bosses'. Their imagery ('godfather') seems rather fanciful and may simply represent an attempt to explain informal recruitment practices which were unfamiliar to them (3). Yet if management did not want to delegate control for fear of loosing it, how were they to obtain the extra leverage on their Asian workforce which they seemed to think was necessary? The answer lay in the <u>character</u> of supervision. One respondent reported that his firm had recruited a (White) overlooker with experience of supervising Asians prior to establishing a night shift which would be staffed by Asian workers. Indeed, several respondents thought that special qualities were required of those White workers charged with supervising Asians. Overlookers, for example, were required to exercise <u>physical</u> control where necessary:

> 'We had one lad here, D---, he threw one /Asian/the length of that frame.'

But such excesses were not usually required:

> 'Of course we have good relations with the immigrants -
> you see we've got a firm but fair general manager who
> knows how to treat them. He won't stand any nonsense.'

While supervision seems an obvious locus of control, the same cannot be said of 'language problems'. In fact, some respondents showed little interest in this area. The greatest anxieties were shown by <u>junior</u> managers who had day to day involvement with problems of control. Junior managers in personnel and production suspected that Asian workers pretended ignorance of English in order to refuse orders. It was this group who were most likely to think that 'language problems are exaggerated' and to believe that communication problems were manufactured by the workforce in order to lessen their workloads: 'they <u>pretend</u> not to understand.' (c.f. Allen et al., 1977, p.119). Junior managers wished that they had never been put in a position where their 'right to manage' could be challenged in such an unfair manner:

> 'They shouldn't let anybody into the country to work who
> can't speak the language.'

On the other hand, they did not want the problem to be solved in the most obvious way.

West Yorkshire Language Link (WYLL) had done pioneering work in language training <u>inside</u> companies in the area. This organisation, based in Bradford, had concentrated much of its effort in the wool textile industry and, especially in the early years, had provided its services free of charge. Yet several junior managers described WYLL training as 'preferential treatment':

> 'They shouldn't have to do it in our time. I did my
> learning to get where I am at nights.'

Suspicion of favouritism was not, however, the sole reason for junior managers' dislike of language training. Firstly, they felt that language tuition during working time usurped their control on the shop floor. Secondly, they feared that the training would be <u>successful</u>!

As in the case of 'straw bosses', respondents had mixed feelings about 'language problems'. Their ambivalence resulted from the fact that they could never be sure when ignorance of English was a pretence. If 'language problems' were real then language training might actually erode managerial control. A real lack of understanding might be a good thing since it could make management's job easier: how could management policy be challenged if it was not understood? For example,

> The theory is that more production means more money but
> it isn't that simple. It depends on the machines and
> it gets complicated explaining why wages aren't increased.
> At a certain stage it gets beyond all of us but because
> of the language barrier they will accept what you say on
> trust.

> We have a very profitable company here. We have had no
> short time for fifteen years. We must be doing something
> right. Language Link may produce some benefit but may
> also produce problems - a little bit of knowledge can be
> more dangerous than none at all.

Most respondents thought language training justified only where management was 'having trouble' with its Asian workers and the respondent quoted above only thought it advisable where dealing with a persistent 'industrial relations' problem, i.e. where it might reinforce control. If it were not for the Health and Safety at Work legislation and the demands of the industrial training board, he would be better off with Asians who could not speak English.

Of course these last two factors might influence employers and senior managers as well as the junior managers who saw 'language problems' as control problems. WYLL's efforts to 'sell' - even where no charge was made - language training as an adjunct to control did not persuade employers and senior managers unless production was visibly suffering. Only in these circumstances might they respond to WYLL's claims that language training could be a profitable addition to normal personnel work since it would eliminate 'lack of communication' on the shop floor. Respondents were usually inclined to think that these claims were exaggerated and to require proof. Thus I was told by an informant at WYLL that one firm - probably one of the responding companies - had only considered language training after an initial approach to WYLL was made by a South African subsidiary which also employed Black workers.

Those who see language training as a solution to problems of racial disadvantage might do well to remember the attitudes of wool textile managers and employers, and to note the responding firm which reacted to a report which highlighted 'language problems' by deciding to reduce the Asian workforce rather than by arranging language training. Other firms had taken similar but less drastic action. For example, some had resolved only to recruit Asians who were fluent in English. For junior managers, however, this raised the same problem as language training: 'more knowledge would mean less acceptance on trust.' Fortunately, there was an alternative solution which allowed them to escape from this double bind. Thus one manager explained that he would only hire Asians without a command of English if his next 'trainer' was Asian.

Employing Asian 'trainers' or 'instructors' might mean using Asian workers who, as was frequently the case, introduced new recruits, to train the new workers (to mind combs or frames). But this raised the problem already encountered in the discussion of 'straw bosses', the risk of loosing control to an intermediary. If there were to be intermediaries, they should ideally be selected from those who owed their elevated position entirely to management and remained under managerial control. Thus the use of 'instructors' selected by employers and trained by the industrial training board was increasingly common. As one respondent pointed out, the introduction of 'instructors' made it unnecessary to accept employees with good English as 'self appointed leaders'. The training board's courses allowed this respondent to choose the 'communicators' he wanted and improve their English. It should therefore be no surprise that the training board thought the 'instructor' courses they provided were the only ones on which positive discrimination in favour of Asians might exist, and it is worth noting that employers said they would not necessarily choose UK educated Asians for these courses since they could be 'too much trouble'.

'ECONOMIC MEN'

In spite of, or possibly because of, the resistance of Asian workers, employers liked to think they could exercise total control. The following comments were made by a respondent after the author had visited one of his employees:

> 'If you had gone to see anyone else than S_____ - who is
> quite westernised - they would have probably left the
> country. The only people who are likely to take an
> interest in our Asian workers are the local constabulary -
> let's face it, not all of them have their papers in order.
> It would have been far better to go through me - that's
> the only way they could have been put at ease.'

While it is undoubtedly true that, for Asian workers, control is not limited to the workplace, the respondent saw this as an opportunity to enhance his position by posing as protector. He portrayed his workforce in paternalist terms, dependent on their employer as their only friend. This was not an isolated view.

Given our discussion of respondents' views on 'managing Asian workers', it comes as some surprise to discover what they thought were the general characteristics of these workers. (c.f. Allen et al., 1977, p.351). Firstly, the managers and employers I interviewed thought that, in their general 'attitude', Asians showed themselves 'docile' and 'willing'. By 'docility' they meant that the Asians complained less, in particular about conditions, and were 'servile'. Most importantly, respondents thought the Asians were 'like children' and should be treated as such. By 'willingness' the Asians, and to some extent the earlier migrants from Europe, were meant to be willing to work any hours and take any menial job. Secondly, respondents commented on the physical characteristics of their workforce: they thought that the Asians were 'small', 'thin' and 'nimble fingered'. Finally, respondents summed up the Asians' intellectual characteristics in this way: 'uneducated', 'unintelligent' and 'inarticulate'. While these opinions do not differ significantly from those held more widely, held even by those managers and employers in firms or industries without Asian workers, wool textile managers and employers seemed to value such 'characteristics'.

For instance, respondents thought that Asians were physically suited to textile work:

> 'The Pakistanis had smaller hands than the locals, like
> the women they were suited to dealing with the small frames'.

'You need nimble hands for spinning and weaving - women
and Asians are good at it'.

Of course this is not an entirely new idea.   The descriptions used by
respondents to emphasise Asians' suitability were, as one of the quotes
demonstrates, those usually associated with 'women's work'.   Furthermore,
research in the late 60s turned up the idea that Indians were physically
suited to furnace work because they were accustomed to working in high
temperatures!   Even within wool textiles, Eastern Europeans had always
been labelled 'bloody hard workers', yet there is a <u>degree</u> of difference
since the characteristics the Asians were believed to possess seemed to
form a perfect fit with the characteristics of the work they were
required to do.

In previous chapters we have discovered that there was change in the
nature of work in wool textiles and that employers thought that different
characteristics were required in the jobs performed by Asians as against
those performed by the traditional female workforce.   To begin with
'attitude', when conditions are being changed for the worse it is of
course an advantage to have workers who are 'docile' and 'willing', however
my respondents actually claimed that the Asians <u>preferred</u> work under the
new system.   For example, they thought the Asians were only interested
in take home pay and were prepared to work 'any hours' in order to increase
their income, i.e. Asians actually wanted to work long, unsocial hours.
Their intellectual capacity (or lack of it) was also believed to 'suit'
the Asians to the new work organisation.   We know that the bulk of the
jobs which, in the racial division of labour, became the Asians' preserve
were also defined as 'minding' with the skilled element of the operative's
work eliminated or simply unacknowledged.   Asians occupied the only
jobs for which they were considered suitable.   Their's was the kind of
labour required in the transformed labour process, where a worker should
be willing to 'listen to what he's told and to work hard ... /and/ ...
be able to put his imagination out of gear.'   Thus,

'For comb and gill box minding, in fact for any operative's
job, the ideal worker's main qualification is the capability
to cope with boredom for twelve hours - the immigrants do this
best.'

Lack of intelligence was an advantage rather than a handicap where the
job was 'machine controlled' and Asians were acceptable in repetitive
work - only 'children' after all.

Other researchers have asked wool textile managers and employers what
they thought of their Asian workforce.   From the answers they received
Cohen and Jenner concluded that the 'culture' of the Asians made them
closer to the economists' ideal of 'economic men'.   They were thought
to be interested simply in take home pay, they had not learnt about the
effort bargain with employers.   Furthermore, the Asians had not 'unlearnt'
habits of deference and cooperation.   Cohen and Jenner thought that the
Asians' 'culture' might make them 'adaptable' where the employers valued
adaptability more than usual (Cohen and Jenner 1968, pp.55-6).

There are two faults in this thesis.   Firstly, Cohen and Jenner assumed
that, when they were told that the Asians were 'docile' and 'willing',
they were being given accurate descriptions of the Asians 'cultural'
characteristics.   Although my respondents made similar comments to those
of Cohen and Jenner, it was clear that they were simply <u>ascribing</u>
characteristics which were far removed from any real cultural
characteristics Asians might possess:

'The Indians are best - British rule, the Pakistanis
didn't have that - and a lot of them were in the army
so they were used to the discipline and our way of life.
The Pakistanis are much slower - have you ever walked
behind one in the street? Their natural pace of life
is much slower and it's just the same in the factory.
The Bangladeshis are somewhere between the two (as
regards performance). They had British rule too, and
most of them are Hindus, aren't they?'

Some of these stereotypes were generated, as the misinformation they
contain suggests, by the managers themselves, but they also owed a great
deal to the educational activities of that sector of the race relations
industry which is concerned with the 'multi racial workplace'. This was
particularly true of the fine tuning of stereotypes which parallels the
'ethnic school' of race relations described by Jenny Bourne (1980).
We are primarily interested in stereotyping of 'Asians' rather than in
the 'cultural' sub groups respondents identified, however it is worth
noting that most respondents differentiated the three groups identified
in the quote above. They were not, however, always ranked in the same
order or with the same explanations.

The second mistake in Cohen and Jenner's account lies in their
assumption that the existence of 'cultural' characteristics helped to
explain why Asians were concentrated in certain jobs. Of course it is
possible that managers acted as if their stereotypes had some substance:
they might believe that Asians were suited to certain kinds of work and
make sure that Asians were hired in these jobs. Furthermore, it has to
be admitted that some of the explanations given by respondents for the
racial division of labour seemed to suggest this was exactly the
course they did pursue:

'Asians are plodders so you put them in combing where you
need plodders.'

Nevertheless, the impression is misleading: these and other similar
comments simply amounted to attempts to rationalise events over which the
respondent had exercised very little control.

Cohen and Jenner remarked that some managers had been less than
convincing when they described how they had weighed up the qualities of
various sub groups of Asian workers and allocated them to the work in
which they would prove most useful. I also found that where such and
such a sub group was said to be 'good at' the work in a particular process,
I invariably found that the workers from that sub group were concentrated
in the relevant department. We require an extension of this scepticism
to cover all of those occasions on which employers or managers attempted
to claim the racial division of labour as their own work; for example
when they claimed that Asians were over represented on night shifts
because they preferred to work at nights! The people I interviewed had
neither the time nor the inclination to do what was in fact impossible (4),
i.e. to carefully allocate workers to different parts of the labour process
according to criteria which accurately indicated their suitability for
particular kinds of work. Their rationalisations represented an attempt
to persuade the interviewer, and perhaps themselves, that they had made
the effort and succeeded, just as they imagined a good manager should.

It has long been contended that managers use arbitrary criteria to
select and allocate workers in the belief that these criteria bear some
relationship to the qualities they believe the work requires. Now it is

112

true, in part, that skin colour was used as a screening device in wool textile mills. There is overwhelming evidence that Black workers were screened out of recruitment procedures for better jobs, i.e. those in which they faced competition from White workers, but there is little proof that Black workers received more positive treatment in screening. While it is true that an Asian applying for work in a combing mill was usually asked one question - 'can you work a French comb?' - the manager's disinterest in his qualifications did not stem from a belief that Asians made good comb minders but from the belief that Asians made bad accountants, laboratory technicians or even warehousemen. In fact the managers would have preferred to exclude Asian workers from all jobs. That they could not do so reflects the fact that in some areas of recruitment there was simply no other labour available. Employers who were believed to express a preference for Asians (see, for example, the quotation from The Times in Chapter One) had merely made a pragmatic decision about recruitment costs. They had established through their experience that the attempt to recruit White workers was, at least temporarily, a waste of time. Thus several respondents reported that any Whites they did manage to hire left within the day or refused to work and were dismissed.

We have noted that wool textile respondents' views on Asian workers did not differ significantly from those held by other employers who did not employ Asians. The difference lay in the value which respondents attached to those characteristics. Respondents explained that what other employers might consider a vice in their workforce, for example lack of intelligence, they saw as a virtue. When they explained that unintelligent workers were 'best suited' for work in the transformed labour process, they were justifying their patent inability to discriminate against Asians in these jobs. Their statements were in fact apologies for non discrimination: they could use workers that common knowledge dictated were second class because the work they offered was inferior. Thus their stereotypes of Asian workers did not only consist of ascribed 'cultural' characteristics but also of the characteristics of the work that the Asians performed (c.f. Allen 1977, p.115). In large part these characteristics referred to the behaviour that any group of workers who did such jobs would be forced to exhibit. For example, workers on night shift are, by definition, willing to work at night. Employers and managers simply extended this logic to claim that Asians preferred the jobs they occupied and that they were good at such work. Nevertheless, the refinement of these stereotypes did not prevent respondents from using the same set of ascribed characteristics to explain those cases where they were able to discriminate. This can be illustrated with the views of an employer with an old fashioned worsted spinning mill.

This man shared the general view of Asian workers' characteristics but in his firm such characteristics remained vices and not virtues. Of course he had an idea that if his firm were modernised, i.e. if the labour process were transformed, then things might be different. He said that Asians were 'O.K. for repetitive jobs like combing' and 'good on the big machines' but were not suited to the jobs or technology in his mill and so he did not employ them. We then toured the shop floor and watched two young Asians maintaining a loom! This employer had a small workforce and he knew he employed the two young workers I saw but he did not consider them sufficiently important to demand an explanation (or even recognition). They simply weren't sufficiently visible enough for him to have to justify his inability to discriminate. The White faces around the mill demonstrated that he could afford to discriminate when he wished and so the characteristics he believed Asians to possess remained vices and not virtues. In other words, he was able to draw on a common set of stereotypes in order to 'explain' discrimination.

It seems illogical that respondents should wish to simultaneously justify non discrimination and discrimination, but the paradox is not too difficult to explain. In the first case they were justifying their circumstances to themselves, i.e. finding the most pleasing account for their inability to behave like other employers. In the second case respondents were concerned to justify their actions to a (presumably sceptical) observer. As the case recounted above illustrates, there was no inconsistency in the explanations offered to explain non discrimination and discrimination. For example, if Asians actually preferred to work at night then one had an 'explanation' for their absence from day shifts. Similarly, respondents were able to use their common stereotypes of Asian workers where change in the labour process had increased their opportunity for discrimination.

We discovered in Chapter Six that the proportion of jobs in which employers felt able to discriminate was increasing since employment was falling more quickly in those areas of work where Asians were concentrated. Respondents' views of the characteristics required of workers in those areas where the contraction was less marked differed from their views of the ideal worker required in the departments staffed by Asians. Typically, they emphasised the sensitivity of the machinery, its improved productive power and its 'high technology' features. Thus, 'you can't use a big spanner to fix an electronic circuit'. In other words, the workers required by this new machinery should have a new set of skills and aptitudes, and those formally in demand were no longer needed. Similarly, respondents emphasised the high output and quality of production under the latest technology. If workers made mistakes now they would spoil a much larger volume of materials, and thus accuracy and care were required of the workforce whereas these qualities had been of little importance in the past. Finally, the new machinery required much more than 'minding'. Workers should have the ability to diagnose and report faults and understand the logical sequence of processes:

'... the labour must be more sophisticated with regard to the machine.'

'... they must be able to stand back and think what to do, not be doing the things the machine does for them anyway.'

It is clear that the common stereotypes applied to Asian workers did not 'fit' respondents' characterisations of the qualities required in these new jobs, and managers and employers were quick to point out the discrepancy. They were now trying to wait for the 'better calibre' of recruit, and this meant White workers:

'We are trying to be selective about the immigrant jobbers, well all the immigrants really. We try to wait for the better recruit when we can'.

At one firm I was told that the Asians

'are unreliable and we are trying to reduce their numbers ... because the labour is there now. We have White women to do the weaving. We're getting quite a few school leavers - very good, quick to learn'.

'Selectivity' had become a euphemism for reducing Asian employment (5) but helped respondents to justify their discrimination since the Asians did not have the qualities they wished to select. Wool textile employers could now exclude Asians on the same grounds as other industries: 'nimble fingers' were no longer required. The characteristics they had ascribed to Asians became either valueless or positive handicaps. Thus 'plodders' were now seen as 'too slow, used to pushing a plough'. Of course, this does not explain why respondents now felt able to discriminate. The perceived discrepancy between the Asians' ascribed characteristics and those of the jobs from which they were excluded constituted the respondents' justification for discriminating against Asian workers. The explanation for their actions lay in the expansion of the arena within which discrimination had become a possibility. Even the employers' representatives accepted this explanation although, in contrast to our conclusions in Chapter Six, they saw rising unemployment as the primary cause of employers' increased ability to discriminate. Thus one representative agreed that the Asian proportion of employment in his section of the industry was falling - in fact he seriously underestimated the proportion of Asians still working in the industry - since firms could now get labour from the local White community. He cited instances where redundant engineering workers had returned to textile occupations that they had once held, or perhaps had entered textiles for the first time. In fact these workers would, in the main, be entering skilled occupations, i.e. rising unemployment in 1978 had no direct effect on the occupations in which Asians were concentrated. We have already discovered that the decline in these occupations followed from further transformation of the labour process which reduced the number of less attractive jobs rather more quickly than total employment. Hence there was some truth in the employers' conviction that the character of work in their mills was changing. The flaw lay in their contention that Asians were not suitable for the work that remained. The error was repeated in their justification for the exclusion of Asians from nonmanual and skilled or supervisory positions.

It almost goes without saying that the stereotypes of Asian workers did not 'fit' the characteristics which employers thought were required of the workers who performed the more attractive jobs in their mills. However, respondents supplemented their justification of discrimination by reference to an additional set of stereotypes. For example, one worsted spinning respondent explained that they had no Asian overlookers because where they had tried to recruit Asian apprentices in the past these recruits had interrupted their training by returning to Pakistan or India for visits. Furthermore, 'they never come from school on the same basis /as Whites/', i.e. with the required qualifications: 'the Asians who have these kind of qualifications want to be brain surgeons'. This respondent claimed that they had tried, 'really tried', to find suitably qualified Asian recruits. Another worsted spinning respondent claimed to have made similar efforts but employed only one Asian overlooker and one Asian trainee as yet and thought 'the position will change as their education and language improves'. Other respondents thought that the Asian applicants for skilled jobs were suitably qualified but would not recruit them for other reasons:

'... you need loyalty, and the Pakistanis will leave for £1 extra down the road.'

115

'We've advertised for two overlookers now. The
Pakistanis come but they want big money.'

It was also suggested that Asians could not be promoted because of
jealousies amongst Asian workers on the shop floor:

'Unless a Paki is a manager he won't be obeyed by his
mates ... You have to get them all doing the same thing
at the same time.'

Perhaps the most bizarre explanation was offered by an employee of the
industrial training board. He knew of one firm which had refused to
take on any Pakistani apprentices because they had had experience of
such recruits taking the company's trade secret back to Pakistan! More
commonly, however, employers and managers claimed that they were 'forced'
to discriminate against Asians by their employees.

WHO DISCRIMINATES?

The tendency of employers to blame their employees for the existence
of discrimination is already familiar from studies conducted in the 60s
and 70s, and from employers' arguments when formally charged with
discrimination. Wool textile employers used this defence in all cases
where Asians were under represented. Take, for example, their refusal
to hire Asians for the day shift in worsted spinning mills:

'The girls don't like them, they leave other mills because
of them and come here'.

'No Whites /males/ apply for the day turn, coloureds do
but we don't set them on because we have to keep the
girls sweet'.

Employing women on days was 'traditional' and it was widely accepted
that hiring Asians on the day shift led to increased (voluntary) turnover
amongst the White women:

'the Whites voted with their feet ... two Pakistanis
arrived in a spinning shed and pretty soon it was full
of them'.

and the solution was, as at this firm:

'complete segregation; the women finished at 5,
the men came in at 7'.

Respondents also claimed there was resistance to the recruitment of
Asians amongst skilled White workers:

'As a company we are aware that there is resistance from
the overlookers and fitters we already have here. Even
with union cooperation we can't do much about it'.

'The fitters and overlookers threaten, they say they will
refuse to train an Asian taken on as an apprentice ...
You can't force them to part with their knowledge'.

One woolcombing respondent reported that he hoped they did not get any
Asians through the new training scheme for woolcombing technicians (see
below), not because of any personal reasons of his own but because the
existing supervisors would not accept an 'immigrant' as an equal.
Furthermore, he thought the supervisors did not like WYLL's language
training scheme and saw it as 'preferential treatment - there's a lot of
prejudice about!'

116

While managers and employers tended to blame individual workers or groups of workers for discriminating, employers' representatives thought the trade unions were responsible: the craft unions denied Asians access to skilled and supervisory positions through the operation of labour supply agreements and control of apprenticeships. Of course the craft unions did not concur, but there was some support for this view amongst informants from unions representing operative wool textile workers (6), and one craft union official said that his union would like to see wages and conditions improved in order to reduce the number of Asians employed. Nevertheless, one must be wary of accepting the employers' argument on face value. For example, employers' representatives contended that there were more opportunities of promotion for Asians in combing (7) because there was less 'union influence' in this sector. While this may have been true, it was also the case that in combing promising operatives were promoted off the shop floor into positions as jobbers and overlookers, and skilled workers were rarely given apprenticeship training. Since some departments and shifts were composed entirely of Asian workers it was inevitable that this practice would produce some Asian overlookers. Nevertheless, one trade union informant thought that the system of promotion in combing limited opportunities for workers under forty years of age and one employer at least thought that this limitation indirectly discriminated against Asians. This respondent looked forward to the new scheme for training woolcombing technicians introduced in 1978 by the British Wool Confederation (BWC). It was supposed that the new scheme would remove this barrier to the promotion of Asians. This is highly unlikely: the BWC scheme was described by an informant at the industrial training board as the woolcombing employers' attempt to introduce the kind of training given in worsted spinning and weaving 'on the cheap'. In worsted spinning and weaving - where most overlookers were trained by apprenticeship - there were proportionally fewer Asian overlookers than in combing. Evidence from the first year of the scheme's operation seemed to suggest that this change in training practice further limited promotion opportunities for Asians. While there were few Asian overlookers in the woolcombing firms I visited, only one or two of the seventeen recruits to the scheme were Asian.

It is clear that institutional arrangements for access to skilled and supervisory occupations could provide barriers to Asian workers. Thus, the recruitment of apprentices amongst school leavers known to employees is fairly common practice and one woolcombing respondent explained that apprentice overlookers were normally recruited by passing the word around the mill. This arrangement was maintained since they would not consider advertising 'because we would be swamped by immigrants'. Nevertheless, the example of the change in recruitment practices associated with the BWC scheme shows that established arrangements could be modified if they no longer allowed discrimination. In some cases respondents had suspended training altogether in consequence. Thus one respondent explained that the traditional practice had been to recruit skilled and supervisory personnel off the shop floor, but there had been a shortage of recruits

'because there was no English on the shop floor to move up. So we will have to advertise for trained personnel, not apprentices.'

Perhaps the most important point to note about the BWC scheme is that the employers - and not skilled workers or the craft unions - picked the recruits who would be trained as combing technicians. The essential difference between this scheme and the established practice was that

employers were no longer obliged to pick these recruits from the workers
on the shop floor.   An industrial training board employee interpreted
the change in this way:

> 'The Confederation scheme illustrates the standards
> involved in recruiting skilled workers.   If there are
> no Asians on the scheme it is because the firms are
> picking the recruits to the scheme themselves and they
> are looking for a good standard'.

It is clear that, on this occasion at least, employers could not claim
that discrimination was the fault of their employees.   Furthermore,
this could hardly be the case in <u>operative</u> recruitment where employers
had complete control and where the Asians had encountered their most
recent problems.

The opinion that Asian workers were being given better access to skilled
and supervisory occupations was most often expressed by the employers'
representatives and the industry's service agencies.   Nevertheless,
this point was often made with considerable ambiguity:

> 'But what could we do to help the Asians anyway? ...
> would like to help but can't ... they aren't clever
> enough yet and there is prejudice down the line ...
> you can't see the problem in terms of numbers ...
> for example if there is a low number of Asian overlookers
> - there probably is - then you should start looking at
> the problem, pattern, over a number of years ...
> and the figures might indicate other things'.

This informant admitted that 'prejudice' did exist in the industry but
thought that, in the bigger firms, this would be more in evidence nearer
the shop floor than in higher management.   In smaller firms 'prejudice'
might exist at the highest levels.   While I did not have the
opportunity to test this thesis, we have already remarked that junior
managers perceived their position - in relation to Asian workers - to be
different to that of senior managers and employers (8).

It might be thought that <u>junior</u> managers were more likely to see the
Asians as a problem because they had more immediate contact with them,
however familiarity with Asian workers was not the decisive factor.
Rather, day to day contact with the shop floor gave them an appreciation
of problems of <u>control</u>.   This was clearly illustrated in the discussion
of 'language' problems.   Senior managers and employers were much less
likely to be worried about control since it was not their province.
It only caused them concern when it affected their immediate interests:
costs, production and profits.   Thus, junior managers sometimes felt
themselves to be in the front line of a struggle over the labour process
which employers and senior management did not understand.   There was
some truth in this: junior managers were charged, in effect, with forcing
the workforce to submit to an increase in the intensity of exploitation,
and it was their responsibility to deal with any resistance that
developed.   Of course they did not see the problem in quite these terms,
rather, they complained that their superiors simply did not appreciate
the difficulties that the employment of <u>Asian</u> workers created in the
exercise of a junior manager's responsibilities.   Thus one woolcombing
personnel manager explained that he was concerned about the rising
percentage of workers in his firm who were 'immigrant':

'This is what I'm concerned about ... we are getting
too dependent on them ... it's just a bit frightening'.

He had tried to communicate his fears to senior management and had
produced reports containing 'ethnic' breakdowns but felt that senior
management were too concerned with keeping wages down and conditions poor -
and thus maintaining profits - rather than sharing his concern about
'dependence on immigrants' (9).   Similarly, one worsted spinning manager
wanted to reduce the number of Asians in his charge but complained that
he got no help from senior management because they were only interested
in production and not in 'industrial relations'.   His use of the term
'industrial relations' was revealing: he saw that a generalised fear of
'dependence' on Asians in fact reflected anxieties over loss of control.
His colleague, a personnel officer, had similar feelings:

'The blinkers on people outside textiles keep them from
seeing that the worst trouble is between immigrants,
not just Indians against Pakistanis but village against
village. Blocs develop so easily and you don't know
until it's too late when you put a lad in and they won't
work with him, a fait accompli'.

Despite the anthropological cast of this comment, it is clear that the
personnel officer was worried about control. He also used the term
'bloc' to describe workers who had been organised into a trade union.
In both cases he was concerned about his 'right to manage'. He felt
that, as a personnel officer, he should have the power to allocate workers
wherever he pleased and thought that his job became impossible when the
workforce effectively removed this perogative. Several respondents
thought that their jobs were made harder by the presence of the Asians
and the anxiety of this manager was shared by others. As a trade union
official pointed out,

'It's this lot that are scared of the younger immigrants
questioning their authority. Overlookers, mill managers,
personnel managers don't like being questions.'

It may be that the anxieties of junior managers were receiving some
attention by the end of the 70s. We have already recounted some
respondents intentions to decrease Asian employment by increasing
selectivity. Some of these respondents were quite senior. Indeed,
employers' representatives explained that Asians were not up to the
standards firms now required in their 'more selective' recruitment
policies. An employee of the industrial training board referred to
'objective tests' conducted at one Bradford woolcombing firm which had
shown that Asians weren't good enough to take up 'responsible' jobs in
the new employment structure the company was trying to create:

'... not every firm discriminates you know, T_____ for
instance ... But you see the Asians weren't as good as
the others. The tests at T_____ showed this. T_____
were disappointed at the Asian standards in the tests,
especially in combing, whereas there are more women in
spinning ... anyway are the Asians all that important?'(10)

As in non textile recruitment (see following chapter), the only formal
(new) standard of which I could find evidence was language. Informants
at West Yorkshire Language Link saw 'language difficulties' as the main
barrier to the continued employment of Asians, as well as to their chances
of better jobs. This was a growing problem given that by 1978 most

employers could afford to refuse any applicant without competence in
English and without textile experience. The argument seems to be
plausible until we remember the significance attached to language.
For example, fluency was not always desired. Furthermore, respondents
had never considered language screening for European workers yet many of
them remarked how it was 'funny' that these migrants had never learnt
English.

It is possible that the 'new concern' for language competence followed
changed requirements in the labour process (and from Government legislation)
but this does not immediately explain why <u>Black Britons</u> fared no better
than other Asians. One of my WYLL informants claimed that even Asians
with three quarters of their education in this country needed language
training and that it would be a mistake for firms to use these young
workers as 'instructors' or 'interpreters'. The managers agreed: one
told me that the UK educated Asians he employed

> 'can just about communicate what's wrong with a machine
> but their general English - spoken and written - is
> devoid of detail and their arithmetic is poor.'

If this is true, it reflects very badly on the standards of education
provided by a local authority which prides itself in being a pacesetter
in 'immigrant education'. On the other hand, it may be that language
was being used as a (flimsy) excuse for the exclusion of Asians rather
than an objective selection criterion. It is worth noting that it was
often the junior managers, with their worries about control, who enforced
the new 'selectivity' through standards of language competence.
Furthermore, formal testing arrangements were not typical practice.
More often there was an explicitly subjective assessment of employees'
capabilities. One woolcombing respondent - in fact one of those who
blamed discrimination on his overlookers - simply told his overlookers
to refuse any applicant 'they can't get through to.'

This last example would seem to suggest that a great deal of
discrimination in wool textiles occurred without the <u>active</u> participation
of employers. This reflects the fact that they did not take part in
day to day selection and recruitment procedures. It is therefore very
difficult to establish to what extent the employers were themselves
responsible for discrimination against Asians. Further difficulties
arise because, unlike junior managers, there is no doubt that employers
were prepared to take labour from any source if they needed it.

On the other hand, the power of employees was generally limited: they
had few sanctions which might be used to force their employers to exercise
their greater power (to discriminate) as they would wish. Take, for
example, the employers' contention that Asians were segregated by shift
to please White female employees. The only realistic sanction available
to these women was <u>quitting</u> and we have seen that they exercised this
sanction in response to an increase in the intensity of labour (see
Chapter Five). The women 'voted with their feet' against the
transformation of the labour process and not against the recruitment of
Asians. At an early stage of the research on which this book is based,
it appeared that the 'disadvantaged' position of Asian workers might, in
part, have resulted from Whites' attempts to protect themselves against
the initiatives of employers. However, we can be sure that White worker
resistance had only an <u>indirect</u> effect: women workers protected themselves
by quitting and this permanent withdrawal of labour created the
possibility of the creation of a racial division of labour. Nor did

White worker resistance have an effect on employers' decisions in other areas of employment. The craft unions <u>were</u> protecting their White, male members by the use of labour supply agreements and control of apprenticeships, however any racism amongst these unions did not explain why Asians were largely absent from the jobs they hoped to control. Asian workers were absent because alternative White labour was available and thus employers had no reason <u>not</u> to discriminate.

In sum, expressions of resistance and discrimination against Asians were both functions of a third factor: the availability of more attractive employment. Although it is not considered a defence in law, employers and managers used White worker resistance to justify discrimination. Their complaints of pressure from their White employees simply represented attempts to transfer the blame for discrimination against Asians onto other workers.

BLACK BRITONS

Perhaps the most remarkable conclusion to be drawn from the evidence presented in this chapter is that British managers' and employers' stereotypes of Black workers underwent little change in the 1960s and 70s. There are many similarities between the comments reproduced above and those recorded by Allen et al., (1977, p.95-135), Patterson (1968, for example p.64) and Wright (1968, p.64, 75-6, 95, 109-92) (11). Nevertheless, there was also some suggestion of change in these stereotypes.

In an earlier section, we discovered that junior managers identified Asian workers as a cohesive group which, if it became too large, would threaten their control over the labour process. But while some respondents were clearly worried about a threat to their 'right to manage' others were unable to articulate their fears beyond a generalised anxiety about 'dependence' on Asians. Nevertheless, most respondents thought that special measures - even extending to coercion - were necessary to control Asian workers and it seems that they felt that the employment of 'too many' Asians was a risk. Now it may be that this element of risk was increasing, at least in the eyes of managers and employers.

Cohen and Jenner predicted that 'cultural' changes and the development of 'institutional constraints' within the Asian workforce might make Asians more like other workers. They would, therefore, be less attractive to wool textile employers (1968, p.56). There is some evidence which appears to support this view, in other words there is evidence for increased <u>resistance</u> amongst Asian workers:

'... during the 60s the Asians were becoming increasingly aware that hours were as important as cash. In 1968 the going rate demanded by the Asians was £25 for sixty hours but they were finding out that other industries paid the same or similar money for less hours. They were also increasingly aware of conditions, how they were worked and so on.'

Although several respondents remarked that 'the longer they /Asians/ have been here, the less hours they want to do,' this manager's view (certainly this time scale) was not typical. However, respondents were much more likely to make comments of this kind when they were asked directly for their opinions of <u>Black Britons</u>, i.e. the very group, born and educated in the UK, amongst whom we might expect Cohen and Jenner's 'institutional constraints' to make their initial appearance.

We have already seen that junior managers singled out Black Britons as too much of a threat to control to be tolerated. Although there were relatively few Black Britons in the industry (see Chapter Eight), managers were adamant that they did not want more since they held a much lower opinion of Black Britons than of any other group of workers. It may be that respondents distrusted Black Britons for the same reason that they saw Asians with a better command of English as dangerous. In other words, their dislike of Black Britons was genuine and based on their habitual distrust of the more articulate Asians. On the other hand, we have already noted that some managers denied Black Britons' fluency. Furthermore, we must remember that those who complained about Black British workers were the very managers who hoped to eliminate Asians from the workforce. If Asians were still to find work in wool textile mills then Black Britons would soon comprise the majority of new Asian recruits. By portraying them as inferior to the existing Asian workforce, managers justified future discrimination. Since they could not ascribe the general stereotypes of 'Asian' workers to Black Britons, new stereotypes were adopted. There can be no doubt that Black Britons are <u>not</u> 'docile' and 'willing' (12), the doubt is that their fathers and mothers were ever the timid workforce which respondents portrayed.

That Asians were capable of resistance was not simply admitted in the case of Black Britons, it was <u>proclaimed</u>. Black British recruits were rejected because they

> 'are usually worse in attitude to their work ... more Bolshie.'

> 'have the worst characteristics of both the English and their own race, and they are not as good as their parents.'

Of course respondents almost always neglected to add that young <u>White</u> workers might also be considered less reliable, or more lazy or more 'bolshie' than their parents.

As in the case of general stereotyping, the most illuminating evidence comes from an exceptional respondent, in this case a manager who had charge of several Black Britons. He admitted that he would rather not have any Asians in his department but justified the presence of Black British workers by claiming that they were 'different', perhaps not even Asians but honorary Whites:

> 'None of this garlic nonesense, fish and chips and a teacake for them.'

This young manager explained that he would take on young Asians without textile experience if they were 'smart', i.e. dressed and behaved like him, and he went on to explain that his policy had worked:

> 'Their English is much better and they have never worked before therefore they have nothing to compare our wages with ... The young Pakis are better than their fathers. Young Whites don't care.'

He claimed that, as a result of his good judgement, he had the best production record in the company and the praise of senior executives for the way he ran his department.

This is, once more, an example of a respondent justifying his <u>inability</u> to discriminate. Just like some of the managers interviewed by other researchers in the 1960s, this respondent claimed that he could pick the 'good ones'. Yet he admitted that he would rather not have

employed Asians <u>at all</u>. 'All Italians' would have been the best;
'all White, English' was too far fetched to contemplate. In fact, he
admitted that he even experienced problems in recruiting older Asians
since average wages in his department were depressed by a 'short'
(i.e. eight hour) shift system. This limitation on earnings was, of
course, the real reason why his department was staffed by young Black
Britons.

CONCLUSIONS

In the first section of this chapter we established that some wool
textile managers saw Asian workers as a threat to their control over the
labour process. We also discovered that many respondents thought that
special measures were needed in order successfully to manage Asian
employees. Yet resistance was not part of the general stereotypes
applied to Asian workers. These stereotypes consisted of ascribed
'cultural' characteristics and the characteristics of particular jobs,
and were used by respondents to <u>justify</u> their own position.

Where Asians were <u>not</u> excluded, these stereotypes were employed to
explain <u>non discrimination</u>. When an employer said, like this man (who
had recruited a workforce of Asian women for a new plant)

'They like the job, couldn't speak much English but they
fitted in with what we wanted'

they were rationalising <u>after the fact</u>. 'What we wanted' turns out to
have been simply <u>labour</u>, not some particular group of workers who
possessed special qualities. It is very doubtful that Asian workers had
particular characteristics which were highly valued by their employers.
Their reluctance to leave wool textiles hardly seems to justify calling
the Asians 'economic men', but even if the term is valid, their behaviour
was not a reflection of their culture (c.f. Cohen and Jenner 1968, pp.55-6)
but of their inability to gain access to alternative employment. This
is properly the subject of the following chapter and it will suffice to
say that the present chapter has established that 'economic men' were no
longer needed by wool textile employers. This suggests that all the
employers had ever required of the Asians was an alternative source of
labour when others were reluctant to work in wool textiles.

Where Asians were <u>absent</u>, stereotypes were used to justify
<u>discrimination</u>. Thus change in respondents' ideas of the qualities
required of workers employed where very recent changes had been made in
the labour process no longer corresponded to the (ascribed) characteristics
of the Asians. In fact, several respondents frankly admitted that they
wanted to reduce the proportion of Asians employed in their companies.
The discrepancy between stereotypes and the qualities required of the
'new' workforce was meant to justify this discrimination. Employers
generally preferred to blame discrimination in <u>skilled and supervisory
jobs</u> on their employees, however this was not possible, for example,
where institutional arrangements for recruitment or promotion had been
modified in order to allow discrimination and/or to give employers greater
control over selection. Then a whole array of stereotypes were employed
to justify discrimination: which stereotype was used seemed to depend on
the method of recruitment. If vacancies were filled by workers the
company had trained then respondents were more likely to think that Asians
did not have the qualifications required of young apprentices. If the
firm was 'poaching', i.e. seeking ready trained labour, then this
explanation could not be used. Instead respondents thought Asians were

disloyal or wanted too much money. Where the tradition had been to
recruit trainees from the shop floor, respondents could not explain their
decision to change this practice in any of the foregoing ways and
therefore called into question the Asians' ability to control other
Asian workers.

When justifying discrimination against <u>Black Britons</u> respondents were
not always able to employ the same stereotypes which had been applied to
other Asian workers.   Instead they made explicit their fears of resistance
from Asians.   Nevertheless, even if we accept that resistance grew,
the fact remains that Asians continued to apply for jobs in wool textile
mills.   It must be admitted, moreover, that Asians did not leave the
industry when work was intensified or when they found they had to work
long hours in order to earn a living wage.

We should not assume that respondents' 'explanations' of the
unsuitability of Asian workers betrayed their reasons for discriminating
against them.   Their justifications often relied on the assumption of
various characteristics on an <u>ad hoc</u> basis and the resulting
stereotypes did not always bear a close relationship to the beliefs
(racism) which led them to discriminate.   We began this chapter by
assuming the existence of racial discrimination.   It should now be added
that discrimination is not simply an example of a more general practice
in which employers 'screen' groups of workers instead of assessing the
attributes of individuals.   While it is true that discrimination results
from a belief in the inferiority of Black workers, this inferiority is
<u>absolute</u>: managers therefore feel they have to justify <u>non</u> discrimination,
even when they employ Black workers in the least attractive jobs.
Black workers are thought to be unsuitable for any jobs, even the most
menial.

NOTES

(1)   Earlier attempts to make sense of the information presented
      in this chapter were unsatisfactory in many respects.   For
      example, I now find most of the analysis presented in a
      paper of the same title to the 1981 Sociologists in
      Polytechnics Conference is inadequate.

(2)   There is no doubt that racism in the UK frequently takes
      a different form in respect of different groups of Black
      workers.   Although the end product in all cases is racial
      discrimination, employers may have preferences <u>between</u>
      Black workers classified according to any further racial
      categorisation they might use.   There were, of course, very
      few Asian textile workers outside direct production, i.e.
      where work had not been transformed.   In contrast, West
      Indians could be found in warehouse labouring.   Now it is
      true that a different set of stereotypes (for stereotypes
      of Asian workers see below) were applied to West Indians,
      but the ascription of, say, great physical strength to this
      group of workers was merely rationalisation after the fact.
      This was not why they were able to gain access to slightly
      more attractive jobs: rather, they got these jobs because
      employers preferred them to Asians, if to no other group
      of workers.

(3)   In part these practices represented Asian kinship systems,
      but more frequently the difficulties they faced in finding
      employment through more formal means forced Asians to use
      informal practices, perhaps including bribery.

(4) No manager really knows what is required of a job and what qualities he should look for. All of it - qualifications, aptitude tests, even psychologists - represents the attempt to find a suitable proxy.

(5) Employers' representatives admitted that this might be the case. Although one thought that falling Asian employment might be largely a matter of a reduction in the number of operatives relative to other grades, he did admit that employers were being more 'selective' and that Asians might even be loosing access to operative jobs.

(6) Although some seemed to view the problem with a degree of complacency:

'In time the coloured people will have a chance of any job in the mill.'

(7) This was not, however, the case in woolsorting. Sorters were still given apprentice training and organised - in a closed shop - by a small craft union. To the best of my knowledge, there were no Asian woolsorters in Bradford in 1978.

(8) It might be noted that the founder of the extreme right wing Yorkshire Campaign to Shop Immigration in the 1960s was a junior manager in a wool textile firm (Yorkshire Evening Post 5 November 1970).

(9) Note that this respondent admitted that, of the recruits who did come forward at the existing wage rate, the Asians were the only acceptable workers. This did not contradict his views on the dangers of 'dependence' on 'immigrants'.

(10) This last, throwaway remark was not, I believe, quite as callous as it might appear. I think that this informant was trying to highlight the existence of discrimination against women. As I have already remarked, I have no doubts that sexual discrimination was (and is) prevalent in wool textiles, however this is not the main subject of this book.

(11) For some, more contemporary examples see Anwar 1979 and Department of Employment 1977.

(12) It is interesting to note that trade unions seemed to share the employers' and managers' opinions of Black Britons:

'It's not easy dealing with these people - they think everything should be done on the spur of the moment'.

or, as another official said,

'They come to see me all the time (never the old ones, we never see them) ... but they are not necessarily better trade unionists. They may organise but they can be a nuisance, they come down here for every little thing'.

8 Black workers in the labour market

This chapter is concerned with opportunities, or rather the lack of opportunities, for Asian workers to find employment outside the wool textile industry. As in earlier chapters, no systematic effort will be made to demonstrate the existence of racial discrimination since this has been exhaustively documented elsewhere. Instead, this chapter is concerned with the effects of discrimination on the distribution of Asian workers.

Despite the credence which they gave to managers' explanations of why Asians had come to be concentrated in wool textiles, Cohen and Jenner did suggest that discrimination elsewhere in the labour market might have been instrumental in limiting Asians to wool textile work (1968, p.54). This chapter will establish that this was indeed the case: discrimination against Asian applicants for more attractive work confined them to those jobs which other workers found unattractive, i.e. jobs in the mills. Unlike White workers, Asians did not benefit from the growth of attractive alternatives to millwork which accompanied expansion elsewhere in the labour market.

At this point it might be of use to define what is meant by the term 'labour market', or, more specifically, 'local labour market'. The confusion which has arisen around the idea of a labour market largely follows from the uncritical acceptance by empirical researchers of an abstraction developed by economists in order to explain how labour is bought and sold. As in other economic theories of resource allocation, the market concept is given a degree of prominence which is difficult to justify in empirical research. It remains to be seen how the confusion will be resolved. We might speculate that sociologists will eventually decide that very few workers sell their labour under market conditions but we need not pursue this argument for the purposes of this chapter. Instead, we will simply define a (local) labour market in a way which reserves the question of how labour is bought and sold. Thus a labour market is the geographical area within which the majority of residents sell their labour and the majority of resident firms buy their labour (c.f. Harris 1981, passim). This approximates to the Department of Employment's 'travel to work area' and in what follows most statistics on the local labour market will refer to the travel to work area for Bradford. This is, in effect, how most empirical studies operationalise the idea of a local labour market. The mistake is to forget that it is only a geographical area, i.e. to assume that we know something about how labour is bought and sold because the area where it is bought and sold is called a 'market'. Chapter Ten will demonstrate that the idea of a market is of little use in explaining the employment distribution of Asian workers.

The foregoing dictates that much of this chapter should be devoted to
analysis of the employment (and unemployment) statistics for Bradford.
In order to spare the reader, these figures are summarised where possible
(a full account is available elsewhere: ASRP, pp.396-455). It should
be pointed out, however, that these statistics share a common limitation:
they do not distinguish Asians from other Black workers. A notable
exception is the information provided by employment and careers offices
on 'unemployment by ethnic origin' (EDS83B returns). Nevertheless, the
analysis below will refer, in the main, to Bradford's Black population as
a whole and not to its (majority) Asian component. Particular attention
will be paid to the statistics on school leavers entering the labour
market since, despite the small numbers involved, these series provide
a key indicator of future trends. Any improvement (or deterioration)
in the employment prospects of Black workers might be expected to make
its first appearance in the employment distribution of young Blacks.

EMPLOYMENT TRENDS

If there was any evidence that non textile work became less attractive
in the postwar period, we would not be able to assert (see Chapter Four)
that millwork amounted to cheap labour. In fact, as we briefly mentioned
in Chapter Five, the evidence suggests that non textile work was becoming
more attractive and that the number of jobs on offer was expanding.
Thus the White, English workers who rejected wool textiles, and even the
European workers who left the mills, found better jobs to go to. As
will become clear below, these jobs were not open to Black workers.
Furthermore, by the time the number of Asians in wool textiles began to
fall - well in advance of the later fall in the Asian proportion of wool
textile employment - there were signs that the growth of attractive
alternatives to millwork had slowed down. Unfortunately, analysis of
employment trends is hampered by the scarcity of official statistics (the
most recent Census of Employment figures available at the time of writing
were those for 1978). Nevertheless, Census of Employment returns for the
1970s show that Bradford was experiencing the same shift from manufacturing
to service employment which was taking place in the rest of the UK, but
trends in the local labour market did not reflect the national pattern
in every respect.

Most importantly, in Bradford's case the decline in manufacturing
employment was not balanced by an equivalent increase in service sector
jobs: only five thousand extra jobs were created in services in the 60s.
Furthermore, from 1976 onwards the pace of the shift to services seems
to have slowed down.

The overall decline in employment in the previous decade was not - at
least until after 1978 - maintained, but several industries did shed jobs.
The textile industry was still the largest employer in Bradford in 1971
with 20.5 per cent of all jobs but by 1978 ten thousand textile jobs had
been lost and the industry accounted for less than 15 per cent of all
employment. Nevertheless, the proportion of employment accounted for by
all the major industries together changed little between 1971 and 1978.
Decline in employment in one industry was matched by growth in another.
In 1978 the largest employer was professional and scientific services with
six thousand more jobs than in 1971. The pattern was repeated in other
industries: service sector employment in miscellaneous services, public
administration, and insurance, banking and finance increased while jobs
were lost in mechanical and electrical engineering and in most other
manufacturing industries (1). Most of these changes were fairly well

advanced by the mid 1970s.   The only significant development after 1976 was a (temporary) increase in employment which was spread fairly evenly over the service industries.   More dramatic changes would be expected in the figures for years after 1978.

While the Census of Employment does not provide up to date information, it does analyse the industrial distribution of employment by sex. Bradford has traditionally had a higher than average female activity rate stemming, in large part, from the extensive employment of women in wool textiles.   We might therefore expect the shift to service sector employment to have had a less pronounced effect on women workers in Bradford than elsewhere.   On the other hand, we know that women's employment in textiles has declined and therefore a considerable increase in service sector jobs for women may have been required to keep the same number of women at work.

In fact women lost jobs in _all_ manufacturing industries, not simply in textiles (where, in fact, women suffered greater job losses than men). For example, women were harder hit than men by declining employment in electrical engineering.   The overall trend, however, was of increased employment for women - four thousand extra jobs between 1971 and 1978 - and of declining employment for men - five thousand less jobs in 1978 than in 1971.   It is clear that both sexes were affected by the loss of manufacturing jobs but that women benefited rather more from the increase in service sector employment.   For example, five thousand extra jobs for women were created in professional and scientific services alone between 1971 and 1978.   Nevertheless, while the proportion of women in manufacturing was steadily falling there was some suggestion that women's monopoly of new service sector jobs might be challenged.   Women gained rather less than men from increased service sector employment, 1977-8 (2) but they nonetheless still outnumbered men in service sector jobs.

At the beginning of the 70s Blacks in Bradford were clearly concentrated in manufacturing, i.e. where employment was declining most rapidly, and they were under represented in those sectors where employment was increasing (March and Lomas 1975 quoted by Jones 1979).   It is difficult to establish whether this distribution persisted throughout the seventies, but a survey conducted in 1978 suggested that there had been little change. Nearly half of the fathers of Campbell and Jones' sample of young Asians either worked in the textile industry or were unemployed textile workers. Mothers were almost as concentrated in textiles and clothing (Campbell and Jones 1981, p.24).   But these proportions were derived from a small sample and a more comprehensive guide to the industrial distribution of Black workers is required.   This is provided by the statistics on school leavers in Bradford collected by the Careers Office (see ASRP, pp.408-18).

The industrial distribution of male school leavers bore some relationship to the industrial distribution of all male workers in 1977 but with the following differences: textiles was a much less important, and distribution a more important, source of employment for school leavers. In fact male school leavers were more likely than all male workers to find jobs in industries where employment was expanding, especially in miscellaneous services and public administration.   Although they were under represented in professional and scientific services they were, moreover, less likely than all males to be working in the (declining) manufacturing industries.   But in the years after 1978 - for which no overall figures on employment are available - the pattern changed dramatically.   While the proportional shift into distribution and public

128

administration - and the shift out of mechanical engineering and, especially, textiles - might have been expected, the increased importance of construction and of smaller manufacturing industries could not have been predicted. However, the most dramatic change between 1979 and 1981 was the overall decline in employment of any kind. The number of jobs for male school leavers in 1981 was less than forty per cent of the 1977 figure and all the individual industries employed fewer boys in 1981 than 1977.

It is a matter of conjecture as to how well the school leaver statistics represent overall changes in the industrial distribution of employment after 1978 but it is probable that a comparison of trends for Black leavers and all leavers will give a guide as to the trends for adults. It is therefore significant that Black boys suffered an even more severe decline in employment between 1977 and 1981 than all male school leavers. Furthermore, whereas the distribution of all boys bore some relationship to the distribution of all male workers, this was not the case with Black boys. Blacks were <u>over</u> represented in the declining manufacturing sector, especially in textiles, whereas all school leavers had been <u>even less likely than adults</u> to find work in these industries. Moreover, as employment in manufacturing declined after 1978 there was no shift of Black leavers into service sector jobs, indeed the proportion of Black boys finding work in distribution actually declined up to 1980. Meantime the number of jobs in textiles had fallen from forty three jobs for Black leavers in 1977 to one in 1981 (3).

All girl school leavers were rather less likely than all female workers to find work in professional and scientific services and rather more likely to get jobs in distribution. Nevertheless, the remainder of their industrial distribution approximated that for all women with textiles and other service industries figuring prominently. But it may be that, as with boys, girls were more concentrated in the service sector and under represented in areas of declining (manufacturing) employment like mechanical engineering (4). The exception was clothing and footwear but here employment declined by a substantial amount between 1977 and 1981. This, together with a shift out of textiles (5) led to an increasing proportion of girls finding jobs in the service sector despite a decline in the proportion going into miscellaneous services. Other service industries - for example insurance, banking and finance - increased in importance and only paper and printing, of the manufacturing industries, took an increasing proportion of girl school leavers. Nevertheless, the overall trend was of declining employment. As with boys, employment for girl leavers in 1981 was less than forty per cent of the 1977 figure, and all but one industry (6) offered substantially fewer jobs to girls in 1981.

The numbers of Black girls finding work in any year between 1977 and 1981 were very small but, as with Black boys, clear differences emerge between their distribution and the industrial distribution of all girl leavers. Black girls were more likely to find work where employment was declining most rapidly - in particular in clothing and footwear - and to be under represented in services. Clothing and footwear took 26 Black girls in 1977 and only 1 in 1981 while distribution and miscellaneous services took 22 Black girls in 1977 and 4 in 1981. Since the numbers of Black school leavers, especially girls, were small, it is advisable to seek confirmation of these findings. Campbell and Jones' study showed a considerable concentration of Bradford's Asian youths in manufacturing employment, even if not always in textiles and clothing (Campbell and Jones 1981, p.55).

129

We now turn to the occupational distribution of Black workers in
Bradford.   In 1971 Bradford's Blacks were concentrated in manual work
and, within this category, in semi and unskilled grades.   Black men were
massively under represented in skilled and nonmanual work and Black
women were just as seriously under represented in junior nonmanual
occupations (March and Lomas 1975, quoted by Jones 1979).   These
differences persisted in spite of the fact that Bradford had a much higher
percentage of manual workers than the average for England and Wales
(Jones 1979).   Furthermore, even within manufacturing - where Black
workers were concentrated - there was no evidence of a more equitable
distribution of occupations between Blacks and Whites.   Like Black adults
in 1971, Black boys leaving school in the late 1970s were much less likely
to get nonmanual or skilled jobs than White boys, and this despite the
fact that school leavers as a whole were more likely to be in manual and
unskilled occupations than adults in 1971 (7).   It is difficult to
distinguish trends within the period 1977-82 because of the overall
decline in employment.   For example, proportionately more Black boys
got apprenticeships in 1980 than in 1977 but the actual number of boys
was reduced from thirty five to nineteen (8).   The number of all leavers
getting apprenticeships declined rather more slowly.

Girl school leavers were rather more concentrated in manual work than
women had been in 1977, and again this was emphasised amongst Black girls.
The occupational distribution of Black girls in 1977 was very close to
that of all Black women in 1971 but with an even smaller proportion in
nonmanual work and a consequently higher proportion in unskilled manual
occupations.   The proportion of Black girls in the latter increased
after 1977, and at a much faster rate than amongst all girl leavers.
It is interesting to note that for girl leavers the 1977-81 period seems
to cover two distinct, and opposing, trends.   The movement of girls into
nonmanual and more skilled manual occupations persisted up to the end of
the decade but was then reversed.   Something similar happened in the case
of Black girls but here the subsequent decline in nonmanual jobs was
much greater and throughout the period no girls found skilled manual
jobs (9).   Furthermore, Black girls fared badly even within the broad
occupational categories of the Careers Office statistics.   For example,
in 1977, seven per cent of all girls went into professional, rather than
clerical employment, but only one Black girl did so.

CASE STUDIES

By examining two case studies of major employers (for further,
statistical analysis see ASRP, Appendix Three), we can make some attempt
to understand both trends in the local labour market and the varying
effects of these trends on Black and White workers.   Both case studies
were conducted in 1981.   We will begin with a large mail order firm.

Distribution was the third largest employer of all adults and the second
largest employer of all women in Bradford in 1978.   It was also by far
the largest employer of school leavers in 1977-81 but Black leavers of
both sexes were under represented.   In most local labour markets
conventional retailing would provide the great bulk of jobs in
distribution but Bradford is the home of two mail order companies.
Between them, these two firms employed about seven thousand workers in
Bradford in 1980-1 (10).   The vast majority of these jobs were
nonmanual and mail order represented one of the most important employers
of female clerical workers.   Throughout the 1970s employment in mail
order was stable, occasionally even expanding, but at the end of the

decade both firms began to shed jobs.   In the company chosen for the
case study, employment fell from 3,710 to 3,590, 1979-80, and by a
further 227 in the eleven months up to the end of June 1981.   The majority
of workers at this company in 1981 were women and women had been
particularly hard hit by the loss of jobs.   The same applied to young
workers and, by implication, especially to young women.   But while the
proportion of women and young workers had recently fallen it remained
higher than in textiles.   Furthermore, even though women, especially
young women, tended to be concentrated in the worst paid jobs and those
which were more likely to disappear, wages at the mail order firm were
relatively good in comparison to those paid elsewhere in the local labour
market.   Basic weekly rates for a thirty six hour week in 1980-1 were
£58 up to £71 (11) for senior clerical workers and £78 up to £95 for
supervisors and 'controllers'.

Recruitment was centralised and initial selection was conducted by the
personnel department.   The company aimed to fill its requirements in
April and July of each year and bulk recruitment of school leavers
provided the majority of entrants to clerical jobs.   Most of these
recruits were taken at sixteen or seventeen years of age and younger
recruits were preferred.   They were expected to be taking C.S.E.s but
only the higher grade clerical applicants would have '0' level passes.
New recruits were tested by personnel and at the departmental level.
There were a series of 'clerical tests' which evaluated literacy and
numeracy and these were followed by a standard IBM aptitude test.   The
training officer concerned with recruitment of Visual Display Unit (VDU)
operators to 'data entry' explained that the aptitude tests graded recruits
into A's, B's and C's.   In the early stages of the company's programme
of computerisation they looked for B, and even A, passes from potential
VDU operators but as they gained experience of work after computerisation
management lowered its requirements.   They channelled the recruits who
performed well on the aptitude test into other work and took low B's
and high C's for VDU operation.   This preference for young recruits who
performed less well must be explained:

'The girls leave at 20 to get married so we go for 16 year
olds because this means that we keep them for up to four
years ... it is quite deliberate'.

'If you take someone with an A pass and they get bored
and leave, this increases turnover and training costs'.

Outside 'data entry', clerical workers - including VDU operators - were
generally more successful in aptitude tests and older.   How did these
recruitment practices affect Black workers?

A major problem in assessing the employment of Black workers in the
mailorder company was lack of information.   Despite pressure from outside,
the company had consistently refused to count Black workers.   The
personnel manager defended this attitude on the grounds that they 'do not
discriminate' and that counting might lead to 'an American-style quota
system' (i.e. the company might be forced to hire a certain proportion of
each ethnic group).   He informally estimated the number of Black workers
at 'hundreds, well over a hundred anyway'.   If we take this as meaning
between 100 and 200 then less than six per cent of the firm's workforce
was Black.   Observation supported this estimate and it is certain that
the proportion of Black workers in 1981 was no higher than six per cent.
There was, however, no evidence of a racial division of labour and there
were few cases of racist stereotyping.   I was told that Black workers

131

were indistinguishable from White in terms of distribution throughout staff and departments, performance or turnover. The exception was the personnel manager's view of Asian VDU operators. He thought they worked harder and better at this - 'they get their heads down, get on with the job ... nothing to distract them' - than any other group, but this view was not confirmed elsewhere. Furthermore, there was no <u>obvious</u> bar on the promotion of Black workers to the more senior jobs. It is possible that there were hardly any Black workers outside junior clerical grades but this could be explained by the (likely) preponderance of very young women amongst the Black workers.

Yet if there was no racial division of labour at the mail order company, there certainly was a sexual one and Black women at the company had their opportunities - for example, of promotion - circumscribed by their sex if not their race. More importantly, if the company had no racial division of labour, <u>this might have been because they did not have many Black workers</u>. Allen and her colleagues remarked that Black workers were almost completely absent from Bradford's mail order firms (1977, p.92; see also Department of Employment 1977, p.205) and, although there had obviously been some improvement in the 1970s, it is possible that these companies had continued to discriminate against Black applicants.

It is likely that the mail order firm's tests were being used as an <u>excuse</u> to exclude Black workers. The training officer thought that Black applicants might fail the clerical, but not the aptitude tests. The personnel manager was sure there was no difference in failure rate between Black and White applicants <u>but did admit that the clerical tests for new recruits were originally introduced in order to exclude Asian applicants who, it was assumed, would fail certain parts of the tests</u>. These tests were still being used in an unmodified form in 1981.

While it is difficult to know to what extent management considered them to be objective assessments of relevant criteria, the mail order firm's tests were reminiscent of the use of language tests to enforce 'selectivity' in textiles. In Chapter Seven we noted that even senior wool textile managers did not seem to be genuinely interested in improving the language skills of their Asian workers and some respondents claimed that they actually preferred the workers who were the least fluent. Nevertheless, lack of fluency was given as the respondents' explanation for their exclusion of Asian workers. Junior managers were increasingly successful in achieving their stated aim of reducing their firms' 'dependence' on Asians and the spurious issue of language competence had been chosen as the criterion which would make this possible. I asked the mail order firm's personnel manager if he thought his company's tests might still be 'culturally biased' (as had been the original intention). He agreed that this was possible but suggested that tests might be less discriminatory than 'subjective' assessment. He went on, however, to say that if the tests were 'culturally biased' then this was not a bad thing since, if the applicants were accepted,

'... in actual fact everything they then handle in this
business is culturally biased'. (Personnel manager)

It is just possible that these tests were, nevertheless, no longer intended to facilitate <u>racial</u> discrimination. The personnel manager was very proud of the fact that the majority of Black employees appeared to be either Black Britons or to have had a substantial part of their education in the UK:

'We have some third or fourth generation West Indians -
more tyke than me.'

Yet if the tests were intended only to exclude Blacks without British
education, we might have expected larger numbers of Black recruits.   It
is more likely that the high proportion of Black Britons amongst the
company's Black workers simply reflected their preference for sixteen
year old school leavers: the majority of Black employees were under
twenty years of age and it may be that all of them were recruited
straight from school.

Even if management is given the benefit of the doubt in regard to the
intention of its recruitment practices, it is more than likely that the
mail order company's tests contravened legislation concerned with the
prevention of indirect discrimination.   The terms of the Act are very
narrow but they do seem to cover instances such as this.   The tests
were used to select applicants for, in the main, work as VDU operators,
i.e. for work exclusively with figures.   Special competence in language
was unnecessary since, as the training officer said, the work simply
required coordination.   If the tests operated to the detriment of Asian
applicants with less language fluency they amounted to indirect
discrimination since the recognition of numerical symbols, codes and
figures was all that was needed for the job.   Yet management refused
applicants who did not come up to the required standards in all aspects
of the tests.   Indeed, the personnel manager told me that he put more
weight on these tests than on applicants' qualifications.

Ironically, there was some suggestion that the offending tests might be
modified for another reason.   The training officer was committed to a
further lowering of required levels of aptitude and thought that this
might involve the separation of tests in numeracy and language.   The
former, alone, would be necessary for VDU operators in 'data entry'.
But if this change was made some problems would remain: for example,
the personnel manager emphasised that interviews allowed as much
opportunity for discrimination as formal testing.   Language might just
as easily be used as an excuse for discrimination in interviews (see
Chapter Seven).   Furthermore, a two tier test system might actually
produce a racial division of labour.   One test would exclude Asians and
give entry to higher level clerical jobs, the other would lead to the
worst of the VDU jobs and would condemn successful Asian applicants to
work which was given little credit in the company's grading system.

The mail order firm held a favoured position in Bradford's labour
market in the seventies.   Like its competitors, the company was able to
take its pick of female school leavers.   Even before the recession, it
promised reasinable wages and, perhaps inaccurately, the conditions and
status expected of office work.   When this priveleged position was
threatened by expansion, computerisation was introduced and mail order -
unlike textiles or electrical assembly (see below) - avoided increasing
labour demand in excess of its potential labour supply.   Furthermore,
the mail order industry actually introduced technology which enhanced its
labour market position: management had found that new recruits

'can tell their friends they are working with computers,
of course its nothing like that at all'.   (Senior Executive)

In sum, the mail order firm was always in a position where it could
discriminate between applicants for work.   Mail order provided one of
the areas of expanding employment in Bradford in the 1970s and it
provided jobs for young women at relatively good wages.   In

133

consequence of discrimination, Black girls did not get their fair share of these jobs.

We now turn to the second case study. Perhaps surprisingly, the assembly of electrical consumer goods - for example, loudspeakers and TV sets - has been a major source of employment in Bradford. In the 60s and early 70s this industry had a reputation for growth potential but in the later 70s it shrank at a faster rate than wool textiles. The largest single loss of jobs occurred when one of the TV plants closed. The firm concerned employed 5,000 workers in Bradford in the early 70s (12) and at this time the firm was almost unique in that it offered large numbers of jobs for women and young workers in manufacturing (13). Furthermore, like the mail order company, the TV assembly plant offered <u>relatively good</u> jobs for women and young workers: less than sixty eight per cent of women were unskilled or semi skilled (twenty seven per cent for men) and in 1978 unskilled production workers earned £60 for a 40 hour week. Skilled (not apprentice trained) workers earned £72 a week. These levels had not been reached by the equivalent grade of wool textile worker in 1981 and in 1978 wool textile workers were getting up to thirty per cent less than their equivalents at the TV plant.

At the closure, at least four hundred employees, i.e. a fifth of the plant's workforce, were Asian. Furthermore, probably a third of the workforce was Black or immigrant (including European immigrants). The proportion of male employees was higher amongst the Asians than amongst the Whites. This suggests that White males were restricted to nonmanual or higher grade technical or supervisory jobs while Asian men occupied a larger number of lower grade technical jobs. The personnel manager - who had also lost his job when the plant closed - denied that Asian men were recruited into routine technical work but not the more complicated jobs although he did explain that there were 'culturally biased' tests for recruits and for people seeking promotion off the shop floor. These tests were approved by the industrial training board for electrical engineering. A 'vast number' of young Asians failed these tests. It is likely that here, as elsewhere, the use of tests based on language ability constituted a barrier to the promotion of Asians. West Yorkshire Language Link made the following comments in a report (1977) on the TV plant:

> 'Although this was never stated in so many words, there would seem to be a deep-rooted assumption that less than adequate performance in the use of English is necessarily a sign of a degree of intelligence which does not conform with promotion from for example insertion to inspection or test'.

> 'If this is so, then recruitment from the 40% or so of Asian operators in insertion whose language performance is "intermediate" may well be more accidental or haphazard than anyone has appreciated. Characteristics of "intermediate" speakers is that their potential as well as their problems are not always identifiable by conventional criteria'.

Furthermore, WYLL found widespread evidence of stereotyping - which they assumed to be a consequence of the lack of communication between Asians and others - which, it was thought, might affect both the kind of work Asians were given to do and their treatment at work. In another report on the plant, for example, WYLL quoted a respondent who claimed that

> 'Asians respond more readily to hard discipline than local people'.

WYLL also thought that the plant had ethnic work groups, for example Hungarian supervisors. In addition, Asian technical supervisors may have been more common than Asian production supervisors. The personnel manager agreed and pointed out that technical supervisors spent more of their time solving technical problems rather than supervising, and that both groups of supervisors were recruited from the shop floor. WYLL found segregated groups of production workers doing the same job and quoted an employee who claimed that "White and coloured are very separate" at the company. Their later (June) report on testers, inspectors and trouble shooters also found 'bunching', but less than on the insertion lines. Certainly Asian women did work together, and there were groups of European migrants. The personnel manager described one department as 'say ninety per cent' Italian, 'for historical reasons I suppose'. He thought that ethnic work groups might be 'not necessarily management policy' but became so: 'it helped with language'. According to the personnel manager,

'It was a genuinely multi racial factory. Both management and union were strong on it'.

In spite of this general commendation, however, he was able to describe one (small) department from which openly racist White workers had been able to exclude all Black workers and an occasion on which a steward had tried to enlist management's help in keeping down the numbers of Black workers in his department. It may be that the relatively 'good' performance of the union can be put down to the efforts of an anti racist leadership, but what of management's attitude? While both WYLL reports accused management of 'complacency', the personnel manager said that the speed at which the Bradford operation expanded made racism in recruitment and promotion impossible. While this may not be entirely true of promotion (see above) it is certain that the company's demand for labour gave it rather less opportunity to practice discrimination in recruitment. This may not have been true of the employers whom the redundant TV workers approached for work after the closure.

From the peak year of 1973, the company's workforce in Bradford was reduced by three thousand in five years until the closure when two thousand were made redundant (14). Between 1971 and 1978 Bradford lost electrical engineering jobs at a much faster rate than the UK as a whole and the TV firm, along with other major employers like Lucas, was largely responsible for this trend. Fortunately, there is some information on the replacement jobs which electrical assembly workers found (15).

The men - who made up twenty five per cent of the workforce - found jobs much more easily than did the female majority. A substantial number, 284, of these women were Asian, indeed seventy one per cent of the Asians employed were women. These workers faced the most severe difficulties in finding alternative work. Asian men took longer to find work than White men and Asian women took longer than White women. While the concentration of women in production work and of men in craft, supervisor and trouble shooter jobs helps to explain differences in the duration of unemployment between the sexes, so the existence of a racial division of labour helps to explain differences between Asians and Whites (16). For example, some of the difficulties faced by Asian men in finding employment stemmed from the fact that their skills were limited to the narrow range of work allocated to trouble shooters. Nevertheless, differences in training and skills cannot wholly explain differences in the duration of unemployment amongst the redundant workers. Since all Asians - i.e. including the sizeable minority of Asian men - took longer

to find alternative jobs than White _women_ (17), it seems clear that
the Asians faced special problems in finding work.

That the TV plant gave Asians some chance of work, especially in this
sector, was exceptional.   Furthermore, wages were relatively good and
the company offered unique opportunities to Asian women.   The loss of
these jobs was more severe for these workers than any others.   In sum,
any reasonable employment to which Black workers in Bradford have gained
access has tended to disappear leaving Blacks with much less chance of
finding replacement jobs than Whites.

UNEMPLOYMENT

More than fifteen years ago, Eric Butterworth suggested that in West
Yorkshire Asian workers might be more susceptible than Whites to rising
unemployment (1967, p.17).   By the end of the 1970s it was accepted that
unemployment amongst Blacks in the UK exceeded the national rate
(Runnymede Trust 1980,pp.55, 64-68).   As we might expect, this was also
the case in Bradford; indeed the figures (from Manpower Service
Commission) for Black unemployment, especially amongst the youngest
workers, are frankly disturbing.   This might explain why the local
authorities in Bradford and Leeds complained so loudly when the Department
of Employment ceased to provide them with a detailed breakdown of
unemployment statistics.   The Department took this action after the local
authority in Bradford had used the figures to highlight the special
problems of Black unemployment in the city.   Without the Department's
assistance they could only guess at the level of Black unemployment,
perhaps seven in ten (_Bradford Star_ 29 October 1981).

Unemployment amongst all of Bradford's workers rose in the 1970s.   In
the 60s the local rate was a fairly stable one or two per cent, well
below the national average, but by the early 70s between three and four
per cent of local workers were _officially_ counted as unemployed.   By
1980 the published rate was 8.4 per cent and it remained above the national
average as unemployment continued to rise in the following years.

A substantial number of Bradford's unemployed had been made redundant
from the wool textile industry.   Textile unemployment was an especially
large component of the total in inner city areas, i.e. where Bradford's
Asians live (City of Bradford Metropolitan Council Unemployment Survey,
quoted by Jones 1979, p.14).   While Bradford's Blacks were concentrated
in those industries (like textiles) where employment had declined most
rapidly, they also seemed to be even more likely than other workers in
these industries to become unemployed.

Black workers made up an increasing proportion of all the unemployed
in Bradford.   Table 8.1 shows how unemployment amongst Blacks, and
especially Asians, increased.   The rate of increase in Asian
unemployment was much greater than that amongst Whites.   Table 8.2
shows that the greatest increase in unemployment took place amongst
Pakistanis (who make up the majority of Bradford's Asians).   Table 8.3
shows that the brunt of this increase was borne by (Asian) men.

We have already noted that the loss of employment opportunities was
particularly severe for _Black_ school leavers.   This might explain why,
between 1977 and 1981, the sixteen to twenty four age group accounted
for between thirty and forty per cent of all Black unemployment in
Bradford.   Only in 1982 did the proportion drop to 29.7 per cent.
There is, however, a discontinuity in the youth unemployment figures in
1979.   In 1977 and 1978 the sixteen to twenty fours accounted for about

forty per cent of Black unemployment in Bradford but in succeeding years this proportion stabilised at around thirty per cent. The explanation for this discontinuity is clearly the special measures introduced by the Government in an effort to reduce youth unemployment. Campbell and Jones reported that seventy two per cent of the Asians who left school in Bradford in 1980 did not have a job twelve to fifteen months after leaving. Over forty per cent of these young Asians were on the Youth Opportunities Programme (YOP) (Campbell and Jones 1981, p.26). The number of young Blacks in Bradford on YOP far exceeded the number in employment by 1982. Campbell and Jones found (1981, p.27) that young Asians were more than twice as likely as young Whites to end up on YOP, however Careers Office figures show that the proportion of YOP places taken up by Blacks was falling, and falling in excess of the fall in the proportion of all school leavers who were Black.

Because Blacks were less likely to find work than Whites they were more likely to be offered a place on YOP, however unemployed Whites got proportionally more YOP places than unemployed Blacks and this was increasingly the case as unemployment rose. Although a YOP place might not improve employment prospects (at least for Asian boys, Campbell and Jones 1981, p.27) it does seem that Blacks in Bradford were being denied access to special provision for the unemployed just as they were being disproportionately excluded from employment.

There can be no suggestion that disproportionately rising Black unemployment in Bradford can be explained by a differential increase in population between Blacks and Whites. This is confirmed by Careers Office figures which show that there was no increase in the number of Black school leavers between 1977 and 1981, indeed the Black proportion of all leavers fell over this period. Nevertheless, Black leavers have suffered disproportionately from unemployment: while Black boys made up thirteen per cent of all boys leaving school in 1977, they made up thirty nine per cent of those leaving school to become unemployed. It was not until after the introduction of YOP in 1979 that the proportion of unemployed male school leavers who were Black began to approach the proportion of all male school leavers who were Black. Furthermore, in every year between 1977 and 1981 Black boys made up a much smaller proportion of those entering employment than of those leaving school. In 1981 they made up nearly 7.5 per cent of those leaving school for employment but only 1.1 per cent of those finding work (despite an especially high proportion of sixth formers amongst the leavers). Indeed, the proportion Blacks made up of all those male school leavers finding work fell in each year from 1977 to 1981, as did their proportion of all boys finding YOP places between 1979 and 1981 (18). Finally, it is interesting to note that Blacks seemed to be more likely than Whites to respond to reduced employment opportunities by staying on at school or going into further or higher education (also see Campbell and Jones: 1981, pp.19-20).

Black girl leavers fared as badly as Black boys: if Black girls had suffered unemployment in proportion to their representation amongst all girl school leavers then only thirty of them would have been unemployed in 1977 and not ninety one! As with male leavers, there were regular falls in the proportion made up by Blacks of all those entering employment and the Youth Opportunities Programme.

CONCLUSIONS

In the 1960s it was established Black workers in the UK were under
represented in better jobs and over represented in those jobs which had
been rejected by the rest of the population (for example, see Daniel
1967, p.97; Peach 1968, pp.74-5). In succeeding years, however,
commentators began to express some optimism about trends in the employment
distribution of Britain's Black workers, especially young Blacks:

> 'Some special analyses of 1966 and 1971 Census of Population
> Data prepared by the Department of Applied Economics at
> Cambridge ... suggest that the socio-economic pattern of
> West Indian, and Pakistani immigrants may be moving nearer
> to that of the population as a whole. In particular, the
> proportion of males who are in the unskilled manual groups,
> which is the most likely to include unattractive jobs, fell.'

> '... there are indications that as a growing number of
> Black young people with substantial education in Britain
> enter the working population and as first generation
> immigrants gain more experience of life in this country,
> there will be an increasing number and proportion of Black
> workers with the qualifications and aptitudes needed for
> higher grade jobs.' (Department of Employment 1977, pp.82-3).

This chapter would seem to suggest that this optimism was misplaced.
For example, while Black workers' qualifications improved (see below),
they did not end up with better jobs but rather with no jobs at all.

Obviously, there must have been some diversification in the employment
opportunities available to Blacks in Bradford since the number of Blacks
working in textiles fell without creating substantial unemployment, for
much of the 70s. Blacks must therefore have been finding work outside
the wool textile industry, for example in electrical assembly. Work in
the TV plant was clearly preferable to work in the mills. Furthermore,
there is some limited evidence that young Blacks were gaining access to
other desirable occupations. Campbell and Jones found that a small
number of Asian boys were achieving their ambition of becoming car
mechanics (1981, p.55). On the other hand, these few examples of
improvement must be balanced against evidence of continued discrimination.
Thus the school leaver statistics from the careers office suggest that
while Black girls were more likely to go into manufacturing, comparable
groups of White girl leavers found jobs in shops. Similarly, where a
White male leaver might find work in the construction industry, his Black
counterpart ended up in textiles.

There can be little doubt that young Blacks did not want to go into
textiles but rather shared the ambitions (car mechanic, hairdresser)
of other young workers (Campbell and Jones 1981, p.30). This was the
element of truth in wool textile respondents' claims that they were not
recruiting young Asians because Black Britons wanted better jobs. But
surely we do not believe that other Asians did prefer wool textile work?
It must be obvious that no group of workers would prefer the least
attractive alternatives in the labour market. Whatever their desires or
expectations, young Asians had to go into wool textiles:

> 'They can only go into this trade ... they are getting well
> educated in Bradford but all the same they are coming ...'
> (Union official)

This was confirmed by the local careers office: young Black school leavers had to be made aware that textile work was their only realistic expectation.

We know that the numbers of Black school leavers entering wool textiles dropped off almost completely towards the end of the 70s, but this does not suggest a new impulse to the diversification of Blacks' employment opportunities since the young Blacks who would have gone into wool textiles were now unemployed. Similarly amongst older Black workers: with quickly rising unemployment it was now possible for the numbers of Blacks in wool textiles to fall without any new jobs being taken by Black workers elsewhere.

The Unit for Manpower Studies at the Department of Employment had expected the employment patterns of Blacks 'with substantial education in Britain' to more closely resemble those of other workers. The majority of Blacks leaving school in Bradford, 1977-81, had been wholly educated in the UK: sixty four per cent of Campbell and Jones' sample of young Asians had received all of their education in the UK and a further nineteen per cent had undergone all of their secondary education in this country (1981, p.25 (19)). Nevertheless, there was no evidence in the school leaver statistics of an improvement in the employment opportunities of young Blacks which might correspond to their UK education. In fact those with the longest period of education in this country, the Blacks born in Britain, seemed to fare worse than most. Figures from the Manpower Service Commission show that unemployment amongst Black Britons in Bradford rose even more sharply than total Black youth unemployment and at a much faster rate than total Black unemployment. A part of this differential might be explained by an increase in the proportion of Blacks leaving school who were born in Britain, nevertheless it is clear that Black Britons were not helped by their English education. Campbell and Jones concluded that, in their survey of young Asians,

'There is no relationship between job status and whether or not the youth was born or educated in the UK, i.e. this is not an important determinant of who gets the jobs that are available.' (Campbell and Jones 1981, p.52).

The Unit for Manpower Studies suggested that improvement in Blacks' employment opportunities might follow from their acquisition of 'the qualifications and aptitudes needed for higher grade jobs'. Perhaps these young Blacks with British education and sometimes British birth were lacking in qualifications? In fact, Campbell and Jones found no difference between the educational achievements of their sample of young Asians and those of all Bradford youths (Campbell and Jones 1981, p.19). While better qualified Asians had more chance of finding work than less well qualified Asians as unemployment rose, Asians as a whole suffered disproportionately from rising unemployment despite the similarity of their qualifications to those of Whites (Campbell and Jones 1981, pp.40-2, 51-2). Forty one per cent of Campbell and Jones' sample were still unemployed twelve months after leaving school, as opposed to only nineteen per cent of all leavers contacted in a parallel survey. Furthermore, only twenty eight per cent of the Asians were in employment as against sixty four per cent of all leavers (Campbell and Jones 1981, p.27).

In sum, discrimination against Black workers continued to be a feature of the labour market in Bradford throughout the 1970s and into the recession. But this chapter has also highlighted a further factor which operated to limit the job prospects of Blacks: <u>industrial change</u> took place in those few areas of employment to which Blacks had gained access. We have already remarked that this was the case in the wool textile industry, but we can now add that, in the later 70s, industrial change began to remove those few areas of employment outside textiles where blanket discrimination was not practiced. The electrical assembly case study showed that even when - as was rarely the case - Blacks gained access to relatively 'good' jobs, these jobs were more likely to disappear. Of course, when redundancies did occur Blacks faced more difficulties than Whites in finding alternative employment. As we might expect, this was also the case amongst redundant textile workers. Even in the depths of recession, White textile workers had better access to alternative employment. Thus with unemployment rising to thirteen per cent in 1980-1, seventy per cent of a sample of largely White textile workers found new jobs nine to twelve months after they had been made redundant. Only six per cent of the redundant workers found jobs in textiles (Bradford Metropolitan District Council, 1981 (a)), i.e. they found alternative jobs in areas of employment from which Black workers were largely excluded. While the overall decline in employment affected White as well as Black workers, Blacks were harder hit on two counts: they were more likely to be employed in industries where employment was declining most rapidly <u>and</u> they suffered discrimination when they sought alternative work. Similarly amongst school leavers: the drastic overall decline in jobs was a major theme of the careers office statistics, but we also observed that Black leavers were not getting their fair share of the (diminished) total of jobs which were still available, even in wool textiles (20).

Asians left the wool textile industry under very different circumstances to the workers who had preceded them. White, English women and Eastern Europeans had left wool textiles for better jobs but the Asians left for the dole. Asians had not benefited from the earlier expansion of alternatives to textile work, nor did they benefit from more limited expansion in later years. It was, for example, mainly White women who gained from the sectoral shift to service sector employment in the 70s. Both White women and Black workers were moving out of manufacturing, but the latter found no compensating increase in opportunities elsewhere because they faced discrimination. For example, the mail order case study suggested that a major service sector employer discriminated against Black applicants. Those Blacks <u>in work</u> remained in manufacturing employment. Despite significant sectoral shifts in the local labour market, Blacks were still employed in the same industries in which they had found work at the beginning of the decade.

Finally, it should be pointed out that the case studies reported in this chapter suggest that some of the arguments advanced in Chapter Seven can be extended to non textile employment. As in wool textiles, the electrical assembly firm's demand for labour had exceeded the supply of White workers willing to come forward at the prevailing wage rate and so Blacks were recruited, but not to all positions in the company. It would appear that a racial division of labour was established and that this was justified by recourse to stereotypes. By way of contrast, the mail order firm seemed relatively free of stereotyping, and the only reference to Black workers' 'culture' was made in order to justify their exclusion from even the most junior positions. Partly as a consequence of new technology, the mail order company had been able to avoid problems of labour supply which would have prevented discrimination against Black applicants.

NOTES

(1)　There was also some decline in employment in transport and communications.

(2)　But note that this __proportional__ shift concealed an __absolute__ decline in employment in services and that the service sector accounted for a much higher (and increasing) proportion of all jobs held by women.

(3)　In fact the number of White boys __and girls__ entering textiles fell at a greater rate than amongst Black boys after 1978. This reflected the fact that the number of Black boys entering textiles was already very small. Furthermore, the point to note is that Black boys found no compensating improvement in employment opportunities elsewhere.

(4)　Which still employed a large number of women in 1977-8.

(5)　Between 1977 and 1979 textile employment for girls declined more sharply than employment for boys but this trend was reversed after 1979 and in 1981 more girls than boys found work in textiles.

(6)　Other Manufacturing Industry, which offered an extra twenty four jobs.

(7)　This might be a consequence of the inclusion of Blacks in the figures for all school leavers.

(8)　With most of the loss taking place in mechanical engineering. At no stage was textiles a significant source of skilled employment for Black boys. Between 1977 and 1981 only four Black boys got textile apprenticeships.

(9)　Campbell and Jones noted that Asian boys were more likely than Asian girls to receive some kind of training in their jobs (1981, pp. 34-5).

(10)　Mail order employment therefore approached three quarters of the total number of jobs provided by the wool textile industry in the city.

(11)　With additional production linked bonuses for some clerical workers.

(12)　Thus this one plant employed something like half the total number of people employed in the wool textile industry as direct production workers.

(13)　In 1978 seventy five per cent of the workforce was female. This was rather more than twice the proportion of women workers in textiles. Furthermore, the proportion of young workers at the plant was higher for both sexes than in textiles.

(14)　The company had 2,200 employees in Bradford when the closure was announced. Two hundred, probably the more skilled workers, left before the redundancies were implemented.

(15)　Information supplied by Bob Parr, of Bradford College's 'Lift Off' Programme, covering a sample of 500 redundant workers.

(16)　It is very likely that Asians suffered a greater drop in earnings in their new jobs. Certainly women fared worse in this respect.

(17)　In spite of the fact that Asian men had more marketable skills.

(18)　But note that overprecise comparisons of these figures should be avoided since the numbers leaving the area or for whom no information was available were quite large __and__ the proportion of school leavers falling into this category was especially high amongst Blacks.

(19) The proportion of education undergone in the UK was especially high amongst Asian females.

(20) This was pointed out in Chapter Six when we considered several explanations for the fall in the Asian proportion of wool textile workers.   The present chapter suggests that rather more weight might be given to one of the explanations dismissed in Chapter Six.   It may be that, by 1980-1, rising unemployment had persuaded Whites to accept the wool textile work which Asians had performed. It is impossible to be certain, but we might speculate that unemployment began to influence White workers - as the wool textile employers hoped it would - after my fieldwork was completed in 1978.   Thus unemployment would reproduce the effect (a fall in the Asian proportion) of changes in the labour process in those areas of work performed by Asians. The latter would, in any case, have become less important as the recession itself discouraged new investment.

TABLE 8.1 UNEMPLOYMENT IN BRADFORD [a] BY 'ETHNIC GROUP' (QUARTERLY)
1977-82

DATE	TOTAL UNEMPLOYED	WHITES	NON-WHITES [c]		ASIANS [b]	
			No	% TOTAL	No	% TOTAL
1977						
FEB	12,230	10,726	1,504	12.3	1,258	10.3
MAY	11,679	10,325	1,354	11.6	1,165	10.0
AUG	14,398	12,329	2,069	14.4	1,832	12.7
NOV	12,950	10,944	2,006	15.5	1,773	13.7
1978						
FEB	12,860	11,059	1,801	14.0	1,650	12.8
MAY	12,256	10,515	1,741	14.2	1,550	12.6
AUG	15,872	13,553	2,319	14.6	1,949	12.3
NOV	13,019	11,023	1,996	15.3	1,699	13.0
1979						
FEB	13,149	11,236	1,913	14.5	1,668	12.7
MAY	11,829	10,045	1,784	15.1	1,619	13.7
AUG	13,499	11,338	2,161	16.0	1,946	14.4
NOV	12,131	10,167	1,964	16.2	1,796	14.8
1980						
FEB	13,483	11,422	2,061	15.3	1,917	14.2
MAY	14,599	12,270	2,329	15.9	2,176	14.9
AUG	20,267	16,922	3,345	16.5	3,124	15.4
NOV	21,387	17,831	3,556	16.6	3,312	15.5
1981						
FEB	24,051	20,268	3,783	15.7	3,455	14.4
MAY	25,366	21,394	3,972	15.7	3,696	14.6
AUG	28,861	24,428	4,433	15.4	4,123	14.3
NOV	28,116	23,806	4,310	15.3	4,027	14.3
1982						
FEB	28,342	24,041	4,301 [d]	15.2	4,000	14.5

NOTES a Bradford, Keighley and Shipley Employment Exchange Areas
(the latter includes figures from Bingley Job Centre which
were produced separately from February 1979).
   b Persons born or persons with one or more parents born in India,
Pakistan, Bangladesh or East Africa.
   c Asians plus persons of other commonwealth origin.
   d May be an underestimate by 52.
SOURCE: Manpower Service Commission.

TABLE 8.2   UNEMPLOYMENT IN BRADFORD BY ETHNIC ORIGIN (QUARTERLY) 1977-82.

DATE	EAST AFRICAN & INDIAN		OTHER AFRICAN		WEST INDIAN		PAKISTANI		BANGLADESH		OTHER NON-WHITE	
	No	% 1977 FIG	No	% 1977 FIG.	No	% 1977 FIG	No	% 1977 FIG	No	% 1977 FIG	No	% 1977 FIG
1977												
FEB	414	100.0	25	100.0	216	100.0	790	100.0	54	100.0	42	100.0
MAY	375	90.6	21	84.0	161	74.5	726	91.9	64	118.5	7	16.7
AUG	588	142.0	22	88.0	210	97.2	1,156	146.3	88	163.0	15	35.7
NOV	487	117.6	24	96.0	173	80.1	1,192	150.9	94	174.1	37	88.1
1978												
FEB	451	108.9	21	84.0	148	68.5	1,135	143.7	64	118.5	7	16.7
MAY	404	97.6	14	56.0	182	84.3	1,082	137.0	64	118.5	14	33.3
AUG	720	173.9	36	144.0	204	94.4	1,152	145.8	77	142.6	10	23.8
NOV	459	110.9	21	84.0	170	78.7	1,166	147.6	74	137.0	8	19.0
1979												
FEB	539	130.2	18	72.0	169	78.2	1,063	134.6	66	122.2	26	61.9
MAY	470	113.5	16	64.0	140	64.8	1,077	136.3	72	133.3	9	21.4
AUG	600	144.9	15	60.0	189	87.5	1,259	159.4	87	161.1	11	26.2
NOV	497	120.0	10	40.0	147	68.0	1,207	152.8	92	170.4	11	26.2
1980												
FEB	536	129.5	12	48.0	112	51.8	1,292	163.5	89	164.8	20	47.6
MAY	621	150.0	12	48.0	126	58.3	1,452	183.8	103	190.7	15	35.7
AUG	863	208.4	16	64.0	189	87.5	2,132	269.9	129	238.9	16	38.1
NOV	890	215.0	31	124.0	187	86.6	2,271	287.5	151	279.6	26	61.9

TABLE 8.2 Cont....

DATE	EAST AFRICAN & INDIAN		OTHER AFRICAN		WEST INDIAN		PAKISTANI		BANGLADESH		OTHER NON-WHITE	
	No	% 1977 FIG	No	% 1977 FIG	No	% 1977 FIG	No	% 1977 FIG	No	% 1977 FIG	No	1977 FIG
1981												
FEB	916	221.2	24	96.0	193	89.3	2,371	300.1	168	311.1	111	264.3
MAY	935	225.8	19	76.0	203	93.9	2,598	328.9	163	301.8	54	128.6
AUG	1,022	246.9	23	92.0	267	123.6	2,914	368.9	187	346.3	20	47.6
NOV	944	228.0	24	96.0	226	104.8	2,900	367.1	183	338.9	33	78.6
1982												
FEB	900	217.4	35	140.0	213	98.6	2,908	368.1	192	355.6	53	126.2

NOTE: Bradford, Keighley and Shipley Employment Exchange Areas (the latter includes figures from Bingley Job Centre which were produced separately from February 1979).

SOURCE: Manpower Service Commission.

TABLE 8.3   BLACK UNEMPLOYMENT IN BRADFORD [a] BY SEX (QUARTERLY)
1977-82

DATE	BLACK MEN	BLACK WOMEN	TOTAL BLACK UNEMPLOYED
1977			
FEB	1,250	254	1,504
MAY	1,115	239	1,352
AUG	1,703	366	2,069
NOV	1,681	325	2,006
1978			
FEB	1,532	269	1,801
MAY	1,499	242	1,741
AUG	1,808	511	2,319
NOV	1,567	429	1,996
1979			
FEB	1,521	392	1,913
MAY	1,450	334	1,784
AUG	1,685	476	2,161
NOV	1,586	378	1,964
1980			
FEB	1,644	417	2,061
MAY	1,895	434	2,329
AUG	2,699	646	3,345
NOV	2,940	616	3,556
1981			
FEB	3,118	665	3,783
MAY	3,303	648	3,951 [b]
AUG	3,707	726	4,433
NOV	3,616	694	4,310
1982			
FEB	3,700	653	4,353 [c]

NOTES: a Bradford, Keighley and Shipley Employment Exchange areas
           (the latter includes figures from Bingley Job Centre which
           were prepared separately from February 1979).
        b Excludes Shipley Employment Exchange area (21 people) for
           which numbers of male and female unemployed were not available.
        c May be an overestimate of 52.

SOURCE: Manpower Service Commission.

9 Beliefs and reality

A great deal of this book has been concerned with the distinction between structure and form, essence and appearance. It is, indeed, highly desirable that research of the kind reported here should be forced to confront this problem of distinction, since it faces an array of misconceptions which have often served to obscure the central focus of such study in the past. Nevertheless, the preceding chapters have not entirely solved the problem and the purpose of this chapter is therefore to complete the task of distinguishing between essence and appearance.

AN INCLINATION TOWARDS CHEAP LABOUR

Some writers argue that the culture of Black workers leads them to incline towards the jobs which constitute cheap labour. There are two variations on this theme: the first assumes that culture leads Black workers to prefer the jobs the rest of the population finds unattractive.

This is the view taken by American dual labour market theorists (and extended to Black workers in the UK by Bosanquet and Doeringer 1973, see especially p.432). The most easily quantifiable of the characteristics which dual labour market theory identifies is labour turnover. In contrast to other workers (Edwards 1975, p.9-13) the 'secondary labour force' - which includes Black workers - is assumed to exhibit high voluntary turnover (see Doeringer and Piore 1971, passim) and to prefer jobs where this is no handicap. These are the jobs (cheap labour) offered by 'secondary employers'. High turnover may suit certain employers, indeed this has been suggested for the UK wool textile industry (Moor and Waddington 1980, p.46), but can we accept that workers change jobs so frequently because they prefer to do so? Even if we ignore evidence which shows these employers have actually encouraged high turnover (Moor and Waddington 1980, p.46), and assume that they are simply accommodating workers' 'traits' (Gordon 1972, p.128), how are we to explain the workers' preference? It is likely that Montgomery's observation on nineteenth century immigrants to the United States will apply to 'secondary workers':

'The immigrant labourer ... had one standard remedy for disgust with his job: he quit.' (Montgomery 1973, p.13).

Yet this does not mean that Black workers prefer high turnover jobs (c.f. Gordon 1972, p.50), rather the opposite: they leave these jobs in the hope of finding something better.

Turnover amongst 'secondary workers' is no higher than amongst workers with similar prospects of alternative employment and in similar jobs (1). The jobs and not their occupants' culture explain this high turnover. For example, my respondents accepted that Asians in Bradford moved around wool textile firms in search of increased wages. This brings us back

147

to the fundamental flaw in the dual labour market thesis: 'secondary jobs' are distinguished by low pay and which group of workers can be believed to <u>prefer</u> low pay?

✗ The second variation assumes that Black workers have characteristics which lead them to <u>put up with</u> jobs rejected by the rest of the population. Some writers - both dual labour market and 'radical' labour market (see Gordon 1972; passim) theorists as well as European writers on cheap (especially migrant) labour - suggest that Black workers, or 'secondary' or 'target workers', are predisposed to settle for the most unattractive jobs and to accept the characteristics of these jobs once they are in them.

In Bonacich's version of dual labour market theory, the 'split labour market', she assumes that groups of workers have differences in 'resources and motives which are often correlates of ethnicity' (Bonacich 1972, p.547; for examples see Bonacich 1972, pp.549-51; 1976, p.38; and N.d, p.12). Some of these 'resources and motives' are created on the job but others are prerequisites of employment. We will begin by considering the <u>resources</u> of the occupants of undesirable jobs.

There are firstly the <u>yardsticks</u> against which workers compare their jobs: their customary level of living and their information on other jobs and the prevailing wage rate. Thus the absence of yardsticks is thought to lower the (wage) expectations of married women. While lack of information may result from workers' <u>recent</u> arrival on the labour market, so may their lack of 'political resources' and of the 'customs' of an industrial workforce. Wainwright assumes that married women lack political resources (1978, p.195). Castles and Kosack think this also applies to migrant workers (1973, p.121). Fowler and her colleagues extend the argument to Black workers in the UK (1975, p.41), and Friedman (2) takes weak union organisation as the basis of all cheap labour (1978, pp.45,63). But 'worker resistance', to use Friedman's term, is not simply a matter of trade union organisation. Wainwright assumes that married women have 'no established work customs' (1978, p.195). Castles and Kosack observe (3) that

> 'The overwhelming majority of immigrants come from pre-industrial societies. Most of them have worked in agriculture or artisan activities rather than industry, before migration. They are not accustomed to the exercise of authority through formal technically-rational rules and structures, since authority in the home society is usually linked to specific persons. Nor are they accustomed to the practices developed by workers for regulating output and rhythm ...' (1973, p.121).

and Ward concludes that

> 'The migratory workers are often too inexperienced in industrial work to recognise a speed-up, or to know how to resist it when they do recognise it.' (1975, p.27).

But it is not simply the <u>absence</u> of industrial custom which we are asked to consider. Some writers claim that groups of workers have specific customs of their own that lead them to accept jobs others have rejected. Thus Rimmer concluded, from his study of British foundries, that immigrant workers had 'different cultural values and patterns of behaviour.' They might ignore established 'custom and practice' and be willing to increase output and work longer shifts (1972, passim). The 'agricultural background' of Black workers figures strongly in this argument (4). This is complemented by the institutional definition of workers in the cheap labour category as new or alien:

> '... the insecurity of their residence and their vulnerability to deportation, their habits of deference and lack of a collective identity and praxis of self-assertion relevant to their current situation - their orientations, in any case, to another society altogether - makes them malleable and compliant.' (Worsley 1976, p.136).

This leads us to the _motives_ of workers performing cheap labour: their expectations are not seen merely as a consequence of their lack of resources. In particular, Bonacich argues that they will put up with unattractive work if it is temporary and they have an alternative life to return to. More specifically,

> 'The worker's standard of living does not, therefore, depend on his earnings on the job in question, since his central source of employment or income lies elsewhere ... Such a motive produces the "backward-sloping supply function" characteristic of native workers in colonised territories.' (Bonacich 1972, p.551).

Or the migrant worker may be interested in improving status elsewhere and be willing to submit to lower wages and longer hours in consequence. This analysis has been applied to women workers as well as 'sojourners'. In the latter case it is interesting to note that the argument holds even if the 'temporary' stay turns out to be permanent (see Anwar 1979, passim). Nevertheless, some writers expect that workers' motives will change when their occupation of unattractive jobs can no longer seriously be regarded as temporary. Cohen expresses a widely held view when he writes that young Black Britons will not put up with 'shit work' (Cohen 1980, p.25). This argument can be extended to the resources, as well as the motives, of the 'second generation'.

To summarise, it has been suggested that some workers are unable to improve their jobs or get better ones because they have no yardsticks against which to compare their work and that this lowers their expectations; and that they have no 'political resources' with which to achieve any expectations they might retain. Furthermore, they have no customs, or the wrong ones, and this minimises both their expectations and resources. Finally, even with the correct _resources_, these workers would still have peculiar _motives_ which would lower their expectations of improvement.

Empirical support for this analysis is balanced by data which suggests the exact opposite: the workers who do unattractive jobs have characteristics which make them _less_ likely to put up with these jobs. While Rimmer (1972, p.43) observed that Black foundry workers would put up with twelve hour shifts and other characteristics of cheap labour, he also thought that their culture would lead them virtually to ignore threats of dismissal and to propensities for lateness and absenteeism (5). Which part of this conflicting evidence we choose to believe is ultimately of no importance: characteristics peculiar to workers in the worst jobs have little to do with any 'culture' they bring to their work. Williams makes the following comment on the New World slave:

'To coercion and punishment he responded with violence,
sabotage and revolt. Most of the time he merely was
as idle as possible. That was his usual form of
resistance - passive. The docility of the Negro Slave
is a myth.' (1967, p.202).

This is not to say that the slaves were particularly bloody minded;
rather that, as Tabb explains in respect of 'secondary workers',

'There is not much reason to work hard when the reward
for such effort is not advancement, but merely the
establishment of a higher work norm.' (1970, pp.29-30).

If 'resources and notives' mark out cheap labour they are more likely
to be created at work than in the culture of the workers and to be
similar to those adopted by others in comparable situations (6).
Even if we were to accept that Black workers were different would their
'characteristics' explain why they put up with their jobs? If we
consider workers' motives the proposition quickly takes on an absurd
aspect. For example, Black migrants may judge their achievements by
standards in their country of origin but these achievements usually
fall short of their original expectations (7). Furthermore, we can
ignore this evidence and still be forced to admit that Black workers
work very hard to maximise their achievements and would not object
to working for a shorter period and/or minimising the hard work they have
to do to realise their 'limited' goals.

It may well be that the costs of reproducing labour power are lowered
where cheap labour is performed by migrants or peasants (see ASRP,
pp.488-503) but this provides an explanation of why labour is produced
cheaply (see Chapter Two above) and not why it is sold cheaply. To
extend the 'reproduction costs' argument to the latter is equivalent to
'human capital' theory (see below) in that it proposes that labour will
be cheap where it is purchased in an economy which has low productivity.

Any perceived differences in the resources and motives of the workers
who perform cheap labour may well be ascribed. Thus, in Chapter Seven
we remarked on the difference between employers' stereotypes of Black
workers and the behaviour of their Black employees. Allen and her
colleagues noted the same discrepancy between Black resistance and
employers' views of Black workers:

'We were repeatedly assured that the Asian workforce was
"docile": they "always did as they were told." The
evidence now contradicts this belief, but this in itself
is insufficient to dispel it completely and there are
already indications that the Asian workers' militancy
is now becoming explicable within another managerial
belief, namely that the agitator, or its variant
"outside influences", are causing militancy amongst
Asian workers.' (1977, p.351).

and Burawoy has concluded that, in South Africa,

'Behavioural characteristics due to participation in
a system of migrant labour are portrayed by the dominant
ideology as racial characteristics.' (1976, p.1061).

The characteristics we have been considering may fall into this category,
Jenny Bourne certainly thinks so. She criticises Brooks and Singh for
claiming that immigrants' 'own distinctive traditions and their own

150

ethnic identities ... influenced their occupational and industrial
distribution.' (1980, p.343). Instead such differences are more
likely to be ascribed - the same applies to workers' 'preference' for
cheap labour - and to be at variance with any real characteristics of
workers in the category cheap labour.

We must conclude that Black workers do not prefer, or accept,
undesirable jobs because of their (cultural) characteristics. They
want to do any kind of work and are willing to take the best they can get.
The only real difference we have observed between Black and White workers
is that Blacks cannot resist by leaving unattractive work for better jobs.
We must therefore assume that Black workers find only unattractive jobs
open to them, but why should this be the case?

LIMITATIONS ON THE EMPLOYMENT OF BLACK WORKERS

X It has been suggested that certain characteristics make Black workers
only <u>fit</u> for undesirable jobs and not for others. 'Human capital'
theory assumes that workers can be treated (analytically!) like
machines: the more that is invested in them, the more productive they
are. In the 1960s this theory was applied to Black workers in North
American cities. They were assumed to represent negligible human
capital and therefore to be unproductive, hence they were in
unproductive jobs (8). In its original form, the theory specified
education as the mechanism which created differences in productivity.
This assumption was criticised by dual labour market theorists and is,
in any case, inoperative where differences in educational attainment are
not related to employment distribution. There were two responses
to this problem. Dual labour market and 'radical' (labour market)
analyses assume

> '... that secondary male workers (and especially Blacks) will
> realise few, if any monetary returns to many incremental
> levels of educational attainment because they are typically
> channelled into secondary jobs in which educational
> attainment makes little difference, either in their manifest
> productivities or in their (negligible) chances for promotion.'
> (Gordon 1972, p.118).

In the alternative response, culture replaces education as the
mechanism which transmits productivity differences. Whereas the
'poverty circle' described by Moynihan includes culture as the handicap
which leads Blacks to take less than full advantage of educational
opportunities, Lewis gives culture a life of its own:

> 'By the time slum children are age six or seven, they
> have usually absorbed the basic values and attitudes
> of their subculture and are not psychologically geared
> to take full advantage of the changing conditions or
> increased opportunities that may occur in their lifetime.'
> (1969, p.188).

In this view culture becomes part of, or perhaps identical with, the
human capital of Black workers. Whatever variation of human capital
theory is considered, however, it founders on the fact that, in the
jobs we have been considering, pay is not related to productivity.

151

Dual labour market theorists criticised human capital theory but retained the idea that Black workers were only 'suitable' for some jobs and not for others. Labour turnover, while proving a handicap elsewhere, might suit 'secondary employers'. This much we have already accepted, and we might even assume that 'secondary employers' simply put up with high turnover because they have no alternative, but this could only be the case because the jobs they offer are so unattractive that they cause high turnover. There is no evidence of an intrinsic propensity for high voluntary turnover amongst their employees.

There remains, however, one worker characteristic which we cannot reasonably argue was acquired on the job: the prior acquisition of skills or training. It is a common assumption that immigrants who perform cheap labour, including wool textile jobs in Bradford, have been trained in - or, at least, acquainted with - this work in their country of origin (see, for example, Smith 1976, p.73). Evidence to support this view is scarce (9) and it is evident that the assumption owes something to human capital analysis: the (assumed) skills of the workers who do unattractive jobs are thought to indicate that they are inferior workers. Cheap labour is thought to have few, or archaic skills matched to the jobs they are recruited to do. Barron and Norris are probably closer to the truth when they state that, although 'secondary employers' do not offer training since they are not concerned to retain workers,

> 'This does not mean, of course that candidates for
> secondary jobs do not need to be skilful or intelligent;
> many secondary employers depend upon being able to
> obtain workers who are highly adaptable.' (1976, p.60).

Black workers are not confined to undesirable jobs because of their 'capabilities' any more than their 'culture': the characteristics Black workers are supposed to exhibit are characteristics of the jobs, and not the workers, or are ascribed. But does this mean that ascription causes the racial division of labour, i.e. does ascription explain why Black workers find only the rejected jobs accessible?

Most writers concede that race may be used as a screening device and we have certainly found evidence which suggested that

> 'Because blacks traditionally have been hired in certain
> occupations employers have developed stereotypes that
> Blacks are "best suited" for these jobs.' (Marshall 1974, p.867).

But Marshall thinks that employers come to 'prefer' Blacks for certain jobs because they are available for them (1974,p.836),could it really be, rather, that employers 'positively discriminate' in favour of Blacks, in certain cases, on the basis of all the characteristics we have found to be ascribed? In the abstract, this creates an interesting problem. Take slavery for example: 'White meets Black, Black is seen as inferior therefore Black is enslaved' cannot be separated empirically from 'White meets Black, Black is enslaved therefore Black is seen as inferior'. There are similar problems in regard to migrant workers in Europe (Berger and Mohr 1975, p.140). The most obvious explanation for this difficulty is that the object of enquiry is dynamic, i.e. ascription 'matures' as the racial division of labour develops. This is the implication of Sheila Allen's various statements on the subject but a rather less obvious explanation might be that the nature of racist beliefs actually anticipates the racial division of labour:

152

'Thus systems of racial domination depend ultimately on
control over the movements of the oppressed and restriction
of their full participation in society. Although this
may be secured by laws, or by violence or the threat of
violence, the most common and more stable mechanisms reside
in cultural beliefs and psychological adaptations. Here
the notion of _place_ is central. The idea that there is
an appropriate place - or set of rules and activities -
for people of colour and that other places and possibilities
are not proper or acceptable, is a universal element of the
racist dynamic. In America, as in the European colonies,
White people used to say (and many still do): "The Negro
(or native) is all right as long as he stays in his place".'
(Blauner 1972, pp. 37-8).

We have already discovered, however, that employers do not allocate
Black workers to particular jobs in the belief that they are the best
occupants of these jobs. In Chapter Seven it was pointed out that
employers merely _claimed_ that they had done this in order to justify
their inability to discriminate. The interesting logical problem turns
out to be based on an absurd proposition. 'Voluntary positive
discrimination' can be reduced to the idea that employers give Black
workers the worst jobs because they _ought_ to have them rather than
because nobody else wants them. In sum, that Black workers find only
the rejected jobs accessible to them cannot be explained by their
'culture' or 'capabilities' or even by what their employers _believe_
these characteristics to be.

We agree that Black workers are excluded from most jobs and therefore
have access only to jobs others have rejected. Once we have dismissed
analyses couched in terms of 'human capital' or 'culture', discrimination
seems to the obvious explanation (even to neoclassical economists:
see ASRP, pp.517-8). Employers discriminate against Black workers
because they have racist beliefs which lead them to ascribe characteristics
according to skin colour. In particular, employers ascribe
characteristics which make Black workers appear to be unfit for _any_
role in advanced (i.e. Western!) industrial society. Black workers
are not included in jobs they are thought to _fit_ but excluded from those
they are thought not to be _fit for_.

THE LEGITIMATION OF RACIST BELIEFS

Any other explanation (than discrimination) for the employment
distribution of Black workers amounts to mystification, and represents
a confusion of beliefs and reality. One major problem remains,
however. If employers discriminate against Black workers in the _false_
belief that they are inferior, why don't they realise their mistake and
stop discriminating (c.f. Marshall 1974, p.861)? In other words, how
is the confusion between beliefs and reality sustained?

Racist beliefs lead to discrimination: employers discriminate because
they believe Black people are inferior (and not just at work). This
belief is confirmed by the employment distribution of Black workers, or to
be more precise, the 'racial division of labour'. This term has been
used without qualification or comment in preceding chapters but it is
now necessary to specify exactly what it means: it can be defined as
the way in which the employment distribution of Black workers is perceived
once racial categorisation is admitted.

Racial categorisation was in existence long before Asian workers were employed in Bradford's wool textile mills. The best account of its genesis is provided by Jordan (1968) but this does not concern us. Racial categorisation is only relevant in that it is the medium through which employers perceive the employment distribution of Black workers. If employers saw that Blacks were only given access to inferior work, they might then perceive that the employment distribution of Black workers resulted from their own efforts to discriminate against Blacks. But their initial belief in races, i.e. 'myths about human classification' (Gabriel and Ben-Tovim 1978, p.35; see also Miles 1982, passim) leads them to see the employment of Black workers in terms of racial categories. Their perception is mistaken but they behave as if it were not, hence the racial division of labour legitimates the employers' belief in the inferiority of Black workers because it demonstrates that Blacks do inferior jobs. If Blacks and Whites worked together consistently, and in numbers, employers' beliefs would be threatened. It would be much more difficult for them to sustain the belief that Blacks were inferior if their occupancy of superior jobs constantly gave the lie to this belief.

It might be suggested that this explanation for the persistence of racist beliefs is tautological. For example, it might be thought that we are arguing that employers' beliefs are legitimated by a situation which they have intentionally created. This is the thought underlying Beechey's criticism of the 'vicious circle' described by Barron and Norris in relation to women's employment (Beechey 1978, p.180; c.f. Barron and Norris 1976, p.53). But since we know that employers did not set up the racial division of labour in order to reflect their racist beliefs, and that they would rather have excluded Black workers completely (Chapter Seven), the employment distribution of Black workers cannot have been intentionally created by their employers.

Alternatively, the argument would also be tautological if it depended on the assumption that the jobs which Black workers occupy are only seen as inferior because they are held by Blacks. We have concluded, however, that the inferiority of these jobs is independent of the workers who occupy them (see Chapter Seven). For example, pay is one of the criteria on which a job is judged and jobs are not low paid because Black workers do them. Rather, Blacks only gain access to these jobs because they are low paid. In other words, pay is one of the characteristics of the job hierarchy which precedes the recruitment of Black workers. Workers are aware of the job hierarchy - hence their rejection, when possible, of the least attractive jobs - and so are employers. Thus employers describe changing job content independently of any change in the employment distribution of Black workers. Just as the job hierarchy precedes the racial division of labour (c.f. Allen et al., 1977, p.342), so the employers' view of the labour process is independent of the place Black workers occupy within it. Employers do not decide some jobs are inferior because they are done by Blacks rather than Whites (10).

This leads to a further problem, those exceptions to the racial division of labour where Blacks and Whites work side by side. As long as they remain exceptions, employers see the White workers as sub standard or working below capacity, i.e. as inferior workers. Yet this does not mean they are suffering 'a derivative ascription of racial designation' (Baron 1975, p.208). Employers make judgements of these workers' capabilities from their occupancy of inferior jobs rather than 'Black

jobs'.   Similarly, those few Black workers who get better jobs are
judged as superior individuals.

Finally, what of those cases where no Black workers are employed?
In this event beliefs do not conflict with reality precisely because
Blacks are absent.   They have been totally excluded as unfit and so
their absence confirms their inferiority.

CONCLUSION

The racial division of labour seems to reflect employers' racist
beliefs.   Asian workers do unattractive jobs: work which others have
rejected.   Asians do not prefer or put up with undesirable jobs
because of characteristics which are peculiar to them and which have
been broadly defined as 'cultural'.   These characteristics turn out
to be ascribed and we must conclude that Asian workers want to do any
kind of work and are willing to take the best they can get.   It has
been suggested that Black workers' characteristics make them fit only
for some jobs and not for others.   In no respect - i.e. in terms of
'human capital', 'culture' or the prior acquisition of training - is
this true in our case.   Again the supposed differences turn out to be
ascribed.   While Black workers do not get the jobs which constitute
cheap labour because employers believe they ought to have them, employers
do take account of 'race' in their employment policies, but only by
(negatively) discriminating.   There are therefore limits to the areas
of employment to which Blacks can gain access.   Discrimination results
from ascription which is legitimated by the racial division of labour,
i.e. the appearance which racial categorisation gives to the employment
distribution of Black workers.

In this chapter I have tried to explain that actions are justified
by ideas whereas ideas are legitimated by a view of social reality:
discrimination requires justification but racism requires legitimation.
There has been some confusion about this distinction (c.f. Wainwright
1978, p.195; Worsley 1976, p.137), and sociologists and anthropologists
make a mistake when they assume a direct relationship.   When they
make use of ascribed characteristics to explain the employment patterns
of Black workers they simply reproduce the justifications of employers.
Take, for instance, those analyses which rely on the assumed implications
of Black workers being temporary, alien or newly arrived (for example,
Piore 1975, p.144).   It is argued that Black workers accept unattractive
jobs because they judge these jobs in relation to opportunities in their
country of origin.   This should be compared to the wool textile
employer who justified not giving a suitably qualified Black worker
a superior job because his qualifications and experience 'only'
applied 'to home' (11), or to this managing director's view of the
Asians he employed in unattractive jobs in his worsted spinning mill:

'They must like it otherwise they would go somewhere else.
They have done quite well out of it.   From living in the
bush, more or less, to being relatively wealthy.'

The flaw in his argument is, of course, that his Asian workers had
nowhere else to go.   Discrimination had given them no alternative.

NOTES

(1) In fact some British <u>adherents</u> of dual labour market theory
     see 'secondary workers' as relatively immobile (Fowler et al.,
     1975, p.37; see also Jupp and Davies 1974, pp.14-5).

(2) In some respects Friedman anticipates the later work of Miles
     and Phizacklea in which not only the strength but the <u>kind</u> of
     trade unionism is related to ethnicity (also see Bourne 1980,
     passim).

(3) <u>In spite</u> of their earlier statement that
         'Immigrants should be looked at not in the
         light of their specific group characteristics -
         ethnic, social and cultural - but in terms of
         their actual social position.'   (Castles and
         Kosack 1973, p.5).
     In fact Castles and Kosack's conclusion is closer to the
     views of the 'human capital' theorists (see below) and of
     Oscar Lewis:
         'Indeed, it is the low level organisation that gives
         the culture of poverty its marginal and anachronistic
         quality in our highly complex, specialised, organised
         society.   Most primitive peoples have achieved a
         higher level of socio-cultural organisation than our
         modern urban slum dwellers.'   (1969, p.191).

(4) Compare again to Oscar Lewis, quoted above, on the 'anachronistic'
     culture of the workers who perform cheap labour.

(5) Also compare Rimmer's views on the use of output limitations
     (1972, pp.11,43,60).   For more self contradictory evidence
     on the impact of immigrant workers' culture see Jupp and
     Davies 1974, pp.63-4.

(6) Compare to Montgomery's observation on nineteenth century
     immigrants to the United States:
         '... in small mixed groups ... the impulse of peasant
         immigrants to work furiously when an authority figure
         was present and loaf in his absence ... was soon
         exchanged in coal mines or car shops for the craftsman's
         ethic of refusing to work while a boss was watching.'
         (1973, p.15).
     We need not agree, however, that immigrant workers 'caught'
     the (work) culture of indigenous workers: compare to Nichols
     and Beynon's description of management's search for a 'green'
     labour force which was followed by the growth of informal
     practices for limiting output amongst the 'green' workers
     (Nichols and Beyon 1977, p.136; see also Nichols and Armstrong
     1976, pp.71-2).

(7) For example, see Lawrence 1974, pp.39-45; Smith 1976, pp.92-4
     (c.f. Berthoff 1953, pp.34-5).   Also see Chapter Two above.

(8) For a full discussion see Gordon 1972, pp.28-42; for American
     examples see Moynihan 1969; and for the UK see Department of
     Employment 1977, pp.38,41.

(9) A rare exception might be Turkish migrants to the <u>West German</u>
     textile industry (Kayser 1971, pp.123-5).

(10) Nor do they decide this work is inferior because some of it is
     done by <u>women</u> (c.f. Wright 1968, p.192)!

(11) We might also note that sociologists who write about young
     Blacks in Britain make much of their rejection of 'shit work',
     while employers emphasise the same thing <u>in order to justify</u>
     <u>discriminating against young Blacks</u>.

10 The advantages of discrimination

We began this book by asking why large numbers of Asian workers were employed in the UK wool textile industry. We now know that Asians were employed in those jobs which White workers had rejected. According to the definition given in Chapter One, Asians were providing cheap labour (1). They sold their labour cheaply because they suffered discrimination in other areas of employment. Since many employers refused to hire them, Asians were willing to take unattractive jobs. Wool textile employers therefore benefited from discrimination. The 'disadvantaged' position of Asian workers produced advantages for their employers.

These conclusions differ from much of the accepted wisdom and a more lengthy explanation is therefore required. It might be best to confess at the outset that the research on which this book is based was predicated on a simplistic notion of what was happening in wool textiles. It was assumed that the 'disadvantaged' position of Blacks at work resulted directly from capital's need to exploit labour. The research showed that reality was more complex. The key to this complexity lies in understanding the interaction of labour supply and labour demand.

LABOUR SUPPLY AND LABOUR DEMAND

Most writers on the employment of Blacks in the UK have found that Black workers occupy unattractive jobs. There was general agreement with Smith's conclusion that most 'immigrants' were employed in jobs which Whites had rejected because of low pay; low levels of training, skill and interest; poor conditions and unattractive hours of work (Smith 1976, passim). By the time the Unit for Manpower Studies at the Department of Employment conducted its study, this might almost have been thought a commonplace observation (2), however most commentators went on to conclude that Black workers' occupancy of such jobs could be put down to the existence of a general labour shortage (3). It was assumed that Blacks would be excluded under normal circumstances but where labour demand exceeded labour supply most workers were able to move up the job hierarchy leaving vacancies in the least attractive jobs. Blacks were therefore drafted in at the bottom of the hierarchy. If it were not for the shortfall in labour supply Black workers would not be needed.

This argument takes the abstract idea of the labour market too literally. It may be useful to assume, in economic models, that labour supply and demand are fixed and independent, but this assumption is not supported by empirical research. Since the supply of labour is not fixed - for example, activity rates may vary, especially amongst women - employers can influence the supply of labour. Labour shortages can be created when employers allow wages and conditions to deteriorate. Employers can alleviate shortages by making jobs more attractive or by

abolishing them.   In the former case labour supply will be influenced
by the level of labour demand.   In the latter case, where employers
choose to do without labour, labour demand is influenced by the level
of labour supply and employers may choose to substitute capital for labour
or to reduce output.

Since the creation of labour shortages is not inevitable, it is
difficult to accept that the existence of such shortages 'explains'
the employment of Black workers.   In contrast to those who conclude
that Blacks find work because labour shortages are created in the least
attractive jobs, we should agree with Castells that

> '... immigrant workers do not exist because there are "arduous
> and badly paid jobs" to be done, but, rather, arduous and badly
> paid jobs exist because immigrant workers are present or can be
> sent for to do them.'   (Castells 1975, p.54, emphasis in original)

Yet if the workers who provide cheap labour are available to one group
of employers - who therefore decide to create or maintain unattractive
jobs - we would expect such workers to be available to others.   Why
should certain employers choose to employ cheap labour?

It might be thought that the employers' choice is constrained, for
example that wool textile employers did not have the resources to improve
unattractive jobs or to substitute capital for labour (c.f. Harris 1980,
p.45).   But in the 1950s, when Asian workers began to appear in wool
textile mills, the industry was enjoying a boom period and employers
would have been able to support such expenses.   In the 1960s and 70s,
when product demand was less buoyant, changes in technology, hours of
work and work organisation demonstrated that any scarcity of funds would
not prevent employers from attempting to transform the labour process.
Technical change in the 60s and 70s also showed that new machinery was
available (c.f. Briscoe 1971,p.176).   It is often mistakenly assumed that
the technology of the industries which employ cheap labour is static.
This assumption owes much to the view which equates cheap labour with
'traditional' or 'backward' industries (4) and to the promotion, for
example by Hagmann (1968), of a policy of substituting capital export
for labour import where the latter is reduced by immigration controls.
Certainly the promotion of controls was implicit in Sir Keith Joseph's
assertion that immigration had blocked industrial change in the UK
(Guardian 24 January 1980) (5).

In fact the most important limitation on the choices open to wool
textile employers was provided by the history of their industry.   We
have noted that wool textile employers had habitually turned to cheap
labour in the past, especially during crises.   The industry was the
first within which capitalist social relations became general and capital's
relationship to labour in wool textiles had been established for many
generations.   In all industries the relationship between capital and
labour is historical but no other industry has been established as long.
The ground rules for the employers' response to the postwar crisis were
written more than a century before when their predecessors, perhaps
the founders of modern firms, were winning the lion's share of the
international market for wool textiles.   Thus the employers 'opted'
for cheap labour - for example, when they refused to consider increasing
wages - even where this was no longer the most profitable alternative.
As Briscoe points out, textile employers'

'... aim has always been to obtain the cheapest form of
labour - at first children and juvenilles, then women and
immigrants - the price reflecting the ease with which these
categories can obtain alternative employment.'   (Briscoe 1971,
p.174, emphasis added).

The Unit for Manpower Studies at the Department of Employment reported
that employers would make work more attractive and would substitute
capital for labour if cheap labour was unavailable.   The Unit added that

'In some instances, greater capital intensity was seen
not only as a means of reducing manpower requirements but
also of increasing the earnings of the remaining workers
and therefore making it easier for the firm to attract and
maintain labour.   For example, a number of employers and
industrial training boards in various branches of textiles
suggested that the industry would, in any event, have to
become more capitally intensive if it were to meet
competition from overseas producers and this would in turn
make it impossible to increase relative earnings.'   (Department
of Employment 1977, p.88).

Nevertheless, we have noted that the majority of wool textile employers
did not take this route, despite the exhortations of the unions and the
organisations (like the training board) which serviced the industry.
In consequence, they did not solve their difficulties in the product
market.   The nineteenth century solution was no longer useful in the
1960s and 70s.   Indeed, it might be pointed out that the difficulties
of British industry as a whole could be interpreted in this way.   Most
industries in the UK were established before their competitors and it
may be that the long history of British capital has imposed limitations
which are largely responsible for its failure to maintain international
competitivity (6).

If wool textile employers 'opted' for cheap labour because they
mistakenly assumed on the basis of established custom and practice that
this was the most profitable alternative, then it seems likely that those
employers who did not 'choose' cheap labour were adopting a more
profitable course of action.   In fact we have noted that some wool
textile firms made no response to the postwar crisis and that these
were the least profitable companies.   It would therefore be a mistake
to assume that cheap labour did not produce some benefits for its
employers.   Most importantly - and in contradiction to the claim made
by Sir Keith Joseph (7) - it allowed them to reap some of the benefits
of modernisation.   The Unit for Manpower Studies reported that, if
cheap labour were not available, employers would resort to

'Increased productivity not only by replacing labour with
capital but also by using labour more efficiently where
existing plant and machinery was retained.'   (Department
of Employment 1977, p.87).

In fact this was exactly what wool textile employers did when they
recruited cheap labour.   The transformation of the labour process was
designed to increase the intensity of exploitation but, in accomplishing
this, the employers made wool textile work less attractive.   The
modernisation which did take place could not have been undertaken without
access to cheap labour.   In particular, the way in which employers
dispensed with labour led to a deterioration in the jobs occupied by the

remaining workers.   Far from representing an alternative to cheap
labour, reduced labour demand was, in this case, the cause of problems
of labour supply rather than an attempt to alleviate labour shortages.

This emphasis on the relationship between modernisation and the
deterioration of those jobs which remain is absent from most of the
established writings on the subject.   It is often admitted that
industrial change may be stimulated by abundant labour (8) but this
proposition makes little sense without specification of the effects of
industrial change on the nature of work since the employers'

> '... problem is not to increase the supply of labour but
> to increase the supply of labour willing to be employed
> in certain (usually low grade) occupations.'   (Paine 1974, p.10).

In wool textiles, 'low grade occupations' were created in the
transformation of the labour process which occurred throughout the 1960s
and 70s.   Modernisation depended on the ease with which workers could
be found to fill the unattractive jobs which it created.   In other words,
certain types of industrial change require the use of cheap labour.

DISCRIMINATION

It is, however, clear that industrial change and cheap labour are
not always related in this way and we will return to their relationship
below.   For the moment, we should perhaps reiterate exactly why the
workers who provided cheap labour were willing to go along with the
deterioration which modernisation implied.   Some writers, particularly
those who cite evidence interpreted by Butterworth (1964;   1967) and
Cohen and Jenner (1968) from the wool textile industry, argue that change
in the labour process may produce jobs which are suitable for cheap
labour because, firstly, of the characteristics of the workers who
sell their labour cheaply.   Cohen and Jenner point to the Asians' lack
of custom and practice which might have enabled them to resist change
(1968, pp.55-6 (9)).   Secondly, a particular group of workers might be
suitable because the jobs which were created where the labour process
was transformed were fitting to workers with few skills (10).   We have
dismissed both of these arguments in earlier chapters.   We found that
they originated with employers and managers and could be seen as their
attempts to justify hiring Asian workers.   In fact the only evidence of
the Asians' assumed lack of resistance to change lay in their refusal
to reject the jobs which constituted cheap labour.   Similarly, they
were not particularly suited to the deskilled jobs created in wool
textiles but rather unable to reject them.   Thus the workers who
provided cheap labour went along with modernisation because they had no
alternative.   They were denied access to other sources of employment
because most employers discriminated against Asian applicants.

This furnishes yet another corrective to the view that industrial change
encourages the elimination of discrimination (11), nevertheless some
difficulties remain.   In large part these problems stem from confusions
over the nature of discrimination.   Bonacich, for example, denies that
employers want to discriminate and gives credence to the employers'
claim that they are forced to discriminate by their employees.   She is
sure that all employers want to use the cheapest labour, regardless of
colour, but adds that most incur costs arising from White worker
resistance when they hire Black workers (for example, see Bonacich 1976,
p.44).   Thus cheap labour will only be used where White worker resistance
is minimal (12).

Certainly there was no vociferous resistance from Whites employed in semiskilled wool textile jobs and it was to these jobs that Asians were recruited. Furthermore, Asians were not hired where resistance was vocal and organised, for example in woolsorting and in skilled occupations in dyeing and finishing. But, even if we admit of a correlation between White worker resistance and employers' discrimination against Black applicants, it does not follow that the former causes the latter. In Chapter Seven we suggested that both phenomena could be explained in the same way. Black workers suffer discrimination in more attractive jobs and it is here that White worker resistance is strongest. Resistance is manifested where jobs are thought to be worth holding onto, i.e. where employers can, in any case, discriminate against Black applicants since this does not leave them short of labour. Where jobs are relatively unattractive, resistance is expressed by quitting: the incumbents simply leave for better jobs elsewhere. When White workers leave - because they are not prepared to put up with unattractive jobs - employers are not able to discriminate unless they wish to create a labour shortage. In other words the need for cheap labour and pressure for discrimination against Blacks from White employees do not coincide (13).

Bonacich's explanation of the relationship between cheap labour and discrimination must be rejected because her initial assumption, that employers are 'colour blind', is wrong. It makes much more sense to assume that employers want to discriminate and will satisfy this need as long as this does not involve extra costs. Thus those employers who do hire Blacks consider that discrimination would involve costs in the form of labour shortages or wage increases and other expensive alternatives to cheap labour. Their 'choice' of cheap labour makes it impossible for them to find labour while discriminating.

Discrimination has been used in only one sense throughout this book; to refer to those occasions on which employers exclude Black applicants from employment. Some writers have given a different meaning to the term in an effort to make sense of the relationship between discrimination and cheap labour. Thus it is suggested that employers discriminate between those Blacks and Whites they have already hired in setting wages and work rates. This notion of discrimination is not applicable in UK wool textiles.

It has been proved beyond doubt that Black workers are likely to receive lower wages and to work harder than most Whites and there can really be no objection to the statement that Blacks suffer 'super exploitation' (14). There is no need, however, to explain the 'super exploitation' of Black workers by assuming that employers discriminate between Black and White employees. It is unnecessary to claim that employers 'set' a higher level of exploitation in some jobs because they are performed by Blacks (15). Nor is it necessary to claim that employers give particular jobs to Blacks because they know that, once at work, they will be able to extract more surplus value from the labour of these workers. Rather, 'super exploitation' is guaranteed when employers find workers who are willing to perform the jobs which constitute cheap labour.

Once we have dismissed alternative interpretations of discrimination, the relationship between discrimination and cheap labour can be understood. The employment distribution of Black workers results from employers' efforts to discriminate against Black applicants combined with the inability of some employers to exclude Blacks. Black workers

161

find that discrimination leaves them no alternative but to sell their labour to those employers who cannot recruit Whites. The jobs which Blacks do are peculiar in that their pay seems to be unrelated to the level of labour demand in these occupations. Excess demand is not translated into higher pay. Thus Black workers sell their labour as if the labour market did not exist; indeed it does not exist for Black workers since they suffer discrimination. There is therefore an excess supply of Black workers for the unattractive jobs. In borderline cases, where employers have not yet abandoned attempts to discriminate, this produces the apparent paradox of vacancies and high labour turnover while (Black) labour is abundant.

In Chapter One we stated that cheap labour was performed by workers who took the jobs which others had rejected. Any group of workers who perform cheap labour must therefore be excluded from alternative employment (16). By definition, the jobs which constitute cheap labour can only be attractive to those without access to alternatives. There may be any number of reasons for this exclusion. For example, it may be illegal to employ the workers who perform cheap labour in any other kind of work. But, in the case we have been considering, exclusion results from racial discrimination.

In spite of the fact that they would prefer to employ only White workers, some employers benefit from employing Blacks. Employers do not conspire to make Black workers sell their labour cheaply. The employers of cheap labour are not responsible for the exclusion of Black workers elsewhere, and it is this which makes Blacks available as cheap labour. Black workers would not be employed at all if they did not sell their labour cheaply (17); and in this sense the employment distribution of Black workers is dependent on the creation of advantages for employers. But this is not why the employment distribution of Black workers is created. It results, rather, from the accommodation of discrimination in capitalist relations of production.

THE LABOUR MARKET AND THE LABOUR PROCESS

We can now return to the relationship between cheap labour and modernisation. Cheap labour will be recruited with change in the labour process where this change creates unattractive jobs, but change in the labour process can make these jobs disappear or make them more attractive. Furthermore, cheap labour may be recruited where no change has taken place in the labour process. In wool textiles in the 1950s, change in the labour market seems to have been the predominant factor affecting the number of unattractive jobs. At least until 1958, cheap labour was recruited without noticeable change in the labour process. Some jobs became undesirable because their occupants found that better jobs were available elsewhere, i.e. labour market conditions changed. Employers chose not to improve these jobs because they found they could recruit from alternative sources of labour. This was the case in woolcombing and, periodically in later years, in other sections as well.

By 1964, the employers' organisations were deeply concerned with problems of labour supply: the first industrial training board in the UK was created out of the industry's own recruitment and training organisation and the board's first reports emphasised the large number of vacancies in the industry (Wool ITB 1966, p.10). Nevertheless, change in the labour process was also occurring, and in a way which actually made problems of labour supply more acute. Change in the labour process is not a result of the technical requirements of production (Castells 1975, p.44) but a matter of cash flow, competition, the size of the market and so on, as well as technology. The calculation of the most profitable way in which to change the labour process may not involve pressure from the labour market but it can do so (in the form of labour shortages or rising labour costs). Nevertheless, if, after considering all the available labour supply, employers decide the profitable alternative is to create jobs which will probably be unattractive to the majority of workers but will nevertheless be filled, they will take it. Thus wool textile employers degraded labour in the 60s in the knowledge that these jobs would be filled, as had increasingly unattractive jobs in the 50s, no matter that the workers who filled them would be Asians. They could therefore ignore the growth of attractive alternatives in the labour market. In the (middle) 70s this pattern was repeated in respect of skilled jobs. Better opportunities were available for skilled workers and wool textiles suffered selective labour shortages as a result. But instead of making these jobs more attractive wool textile employers degraded them still further. The (semiskilled) jobs for which there was no shortage of labour were, on the other hand, eliminated!

Even if Black workers are available, unattractive jobs may disappear and employers will have more opportunity to discriminate, thus the percentage of Asian workers in wool textiles began to fall in the late 1970s. Unattractive jobs can be eliminated by structural change or by the loss of alternative opportunities elsewhere in the labour market, but in wool textiles unattractive jobs have also been eliminated by change in the labour process. The gap between wool textile work and its alternatives has been too wide to be affected by all but the most severe rise in unemployment and fall in vacancies. As the recession began, White workers found they had fewer alternatives to unattractive jobs, but these jobs had themselves been casualties of the recession and some undesirable jobs were completely eliminated. Employers knew that suitable recruits (Black or White) would be available to take on the remaining or replacement jobs but they now found they could afford to discriminate. They did not change the labour process in order to change the composition of the labour force (18). Employers might have expected to be short of White labour but nevertheless further degraded skilled jobs. Thus more jobs would have been put in the borderline category where employers would have difficulty in discriminating against Black workers (19).

To summarise, the desirability of all jobs will be affected by changes in the labour process and the labour market but the former seems to predominate. It is not simply that the labour process can be changed independently of conditions in the labour market. In fact it should be explained that conditions in the labour market are dependent on change in the labour process. Although there was no premeditation of its effects, change in the labour process in wool textiles in the early 60s reduced the labour force. Numbers of Asian workers were displaced from woolcombing and made available for other industries and wool textile sections. In the next decade redundant workers provided a pool of ready trained labour. These were mostly Asians since Whites were more likely to leave the industry permanently, perhaps after a number of redundancies, because they could find better alternative jobs (the same was true of skilled White workers). But labour supply was affected by other routes than redundancy: wool textile employers reduced training, and hence effective labour supply, to a minimum. They therefore increased their demand for trained workers (20).

163

It seems that employers will put their requirements of the labour process above any consideration of labour market conditions, at least in so far as these conditions affect their ability to discriminate. This was the substance of the junior managers' complaints noted in Chapter Seven. They wished that senior managers and employers would put 'racial' considerations before production and profit. It has been a constant theme of the discussion of the interaction between the labour process and the labour market that change in either can reduce or increase the employers' opportunities for discrimination but that employers' decisions on change in the labour process take the labour market into account only to the extent that it is assumed that workers will be available - even if they have to be imported - to satisfy labour requirements. They do not take into account whether they will thereby be creating relatively unattractive jobs. All employers would prefer to remain profitable and discriminate but the former undoubtedly takes precedence.

In the 1950s wool textile employers may not have known that their refusal to respond to changed labour market conditions would force them to hire Black workers. They may have been surprised when they found they could not discriminate (when White workers left or did not apply for work). But in the 60s they knew a great deal more about the labour market and the jobs they were creating. Employers at least suspected they were going to have to take on Black workers but they did not change the labour process in order to discriminate 'in advance' because this would over ride their primary motive, profit making. Employers may be aware of the effects of planned labour process change on the composition of the labour force but they do not take these effects into account. In the later 70s, as in the 50s, employers may not have had all the information which would allow them to anticipate changes in their labour force. They may not have realised the potential fall in alternative job opportunities in the 1970s and so may have been (pleasantly) surprised when Whites 'returned' to wool textiles - in fact this means only that the net decline of Whites was less than the net decline in the numbers of Black workers - and that they now had an opportunity to discriminate against Blacks. Nevertheless, even if this had been anticipated it would not have been taken into account in decisions on the labour process.

THE FUTURE

We began this book by expressing doubts about the future of Asian workers in wool textiles. Succeeding chapters demonstrated that unemployment rose for quite some time without wool textile jobs becoming noticeably more attractive to the majority of the population. This apparent paradox has been noted in other industries (for example, see Wright 1968, p.213) and in regard to the UK economy as a whole (Bohning 1972 (a), p.36). Harris concludes that

'... the demand for cheap labour does not disappear in
    slump. On the contrary, it can increase.' (Harris 1980, p.5).

and Castells points out that, in the UK, permanent settlement of migrants has coincided with increased unemployment and increased emigration (1975, p.44; see also Shanin 1978, p.284).

Some writers attempt to solve this problem by proposing that the labour market is 'segmented.' Since it is difficult for workers to transfer from one market to the other, cheap labour can go straight into employment in the 'secondary sector' while other workers are unemployed in the 'primary sector' (c.f. Tabb 1970, p.110). But segmented labour market theory explains the existence of separate labour markets in terms of the culture of the workforce and the worker characteristics required by employers. We have already dismissed this argument in Chapter Nine. Other writers have attempted to explain the paradox in terms of Marx's theory of the reserve army of labour (see, for example, Marshall 1973, p.17). It has been suggested that some groups of workers may have a smaller reserve army, thus a given level of (national) unemployment will be less likely to make some workers accept unattractive jobs than others (c.f. Friedman 1978, pp.113,270; see also Beechey 1978, passim). There is some doubt as to whether the reserve army of labour can be differentiated in this way (Anthias 1980, p.53) and in any event this explanation begs the question: why should some groups of workers have a larger reserve army? The answer is, at least in the case we have been studying, that they suffer discrimination and are excluded from most jobs. The existence of discrimination also explains why Black workers may actually suffer less unemployment - as they did in some years in the 1960s - and yet still find unattractive jobs acceptable. While unemployed Whites might expect to find better jobs (than textiles for example) in time, Blacks did not have such expectations. Nevertheless, unemployment amongst Blacks began to rise - and at a greater rate than all unemployment - in the 70s.

We have discovered that employers are more likely to have unattractive jobs - and therefore to employ cheap labour - when their industry is undergoing change. But we also know that employers are more likely to dispense with cheap labour when industrial change occurs. The outcome of such change is dependent on the interaction of labour process and labour market. In any event, their location in those parts of the labour process most subject to transformation makes the workers who perform cheap labour especially vulnerable to change (21). Firstly, part of the reason for their jobs being unattractive to other workers may be that they are insecure (c.f. Anthias 1980, p.53). Secondly, the very fact that cheap labour may allow industrial change to proceed may make it vulnerable. Since the organisation of work structures labour demand, increased exploitation may lead to rising unemployment. In the 70s this meant that Asians in employment worked harder while the numbers of Asians employed in wool textiles fell. By the end of the decade, however, the proportion of Asians began to fall, i.e. the level of exploitation of White workers was increasing. In part this was accomplished through deskilling. As in other industries, skilled workers suffered deskilling while the less skilled (in this case, Black) workers lost their jobs. In sum, rising unemployment amongst Black workers in Bradford was by no means contingent on the appearance of a general recession.

Nevertheless, it may be that in the 1980s unemployment had reached the level at which those workers who did not suffer discrimination were prepared to take low grade jobs in the wool textile industry. It is likely that unemployment amongst Whites had risen to a level at which these jobs had ceased to be unattractive to many workers. The recession had put them in the same position that Blacks had occupied in earlier years: they had no alternative sources of employment. In this event, wool textile jobs ceased, by definition, to require cheap labour and Black workers were no longer needed. While we are unable to monitor this trend in published statistics (see Chapter One), we can assume that it will continue throughout the remaining life of wool textiles as a significant employer in Bradford and the UK.

165

CONCLUSIONS

The jobs which constitute cheap labour exist because (Black) workers are there, or can be imported, to do them. Employers want to discriminate against Black applicants but for some employers the cost of excluding Black workers is too much to bear. They would be forced to make employment in their companies more attractive - and they expect that this would decrease profits - if they were to discriminate against Black workers. Nevertheless, the desire of capital to exploit labour cannot explain the advantages (to employers) which arise from the 'disadvantaged' position of Black workers. Blacks are made available as cheap labour by the prior existence of racial categorisation and discrimination. The roots of discrimination cannot be found in the capitalist labour process.

Since we know that racial discrimination arises independently of any advantages which might accrue to employers, it is no surprise that discrimination persists even after it has ceased to be 'useful' in this way. Discrimination does not produce advantages for those employers who practice it. Similarly, discrimination does not increase profits for those employers who <u>begin</u> to practice it when unemployment rises. Discrimination continues even though it is no longer required in order to allow some employers to fill unattractive jobs. Blacks remain in a 'disadvantaged' position even where this no longer produces advantages for employers. Thus a disproportionately large number of Blacks may suffer unemployment even though there are sufficient unemployed White workers to satisfy <u>all</u> employers' needs (without the persistence of discrimination).

Unlike the sons and daughters of the European migrants who worked in wool textiles, young Asians are unable to escape categorisation and resulting discrimination. Like <u>sex</u> discrimination, racial discrimination is very difficult to evade. In fact the consequences of racial discrimination may be even more severe than those of sex discrimination. It is true that some White workers may have worse jobs than some Black workers, and that this is more likely to be the case amongst White women, but where unemployment is rising it seems that the consequences of <u>racial</u> discrimination are generally more severe. Firstly, kinship to workers who do not suffer discrimination helps to ameliorate the consequences of exclusion for women. Secondly, as employment declines it becomes clear that employers prefer to employ White workers, of <u>whatever</u> <u>sex</u>, to Black workers. In Chapter Eight we saw that Asian men had held more desirable jobs than White women employed in a TV plant but when the plant closed Asian <u>men</u> faced greater difficulties in finding alternative employment than White <u>women</u>. In recession, Black workers of either sex are much less likely to occupy jobs which White women would be happy to take. It seems that, with mass unemployment, Blacks increasingly find that they are denied access to <u>any</u> jobs, even the most menial.

NOTES

(1)   Other writers confirm that it is unwise to define 'cheap labour' simply in terms of wages and to ignore other aspects of the job which help to make it unattractive (see, for example, Bonacich Nd, p.12). Nevertheless, low pay is certainly the most important attribute of an unattractive job (Castells 1975, p.54; Bohning 1972 (a), p.56).

(2)   See Department of Employment 1977, pp.43, 69, 84. Much of sections E and F in the report consist of supporting evidence.

166

(3)   See, for example, Bohning 1972 (a), p.56; Bourguignon et al., 1977, p.30; Marshall 1973, p.71.

(4)   For example, see Franklin and Resnick 1973, p.83; Marshall 1973, p.101; Freeman and Spencer 1979, p.20; Peach 1968, p.94).

(5)   Note that the implication of tighter immigration controls in this respect was examined before the event by Hallett (1970, p.141) and others in Wilson (edit. 1970), and retrospectively by Department of Employment (1977, pp.38, 184, 187).

(6)   I am indebted to Huw Beynon for this insight.

(7)   Also in contrast to the claims of academics. For example, Hagmann claims that migrant labour creates 'over-manning', 'capital-saving' and a 'technical lag' (1968, p.67). Empirical evidence for similar conclusions comes from as far afield as Californian farms (Buraway 1976) and West German assembly lines (Paine 1974, p.10) but much of this generalisation relies on the mistaken assumption that the workers who perform cheap labour have specific, and limited, training and experience which qualifies them to work only at a certain technological level (for example, see Hallett 1970, pp.143-6; see also Kennedy-Brenner 1979, p.98).

(8)   The opposite of the more usual proposition that industrial change will only take place when labour is scarce, see note (7) above. For examples of work which suggests that industrial change may be stimulated by abundant labour see Bourguignon et al., 1977, p.73; Collard 1970, pp.77-8. This view owes something to the macro economic theories of Kaldor (see also Kindleberger 1965; Lewis 1954). Note that _qualitative_ change can only be introduced into this model in an ad hoc manner as _embodied_ technical progress, i.e. a new generation of machinery may be bought to increase capacity but may _incidentally_ be more productive (c.f. Bohning and Maillat 1974, p.96; Castles and Kasack 1973, p.405). An alternative view is expressed by Marshall, who suggests that cheap labour allows industrial change to proceed since it makes profits available for new investment. This view cannot explain cases, such as those Marshall herself describes, where cheap labour and change in the labour process coincide (c.f. Marshall 1973, p.49).

(9)   See also Preston 1969, pp.644-6; Wainwright 1978, p.195.

(10)   See, for example, Bohning 1972 (a), p.126; Bohning and Maillat 1974, p.53; (CDP 1977, passim; CIS Nd. p.16; Ward 1975, pp.29-30).

(11)   This view stems from the assumption that advanced capitalism is incompatible with ascription. This assumption has received substantial criticism elsewhere: Blauner 1972, Blumer 1975; Corrigan 1977; Freeman and Spencer 1979; Stokes 1975; Wolpe 1970 (especially p.152). For criticism which more closely resembles my own, see Hepple (1970, pp.83-4).

(12)   Also see Friedman 1978, pp.45, 63, 75 and Wolpe 1976, passim.

(13)   Compare to Hepple:

> 'In several industries immigrants have provided cheap labour ... the longer he employs cheap labour the more pressure amounts from the immigrants themselves to move up ... This leads to resistance from British workers who feel their positions threatened and this in turn

induces the employer to resolve the conflict by
dispensing with cheap labour and introducing
automation.' (Hepple 1970, p.137).
Bonacich comes to much the same conclusion in regard to the
American New Deal. The 'racially split labour market' which
had developed in some American firms after World War One
generated conflict. New Deal legislation dealt with this
conflict but encouraged technical progress and so put Blacks
out of work. She gives the example of a textile mill where
the 'NRA' meant paying more and operating at a loss or getting
in new machines and paying 'code' wages to fewer workers
(Bonacich 1976, p.47; see also Freeman and Spencer 1979, p.7).

(14) C.f.Nikolinakos 1973, pp.371-2; Roemer 1978, passim.

(15) As we noted in Chapter Nine, jobs are not low paid because
Black workers do them. Rather Blacks do them (only)
because they are low paid.

(16) Undercutting, the special case of cheap labour discussed in
Chapter One, is also explicable in these terms. When workers
undercut they do so because they are excluded at the going rate.

(17) In the absence of effective legislative or trade union
interference in the employers' practice of discrimination.

(18) This change may have begun in the middle 70s when the rate of
increase in Asian representation in wool textiles began to
slow down, although it was not confirmed until the end of the
decade when the percentage of Asians fell for the first time.

(19) And would therefore be forced to compromise. Thus Asians
were recruited as night shift overlookers, i.e. in the least
attractive supervisory positions.

(20) Training initiatives by employers' organisations paralleled
decreased training provision by individual employers.

(21) This was also true of the women workers who preceded the
Asians in wool textile jobs although the women found more
attractive alternatives to wool textile work.

Appendix: wool textile processes

Worsted processing begins with wool <u>sorting</u>, a manual operation in which the wool is classified according to its varying characteristics and qualities. Sorting is followed by <u>scouring</u> in which impurities are removed from the wool by way of a mechanical washing process. After drying, the wool may be carded on a worsted <u>carding</u> machine which opens out and seperates the fibres. If it has been carded the resulting 'sliver' will be straightened in <u>preparing boxes</u> (or <u>gill boxes</u>) prior to combing. <u>Woolcombing</u> is the characteristic process of the worsted section and the aim is to produce a 'top' in which the long fibres lie parallel to one another. This can be achieved by way of Noble or French (i.e. rectlinear) combing. If it is the former then backwashing and extended <u>finishing operations</u> (performed by machines similar to those used in preparation for combing) will be required.

Sorting, scouring, preparation and combing are all usually performed by woolcombers who do not take part in the subsequent processes. Indeed there is rarely any integration between the next stage, worsted spinning, and the final stages of weaving and finishing. The spinner receives tops from the woolcomber together with other materials including synthetics which have undergone 'tow to top conversion'. The topsmay be dyed at this stage (in which case they will require <u>recombing</u>) although the material can also be dyed as yarn or cloth. A number of <u>drawing</u> operations are required to draft the tops, i.e. to pull the fibres as in spinning but without adding twist. Preparatory spinning on <u>roving</u> frames continues the drafting process while adding some twist to the fibre. Drawing, roving and <u>doubling</u> progressively reduce the size of the 'roving' until it is suitable for <u>spinning</u> proper. The number and kind of preparatory operations is related to the kind of spinning which is used. Thicker yarns may be spun on a flyer frame (the descendant of the water frame and the throstle) or by modern rotor spinning methods. Thin yarns can be spun by old fashioned cap frames or on ring frames. Spinning is followed by <u>twisting</u> - a similar process - and by <u>winding</u> in which the yarn is wound into different package shapes and sizes depending on its end use: it may be intended as the weft or warp for weaving, for knitting machines or even for hand knitting.

Worsted weaving firms may <u>rewind</u> the yarn (the weft is wound on to cops or pins) they receive from the spinners. The warp must, at any rate, be prepared for the loom by <u>reeling</u>, <u>reaching-in</u>, <u>dressing</u>, <u>warping</u> and so on. Some of these operations are manual. Weaving may be done on nonautomatic, semiautomatic or fully automatic <u>conventional looms</u>, or on modern <u>shuttleless looms</u> like the rapier or the gripper shuttle. The cloth then undergoes the manual operations of <u>burling and</u>

mending, which are meant to restore any imperfections, and is finally passed on, possibly to another firm, for finishing where the cloth may also be dyed.

Processing in the woollen section is rather less complicated. Here an extended carding process is followed by spinning on ring frames or on mules and then weaving. The more complex woollen process is finishing where numerous operations are required. In contrast to the worsted technique, the aim of woollen carding is to create a matted web of short fibres. When these fibres are woven into cloth a protracted finishing process is required to raise the nap of the cloth and give the desired effect, but modern continuous processing has replaced fulling and shearing in woollen finishing. Furthermore, again in contrast to worsted, woollen processes - from carding to finishing - are usually integrated.

Nevertheless, despite these differences in processing techniques, woollen and worsted products share the same end uses in clothing and household furnishings. There are, however, differences in end use within these categories: while woollen manufactures may end up as blankets or billiard cloths, worsted products may go to make carpets and hosiery goods. Indeed the worsted section has been able to take advantage of changes in (hosiery) knitting techniques by selling yarn to the machine knitters. In general, worsted producers tend to sell more semimanufactures than do the woollen producers (who are, of course, much more likely to be vertically integrated). Finally, the worsted system is better able to produce special products like hand knitting (or even hand weaving) yarn and industrial textiles.

Bibliography

Note: Place of publication is London unless otherwise indicated.

Advisory Conciliation and Arbitration Service (ACAS), (1972), Report on a survey ... labour turnover amongst woolcombing operatives, Mimeo.

Allen, S., (1970), Immigrants or workers, in Zubaida, S., (edit), Race and Racialism, Tavistock/BSA.

Allen, S., (1971), Mounting unemployment and racial minorities, Race Today, Vol.3, No.4, (April).

Allen, S., (1971a), Race and the economy: some aspects of the position of non-indigenous labour, Race, Vol.XIII, No.2, (Oct).

Allen, S., (1971b), New minorities, old conflicts: Asian and West Indian migrants in Britain, New York: Random House.

Allen, S., (1972), Black workers in Great Britain in Van Houte, H, and Melgert, W, (edit), Foreigners in our Community, Amsterdam: Keesing Publishers.

Allen, S., Bentley, S. and Bornat, J, (1977), Work, race and immigration, University of Bradford.

Anthias, F., (1980), Women and the reserve army of labour: a critique of Veronia Beechey, Capital and Class, No.10 (Spring) pp.50-63.

Anwar, M., (1979), The myth of return, Heinemann.

Ascription and Social Relations of Production (ASRP), Author's PhD. thesis, University of Aberdeen, 1982.

Atkins & Partners, (1969), The strategic future of the wool textile industry, National Economic Development Committee/HMSO.

Aufhauser, R., (1973), Slavery and scientific management, Journal of economic history, 33.

Ayattollahi, A., (1976), The implications of introducing shift work and flexible working hours in the clothing industry, Unpublished PhD. thesis, University of Bradford.

Baron, H.M., (1971), The demand for black labour - historical notes on the political economy of racism, Radical America, Vol.5, No.2, March - April.

Baron, H.M., (1975), Racial discrimination in advanced capitalism: a theory of nationalism and divisions in the labour market, in Edwards, R.C., Reich, M. and Gordon, D.M., (edit.) Labor Market Segmentation, Lexington, Mass.,: D.C. Heath.

Barron, R.D. and Norris, G.M., (1976), Sexual divisions and the dual labour market, in Barker, D.L. and Allen, S., (edit.) Dependence and exploitation in work and marriage, Longman.

Becker, G.S., (1957), Economics of discrimination, University of Chicago Press.

Beechey, V., (1978), Women and production: a critical analysis of some sociological theories of women's work, in Kuhn, A., and Wolpe, A. (edit), Feminism and Materialism, Routledge, Kegan Paul.

Berger, J. and Mohr, J., (1975), A seventh man, Harmondsworth.

Berthoff, R.T., (1953), British immigrants in industrial America 1790-1950, Cambridge: Harvard University Press.

Bienefeld, M., (1972), Working hours in British industry: An economic history, Weidenfeld & Nicholson.

Blauner, R., (1972), Racial oppression in America, New York: Harper and Row.

Blumer, H., (1965), Industrialisation and race relations in Hunter, G. (edit), Industrialisation and race relations, Oxford University Press for The Institute of Race Relations.

Bohning, W.R., (1972), Britain the EEC and labour migration, in Van Houte, H. and Melgert, W., Foreigners in our community, Amsterdam: Keesing Publishers.

Bohning, W.R., (1972a), The migration of workers in the UK and the European community, Oxford University Press for Institute of Race Relations.

Bohning, W.R. and Maillat, D., (1974), Effects of the employment of foreign workers, Paris: OECD.

Bonacich, E., N.d., US Capitalism and Korean immigrant small business, Mimeo, University of California, Riverside.

Bonacich, E., (1972), A theory of ethnic antagonism: the split labour market, American sociological review, 37 (Oct), pp.547-559.

Bonacich, E., (1976), Advanced capitalism and Black/White race relations in the United States: a split labour market interpretation, American Sociological Review, 41 (Feb), pp.34-51.

Bosanquet, N. and Doeringer, P., (1973), Is there a dual labour-market in Britain? Economic Journal, 83, pp.421-435.

Bourguignon, F. et.al, (1977), International labour migrations and economic choices, the European case, Paris OECD.

Bourne, J., (1980), Cheerleaders and Ombudsmen: the sociology of race relations in Britain, Race and Class, Vol.XXI, No.4, (Spring), pp.331-352.

Bradford Metropolitan District Council Directorate of Educational Services, School leaver statistics, 1974/5-1980/1, Bradford Metropolitan Council, Careers Office.

Bradford Metropolitan District Council, (1981), District trends.

Bradford Metropolitan District Council, (1981a), Report, untitled, on Associated Weavers closure, Mimeo.

Briscoe, L., (1971), The textile and clothing industries of the United Kingdom, Manchester University Press.

Brooks, D., (1975), Race and labour in London transport, Oxford University Press for Institute of Race Relations.

Brown, R., (1978), Work, in Abrams, P. (edit), Work, Urbanism and Inequality, Weidenfeld and Nicolson.

Burawoy, M., (1976), The functions and reproduction of migrant labour: comparative material from South Africa and US, American Journal of Sociology, Vol.81, No.5, (March), pp.1050-1087.

Butterworth, E., (1964), Aspects of race relations in Bradford, Race, Vol.6, (Oct), pp.129-141.

Butterworth, E. (edit), (1967), Immigrants in West Yorkshire: social conditions and the lives of Pakistanis, Indians and West Indians, Institute of Race Relations Special Series.

Bythell, D., (1969), The handloom weavers, Cambridge University Press.

Cable, V., (1979), World textile trade and production, Economist
   Intelligence Unit Special Report No.63.
Cameron, D.L., Chapman, F.A., Eagle, A.B., Morris, A.L., Thompson, A.R.,
   (1968), A preliminary analysis of labour force at ... ,
   Report prepared for postgraduate diploma in Industrial
   Administration, University of Bradford Management Centre.
Campbell, M. and Jones, D., (1981), Asian youths in the labour
   market: a study in Bradford, EEC/DES Transition to work project,
   Bradford College.
Castells, M., (1975), Immigrant workers and class struggle in
   advanced capitalism, Politics and Society, Vol.5, part one.
Castles, S. and Kosack, G., (1973), Immigrant workers and class
   structure in Western Europe, Oxford University Press for
   Institute of Race Relations.
Castles, S., Jacobson, D., Wickham, A., Wickham, J., (1977),
   Review of 'Die neue internationale Arbeitsteilung', Capital and
   Class, 7, (Spring), pp.122-130.
Clapham, J.H., (1907), The woollen and worsted industries, Methuen.
Cockburn, C., (1983), Brothers: male dominance and technological
   change, Pluto Press.
Cohen, B.G. and Jenner, P.J., (1968), The employment of immigrants:
   a case study within the wool industry, Race, Vol.X, No.I, pp.41-56.
Cohen, G., (1971), Mirpur in Yorkshire, New Society, 2 July.
Cohen, R., (1980), Migration, late capitalism and development,
   Address to the plenary session of the annual conference of the
   Development Studies Association, University College, Swansea,
   16 September.
Collard, D., (1970), Immigration and discrimination: some economic
   aspects in Wilson (edit), Economic issues in immigration,
   Institute of Economic Affairs.
Commission of the European Community, (1979), Consultation on
   migration policies vis-a-vis third countries, EEC: communication
   from the commission to the council, Brussels, 23 March.
Community Development Project (CDP), (1977), The costs of industrial
   change, CDP.
Confederation of British Wool Textiles and National Wool Textile Export
   Corporation, (1982), Quarterly review of UK trade statistics,
   No.3, (Jan - March), Wool Industry Bureau of Statistics.
Corrigan, P.R.D.C., (1977), Feudal relics or capitalist monuments,
   Sociology, Vol.II, pp.435-463.
Counter Information Services (CIS), N.d., Racism - who profits. CIS.
Cressey, P. and Macinnes, J., (1980), Voting for Ford: Industrial
   democracy and the control of labour, Capital and Class II.
Daniel, W.W., (1967), Racial discrimination in England, Harmondsworth.
Department of Employment, (1977), Unit for manpower studies project
   report: the role of immigrants in the labour market, D.E.
Department of Employment, (1980), Time rates of wages and hours of
   work, HMSO.
Department of Employment, (1980a), New earnings survey, HMSO.
Department of Employment, (1981), Time rates of wages and hours
   of work, HMSO.
Department of Industry, (1978), Wool textile industry scheme,
   An assessment of the effects of selective assistance under the
   industry act 1972, HMSO.
Department of Industry, (1981), An investigation into the woollen
   and worsted sector of the textile and garment making industries
   in the United Kingdom, France, Germany and Italy, Department of Industry.

Dobb, M., (1975), Studies in the development of capitalism, Routledge, Kegan Paul.

Doeringer, P.B. and Piore, M.J., (1971), Internal labor markets and manpower analysis, Lexington, Mass: D.C. Heath.

Driver, C., (1970), Tory radical: the life of Richard Oastler, New York: Octagon Books.

Dunn, R. and Hardy, J., (1931), Labour and textiles, New York: International Publishers.

Edwards, R.C., (1975), The social relations of production in the firm and labour market structure, in Edwards, R.C., Reich, M., and Gordon, D.M. (edit), Labor Market Segmentation, Lexington, Mass: D.C. Heath.

Edwards, R.C., Reich, M., and Gordon, D.M., (1975), Labor market segmentation, Lexington, Mass: D.C. Heath.

Erickson, C., (1957), American industry and the European immigrant 1860-1888, Cambridge: Harvard University Press.

Fishwick, F. and Cornu, R.B., (1975), A study of the evolution of concentration in the UK textile industry, Commission of the European communities (Oct).

Fowler, B., Littlewood, B., Madigan, R., (1975), Immigrant school-leavers and the search for work, University of Glasgow Discussion Paper in Social Research No.12 (August).

Franklin, R.S. and Resnik, S., (1973), The political economy of racism, New York: Holt, Rinehart and Winston.

Freeman, M.D.A. and Spencer, S., (1979), Immigration control, Black workers and the economy, British Journal of Law and society, Vol.6, No.1.

Friedman, A., (1978), Industry and labour, MacMillan.

Frobel, F., Heinrichs, J., Kreye, D., (1980), The new international division of labour - Structural unemployment in industrialised countries and industrialisation in developing countries, Cambridge University Press - Editions de la Maison des Sciences de l'homme, Paris.

Gabriel, J. and Ben Tovim, G., (1978), Marxism and the concept of racism, Economy and Society, Vol.7, No.2 (May).

Glasner, A., Kelly, A., Roberts, B., (1981), The labour market and the labour process, Paper to SIP Conference, Bulmershe College, Reading.

Glenn, N., (1963), Occupational benefits to Whites from subordination of Negroes, American Sociological Review, 28, pp.443-448.

Glenn, N., (1967), White gains from Negro subordination, Social Problems, 14, pp.159-178.

Goodrich, C.L., (1975), The frontier of control, Pluto Press.

Gordon, D.M.,(1972), Theories of poverty and unemployment, Lexington Mass: D.C. Heath.

Gorz, A., (1970), Immigrant labour, New Left Review, 61 (May), pp.28-31.

Hagmann, H.M., (1968), Capital to men or men to capital, Migration Today, 5-11.

Hallett, G., (1970), The political economy of immigration control, in Wilson, C. (edit), Economic Issues in Immigration, Institute of Economic Affairs.

Harris, C.C., (1981), The Idea of a Labour Market, Mimeo, University College, Swansea.

Harris, N., (1980), The new untouchables: the international migration of labour, International Socialism, Vol.2, No.8, pp.37-63.

Harris, N. and Hallas, D., (1981), Why import controls won't save jobs, Socialist Workers Party.

Hepple, B., (1970), Race, jobs and the law in Britain, Harmondsworth.

Hird, C., Herman, G., Taylor, R., (1980), The clothes we wear, New Statesman, 3 October.

Hirsh, B.W. and Ellis, P., (1974), An introduction to textile economics, Manchester: The Textile Trade Press.

Hooper, D. and Morgan, G., (1980), Labour in the woollen and worsted industry: a critical analysis of dual labour market theory, Paper to British Sociological Association Annual Conference, Aberystwyth, April 1980.

Hudson, P., (1981), Proto-industrialisation: the case of the West Riding wool textile industry in the 18th and early 19th centuries, History Workshop, 12 (Autumn), pp.34-61.

Inter Company Comparisons (ICC), (1979), Business ratio report: the wool industry - an industry sector analysis, ICC Business Ratios.

Jones, D., (1979), The labour market in Bradford, EEC/DES Transition to work project, Bradford College.

Jones, K. and Smith, D., (1970), The economic impact of commonwealth immigration, Cambridge University Press for National Institute for economic and social research.

Jordan, B., (1982), Mass unemployment and the future of Britain, Basil Blackwell.

Jordan, W.D., (1968), White over Black, Michigan: Ann Arbor.

Jupp, T.C. and Davies, E., (1974), The background and employment of Asian immigrants: a complete training manual for managers and supervisors, Runneymede Trust.

Kayser, B., (1971), Manpower movements and labour markets, Paris: OECD.

Kennedy-Brenner, C., (1979), Foreign workers and immigration policy, Paris: Development Centre of the OECD.

Kenyon, P., (1972), Textiles - a protection racket, World development movement.

Kindleberger, C.P., (1965), Mass migration, then and now, Foreign Affairs, Vol.43, No.4, (July), pp.647-658.

Kinnersley, P., (1974), The hazards of work, Pluto Press.

Kreckel, R., (1978), Unequal opportunity structure and labour market segmentation, Paper presented at the meeting of the Research Committee on Social Stratification at the Ninth World Congress of Sociology, Upsaala 14-19 August.

Lawrence, D., (1974), Black migrants, White Natives: a study of race relations in Nottingham, Cambridge University Press.

Leeds Trade Union and Community Resource and Information Centre, (TUCRIC), (1980), Wool textiles - special supplement to TUCRIC bulletin, Leeds TUCRIC.

Lewis, O., (1969), The culture of poverty, in Moynihan, D.P. (edit), On understanding poverty: perspectives from the social sciences, New York: Basic Books.

Lewis, W.A., (1954), Economic development with unlimited supplies of labour, The Manchester School of Economics and Statistics.

Lipson, E., (1953), A short history of wool and its manufacture (mainly in England), Heinemann.

Marglin, S.A., (1974), What do bosses do? The origins and function of hierarchy in capitalist production, Review of Radical Political Economics, 6 (2), pp.60-112.

Marsh, P., (1967), Anatomy of a strike, Institute of Race Relations.

Marshall, A., (1973), The import of labour, Rotterdam University Press.

Marshall, R., (1974), The economics of racial discrimination: a survey, Journal of Economic Literature, Vol.XII, No.3, pp.849-71.

Maw, L. and Others, (1974), Immigrants and employment in the clothing industry: the Rochdale case, Runneymede Trust.

Miles, C., (1968), Lancashire textiles: a case study of industrial change, National Institute of Economic and Social Research, occasional paper XXIII, Cambridge University Press.

Miles, R., (1982), Racism and Migrant Labour, Routledge and Kegan Paul.

Mishan, E.C., (1970), Does immigration confer economic benefits on the host country? In Wilson, C. (edit), Economic Issues in Immigration, Institute of Economic Affairs.

Montgomery, D., (1973), Immigrant workers and scientific management, Paper to immigrants in industry conference.

Moor, N. and Waddington, P., (1980), From rags to ruins - Batley woollen textiles and industrial change, Community development project (CDP) PEC.

Moynihan, D.P. (edit), (1969), On understanding poverty: perspectives from the social sciences, Basic Books.

National Economic Development Committee (NEDC), (1973), Employment practices in EEC textile industries - report on the visit by members of the wool textile EDC manpower working party to textile employers' organisations and trade unions in France, Germany and Italy, NEDO.

NEDC (Wool Textile EDC)., (1976), NEDC Industrial strategy - wool textiles, NEDO.

NEDC (Joint Textile Committee), (1977), Textile trends 1970-76, NEDO.

NEDC (Wool Textile EDC), (1978), Finance and profitability in the wool textile industry 1971/72 - 1975/6, NEDO.

NEDC (Wool Textile EDC), (1979), Annual progress report, NEDO.

NEDC (Wool Textile EDC), (1979a), Finance and profitability in the wool textile industry 1972/73 - 1976/77, NEDO.

NEDC (Wool Textile EDC), (1980), Annual progress report, NEDO.

Nichols, T. and Armstrong, P. (1976), Workers Divided, Fontana.

Nichols, T. and Beynon, H. (1977), Living with Capitalism, Routledge and Kegan Paul.

Nikolinakos, M., (1972), Economic foundations of discrimination in the Federal Republic of Germany in Van Houte H. and Melgert, W. (edit), Foreigners in our community, Amsterdam: Keesing Publishers.

Nikolinakos, M., (1973), Notes on an economic theory of racism, Race, Vol.XIV, No.4, (April).

Nikolinakos, M., (1975), Notes towards a general theory of migration in late capitalism, Race and Class, Vol.17, No.1, (Summer) pp. 5-17.

Paine, S., (1974), Exporting workers: the Turkish case, Cambridge University Press.

Parsonage, A.C., (1973), An economic and technological study of the competition between knitting and weaving in the UK textile industry, Unpublished PhD. thesis, University of Surrey.

Patterson, S., (1968), Immigrants in industry, Oxford University Press.

Peach, C., (1968), West Indian migration to Britain, Oxford University Press for Institute of Race Relations.

Pinchbeck, I., (1930), Women workers and the industrial revolution 1750-1850, Routledge.

Piore, M.J.(1975), Notes for a theory of labour market stratification in Edwards, R.C., Reich, M. and Gordon, D.M.(edit), Labor Market Segmentation, Lexington, Mass: D.C. Heath.

Pollard, S., (1965), The genesis of modern management: a study of the industrial revolution in Great Britain, Edward Arnold.

Preston, A., (1969), Effects on the economy, in Rose, E.J.B.(edit), Colour and Citizenship, Oxford University Press for Institute of Race Relations.

Pryce, K., (1979), Endless pressure, Harmondsworth.

Rainnie, G.F. (edit), (1965), The woollen and worsted industry: an economic analysis, Oxford: Clarendon press.

Redford, A., (1926), Labour migration in England 1800-1850, Manchester University Press.

Reich, M., Gordon, D.M. and Edwards, R.C., (1973), A theory of labor market segmentation: American Economic Review, Papers and Proceedings, Vol.63, pp.359-865.

Rimmer, M., (1972), Race and industrial conflict, Heinemann.

Roemer, J.E., (1978), Differentially exploited labor: a Marxian theory of discrimination, Review of Radical Political Economics, Vol.10, No.2, pp.43-53.

Rose, H., (1978), A de-skilled town? New Society, 20th July.

Runneymede Trust, (1977), Review of The role of immigrants in the labour market, Runneymede Trust Bulletin, No.86.

Runneymede Trust and the Radical Statistics Group, (1980), Britain's Black population, Heinemann.

Sandberg, L.G., (1974), American rings and English mules: the role of economic rationality in Floud, R. (edit), Essays in quantitative economic history, Oxford University Press.

Schmidt, G., (1971), Foreign workers and labour market flexibility, Journal of Common Market Studies, Vol.IX, No.3, pp.246-253.

Shah, S., (1975), Immigrants and employment in the clothing industry - the rag trade in London's East end, Runneymede Trust (Sept).

Shanin, T., (1978), The peasants are coming: migrants who labour, peasants who travel and Marxists who write, Race and Class, Vol.XIX, No.3 (Winter).

Sigsworth, E.M., (1958), Black Dyke mills, Liverpool University Press.

Statistical Office of the EEC 1975-1982, Labour costs in Industry, (1972-1980), Eurostat, European Community.

Smith, D.J., (1974), Racial disadvantage in employment, PEP.

Smith, D.J., (1976), The facts of racial disadvantage: a national survey, PEP.

Stokes, R., (1975), How long is the long run: Race and industrialisation, International Review of Community Development, No.4 (Winter), pp.123-136.

Symanski, A., (1976), Racial discrimination and White gain, American Sociological Review, 41 (June), pp.403-414.

Tabb, W.K., (1970), Political economy of the Black ghetto, New York: W.W. Norton.

Textile Council, (1969), Cotton and allied textiles: a report on present performance and future prospects, Manchester: Royal Exchange.

Tuckman, A. and Paulding, J., (1981), The construction of labour processes and the labour process in construction, Paper to SIP conference, Bulmershe College, Reading.

Wainwright, H., (1978), Women and the division of labour in Abrams, P. (edit), Work, urbanism and inequality, Weidenfeld and Nicolson.

Ward, A., (1975), European capitalism's reserve army, <u>Monthly Review</u>,
    Vol.27, No.6 (Nov), pp.17-32.
West Yorkshire County Council (WYCC), (1981), <u>Economic Trends</u>,
    No.17 (June), WYCC.
West Yorkshire Language Link (WYLL), Various Reports, 1977-1978,
    Mimeo, WYLL.
Williams, E., (1967), <u>Capitalism and slavery</u>, Andre Deutsch.
Wilson, C. (edit), (1970), <u>Economic issues in immigration</u>, Institute
    of economic affairs.
Wilson, R.G., (1973), The supremacy of the Yorkshire cloth industry
    in the eighteenth century, in Harte, N. and Ponting, K. (edit),
    <u>Textile History and Economic History</u>, Manchester University
    Press.
Wing, C. (1967), <u>The evils of the factory system</u>, Frank Cass.
Winyard, S., (1980), Trouble looming, <u>Low Pay Pamphlet No.13</u>,
    Low Pay Unit.
Wolpe, H., (1970), Industrialism and Race in South Africa in
    Zubaida, S. (edit), <u>Race and Racialism</u>, Tavistock/BSA.
Wolpe, H., (1972), Capitalism and cheap labour power in South Africa:
    from segregation to apartheid, <u>Economy and Society</u>, Vol.I, No.4 (Nov).
Wolpe, H., (1976), The 'White working class' in South Africa,
    <u>Economy and Society</u>, Vol.5, No.2, (May).
Wool (and Allied) Textile Employers Council (WATEC), (1978),
    <u>Manpower analysis</u>.
Wool and Clothing Industry Action Committee (WOOLTAC), <u>Various
    Bulletins</u>, Wooltac.
Wool Industry Bureau of Statistics (WIBS), <u>(Unpublished) annual census
    of personnel figures for Bradford 1965-1980</u>.
WIBS, <u>Monthly bulletins May 1977 - June 1982</u>.
Wool Industry Training Board, (Later the Wool Jute and Flax
    Industrial Training Board (WJFITB)), <u>Annual reports 1966-1980</u>.
Worsley, P., (1976), Proletarians, sub proletarians, lumpen
    proletarians, marginalidados, migrants, urban peasants and urban
    poor, <u>Sociology</u>, Vol.10, No.1 (Jan).
Wright, P., (1968), <u>The coloured worker in British industry</u>, Oxford
    University Press for Institute of Race Relations.

In addition, the following newspapers and periodicals were consulted:

Bradford Black
Bradford Star
Daily Telegraph
Department of Employment Gazette
Financial Times
Guardian
Migration Today
New Society
New Statesman
Observer
Press and Journal
Private Eye
Race Today
Shipley Target
Socialist Challenge
Socialist Worker
Sunday Times
Telegraph and Argus

Time Out
The Times
Womens Voice
Yorkshire Evening Post
Yorkshire Post

Readers may like to note that a lengthier bibliography, covering
many publications not listed here (especially on wool textile history),
is available in ASRP, pp.570-600.